DISCARDED

THE SHAKESPEAREAN MARRIAGE

Also by Lisa Hopkins

ELIZABETH I AND HER COURT

JOHN FORD'S POLITICAL THEATRE

WOMEN WHO WOULD BE KINGS: Female Rulers of the Sixteenth Century

The Shakespearean Marriage

Merry Wives and Heavy Husbands

Lisa Hopkins
Senior Lecturer
Sheffield Hallam University

© Lisa Hopkins 1998

All rights reserved. No reproduction, copy or transmission of this publication may be made without written permission.

No paragraph of this publication may be reproduced, copied or transmitted save with written permission or in accordance with the provisions of the Copyright, Designs and Patents Act 1988, or under the terms of any licence permitting limited copying issued by the Copyright Licensing Agency, 90 Tottenham Court Road, London W1T 4LP.

Any person who does any unauthorised act in relation to this publication may be liable to criminal prosecution and civil claims for damages.

The author has asserted her right to be identified as the author of this work in accordance with the Copyright, Designs and Patents Act 1988

Published by PALGRAVE MACMILLAN
Houndmills, Basingstoke, Hampshire RG21 6XS and
175 Fifth Avenue, New York, N.Y. 10010
Companies and representatives throughout the world

PALGRAVE MACMILLAN is the global academic imprint of the Palgrave Macmillan division of St. Martin's Press, LLC and of Palgrave Macmillan Ltd. Macmillan® is a registered trademark in the United States, United Kingdom and other countries. Palgrave is a registered trademark in the European Union and other countries.

Outside North America
ISBN 0–333–64732–7

In North America
ISBN 0–312–17748–8

This book is printed on paper suitable for recycling and made from fully managed and sustained forest sources.

A catalogue record for this book is available from the British Library.

Library of Congress Catalog Card Number: 97-23091

Transferred to digital printing 2003

For Chris and Sam

Contents

Acknowledgements		ix
Introduction: Shakespeare and Contemporary Marriage		1
1	Marriage as Comic Closure	16
2	Marriage in the Middle	34
3	What Makes a Marriage?	66
4	The Fate of the Nation: Marriage in the History Plays	85
5	Roman Marriage	109
6	Tragic Marriage	133
7	The Wedding of the Daughter: Marriage in the Last Plays	161
Conclusion		188
Notes		192
Index		215

Acknowledgements

Many debts have been incurred during the writing of this book. The Cultural Research Institute at Sheffield Hallam University gave me study leave to work on it; the staff at the Mary Badland Library, Sheffield Hallam University assisted with enquiries and with interlibrary loans. Two final year students, Nicola Connolly and Marcia Layne, helped me track down references and commented interestingly on critical trends. In a small, close department, I have received a great deal of support from several colleagues, but most of all special thanks are due to Ian Baker for the extraordinary generosity of his unfailing assistance, stimulating conversation and willingness to lighten my workload. The members of the Northern Renaissance Seminar have been a very congenial stimulus, as have those of the electronic discussion group Shaksper, and my friend Mike Davis. Charmian Hearne provided the original backing for the project and, as its editor, has been consistently helpful throughout; I was also greatly benefited by the comments of the anonymous reader. My husband Chris has, as always, been invaluable, not least in looking after our son Sam, and for the same reason I would also like to thank our childminder, Josie Edwards, for the work that has made this book possible. Its faults are, of course, entirely my own.

Introduction: Shakespeare and Contemporary Marriage

In recent years much effort has been expended both by historians and by critics of Renaissance drama to increase our understanding of sixteenth-century ideologies of marriage. By and large, a general consensus has emerged that the period during which Shakespeare began writing his plays was one marked by changes in two major aspects of marriage: its ethos and the actual ceremonies by which it was celebrated. Since wedding customs are fairly easy to document – by reference, for example, to the various prayer books produced during this period of rapid religious change – there is little disagreement among scholars about the nature of the alterations in them, though it is of course often less easy to know to what extent theoretical modifications to traditional practice were actually followed through. It seems clear enough that the old models can hardly have made way for the new ones overnight, so that there was considerable confusion over the legal status of many marriages: in her recent study of bastardy in Renaissance England, Alison Findlay comments that 'localised marriage practices and confusion as to what actually constituted a marriage complicated the supposedly absolute distinction between legitimate and illegitimate',[1] and the many instances of litigation over the validity of marriages or alleged contracts to marry tell their own story of widespread confusion and ambiguity.[2]

Nevertheless, there was general agreement over some broad principles. The age of consent was 12 for girls and 14 for boys; marriages could be conducted in private without even any witnesses, but it was vastly preferable for them to be performed in public; contracts could be either immediately effective or deferred verbal promises (which would, however, become instantly binding on consummation); and, although other considerations were often very weighty, the verbal consent of the individual was felt to be of paramount importance and formed an essential part of the ceremony.[3] Though the problems of assembling evidence of consummation or of an unwitnessed, private ceremony could often lead to disputes about whether a marriage had indeed taken place, the criteria which needed to be satisfied to establish that it had were well marked. When it comes to the ethos of marriage, however, there are marked differences in the ways in which the evidence has recently been interpreted.

The principal disagreements centre on the degree of change which we must envisage as taking place over the beginning of the early modern period. The very name 'early modern' encourages us to see it as a time of change and of the emergence of new ideas more recognisable to us than those which they superseded, and this in itself may predetermine interpretation of such transition as we can detect. The most extreme model, whose original advocate was the historian Lawrence Stone, sees a dramatic and relatively sudden swing away from extended kinship groupings towards what we would now recognise as something roughly resembling the modern nuclear family. He also argued that because of the high mortality rates of earlier periods it would simply have been impracticable for parents to make great emotional investments in their children, since so few would be likely to survive, and that indeed all family ties would have been much less affective than those that we ourselves might hope to experience. Similar models of radical shifts lie behind Frances Dolan's claim, in a recent study of representations of domestic crime, that 'many social historians agree that early modern England witnessed a crisis of order, focusing on gender relations, that began around 1550, peaked in 1650, and passed by 1700'.[4] Other historians have contested Stone's views. Particularly influential have been Keith Wrightson and Alan Macfarlane, both of whom, while agreeing that family organisation has shifted, see it as having altered in far less radical ways. Few modern scholars, however, would not accept the argument for at least some degree of change, however minimal, in family structure and ethos between the medieval and the early modern periods, and one of the places where this is most visible is in the institution of marriage, which, it is now almost universally accepted, was being redefined in the late sixteenth century in the wake of the considerable religious changes which had taken place in British society over the previous half-century or so.[5]

Broadly speaking, the momentum for change is seen as coming primarily from the rise of Puritanism, the extreme wing of the new Protestant Church. Catholicism emphasised rituals, the performance of specific actions and a relationship with God which was strictly mediated through the authority of the priest. Protestantism, by contrast, stressed the personal, interior nature of human communion with the divine and the necessity for self-regulation in the case of men, and, for the weaker, more fallible sex, spiritual guidance by husband or father. A Protestant household was conceived of as a small, self-sufficient enclave, a miniature commonwealth, where, in accordance with all models of good government, the paterfamilias would take full responsibility for the moral, physical and spiritual prosperity of his wife, children and servants. The connection between microcosm and macrocosm is made quite explicit in a comment like that of Euarchus in the romance by the militantly Protestant Sir Philip Sidney, *The Countess of Pembroke's Arcadia*:

> marriage being the most holy conjunction that falls to mankind, out of which all families and so consequently all societies do proceed, which not only by community of goods but community of children is to knit the minds in a most perfect union; which whoso breaks, dissolves all humanity, no man living free from the danger of so near a neighbour.[6]

As Elspeth Graham, Hilary Hinds, Elaine Hobby and Helen Wilcox put it, 'the family was a "little church" or "little state"; Calvin saw the subjection of the wife to the husband as a guarantee of the subjection of both of them to God.'[7]

Additionally, where Catholicism, following the lead of St Paul, had treated sexuality with distaste and valorised virginity, Puritanism saw secular love, properly channelled, as a gift from God. Indeed, removing marriage from the list of sacraments (on the grounds that human sexuality was not inherently sinful, and so married sexuality did not need special consecration to be freed from taint),[8] Protestantism effectively removed it from the arena of the spiritual:

> The characterization of marriage as a 'necessary evil', associated with St Paul and the Catholic church, had been modified by Protestant, and more particularly Puritan, commentators, who

instead lauded it as an honourable, dignified, and natural union between men and women, sanctioned by God.[9]

Crucial to the proper functioning of such a family, moreover, was the issue of consent: the Protestant patriarch was no tyrant, but someone whose authority needed to be fully recognised by all his dependants. Foremost among these was his wife, who would so often be called upon to act as his second-in-command in domestic situations. The advocates of the new Puritanism, therefore, placed great stress on the need for consent rather than coercion in marriage:

> Puritans opposed traditional marriages in which parents had bartered their children like cattle, emphasizing conjugal love, through which individuals could better love and serve the Lord... many of these Puritan attitudes towards marriage are reflected in Shakespeare's plays.[10]

At first sight this may seem liberating, and it was certainly so interpreted at the outset of feminist criticism, most notably and most persuasively by Juliet Dusinberre in a famous book, *Shakespeare and the Nation of Women*.[11] There are, however, less positive ways of reacting to the Puritan abhorrence of enforced marriage. In the first place, consent was only one factor among many; although there was to be no pressure on the young to marry a partner whom they loathed, parents still retained a considerable moral authority, with their offspring often envisaged as having merely a right of refusal rather than one of unfettered choice. Moreover, the new emphasis on the benefits of what is often termed 'companionate' marriage served to make marriage even more forcibly promoted and perceived as the only morally acceptable lifestyle; as even priests began to take wives, to be single or, even more unacceptably, to be promiscuous or to be openly homosexual, became radically demonised.

Even the fact that Puritans sought to make marriage more palatable for women could, as Dympna Callaghan argues, have a negative side:

> In its articulation by Protestant (mainly Puritan) churchmen, the paradigm of marriage was profoundly imbued with idealism, stressing less the evils of voracious female sexuality, as earlier

writings had done, and more the benefits of pliant femininity.... The production of female desire is the mechanism whereby female subjectivities were recruited to changing understandings of marriage and society. The Puritan doctrine of marriage requires nothing less than that women are endowed with desiring subjectivity, which can then be actively solicited and controlled by the social order.[12]

It is, moreover, important to remember that even this relatively limited concern for women's happiness within marriage was taking place within a social order that was, by our standards, profoundly misogynistic and preoccupied with a deep fear of female sexuality and its potential consequences. And it is worth noting the tacit assumption in much of this new marriage theory that men need not even be thought to have emotional needs, since their sexual, social and political needs are all seen as being already gratified by the existing structures of marriage. (It is perhaps only fair to point out that this has been a neglect traditionally replicated by some forms of feminist criticism.)

Feminist critics of Renaissance drama have been quick to point to telling examples of a widespread climate of distrust and denigration of women, even after they had been safely married. Catherine Belsey, introducing her comments on domestic tragedy, declares that 'the existing historical evidence gives no reason to believe that there was a major outbreak of women murdering their husbands in the sixteenth century. What it does suggest, however, is a widespread belief that they were likely to do so.'[13] Kathleen McLuskie points to 'the comic treatment of male violence and the oppression of women in such genres as "gadding stories" and shrew-taming tales', and argues that

> popular representations of relations between men and women... construct literary processes in which women are variously the objects of ribaldry, pathos and sentimentality... the popular literary versions of gender relations organised these responses so that they were not in conflict with the ideology of male supremacy.[14]

Lisa Jardine argues that this general climate of misogyny found its correlative even within the apparent liberalisation of marriage:

Justifications for subjugation altered towards sophisticated mutual consent theories, but the actuality of a woman's role in the household remained, as far as one can discover, unchanged. Instead, it sounds suspiciously as if (in common with sophisticated moderates' views on such relationships in all periods) the Protestants maintained that moderation in marital relations made the task of authoritative control of wives simpler.[15]

Our cultural reverence for Shakespeare, and the legacy of centuries of belief both in an unchanging given called 'human nature' and in Shakespeare's transcendent insight into it, have habitually led critics to position Shakespeare firmly on the liberal side of his society's endemic belief in the inferiority of women. It is perhaps a reflection of how deeply we have internalised the 'desiring subjectivity' which we think is natural but which, Dympna Callaghan argues, is socially produced, that there has also been a critical tendency even – or perhaps especially – amongst recent feminist critics of Shakespeare to consider his treatment of his heroines almost exclusively in the light of the marriages his plays arrange for them, since it is, we assume, there or nowhere that they will find happiness. This is perhaps particularly true of British cultural materialists, who, unlike American New Historicists, regard the drama as a genuine site of subversion and liberalism. Thus Graham Holderness argues:

> Almost without exception Renaissance plays express a positive appreciation of free choice, companionate relationship and romantic individualism in marriage, as opposed to parental authority, domestic inequality and impersonal contract. The audience were metropolitan, more likely to be attuned to the more modern currents of contemporary thought: it was certainly illegal in London to batter a wife or even to call a woman a whore.[16]

It is true that marriage is the crucial feature in the lives of almost all of Shakespeare's heroines – even where it is absent, as in the case of Cleopatra and of Cressida, its absence is a powerfully felt one – and indeed it forms a central thematic and structural motif in his dramaturgy in general. His comedies end with marriages; his history cycles are articulated by marriages; his tragedies begin with marriages, his tragi-comedies are involved in complex negotiations with marriages, and both tragi-comedies and problem plays are habitually judged and generically classified in terms of their portrayal of marriages. The importance of marriage in the plays cannot, in short, be overstated; but its role as a generator of 'happiness', I think, can. Indeed Heather Dubrow argues that we habitually misread the meaning of marriage in Renaissance writing:

> Most readers are programmed to associate wedding poetry with unmitigated happiness and serenity and hence are prone to overlook the tensions and ambivalences in the Stuart wedding poem, as well as those in earlier instances of the genre. One consequence of that neglect is misreading popular lyrics.[17]

Other critics sound a similarly cautionary note: Catherine Belsey suggests that 'the theatre...was not quite as optimistic about marriage as the moralists who prescribed it',[18] while David Bergeron points out that 'in most Jacobean comedy, marriages are made in the marketplace, not in heaven'.[19]

To begin to offer a less optimistic reading of the significance of marriage in Shakespeare's plays I would like, albeit briefly, to commit a critical sin. The author has been dead for so long that he is perhaps ripe for a resurrection;[20] and although in Shakespeare's case this is particularly difficult to attempt since so tantalisingly little is known about crucial areas of his life, it is surely possible to speculate just a little on what ideas about marriage his own experience might have brought him and how they might relate to his experience in his plays.[21]

In the first place, there is no evidence to suggest either that his own marriage was a particularly close or happy one, or that it irretrievably broke down. His wife was pregnant when they married, so the young Shakespeare certainly knew at first hand that Puritan ideals about the total containment of sexuality within marriage did not always find their correlative in practice; he seems not to have lived with her for much of their married life, but there was no open scandal, neither of them murdered the other and, perhaps interestingly in view of the pervasive concern in the plays, there is no suggestion at all of infidelity on her part. On his, there is only what can be gleaned from such sonnets as we choose to read as autobiographical (though they, of course, would tell a colourful story enough if we took them all at face value). He seems not to have liked one of his sons-in-law,[22] but that episode occurred towards the end of his life and can have little bearing on his plays.

More tellingly, perhaps, the sonnets can offer us another perspective on the question. It is often claimed that the first 18 sonnets were written expressly to persuade a young man of Shakespeare's acquaintance to marry. The reason they offer for this, though, not only hardly posits marriage as an end in itself, but also proves to be intimately associated with homoeroticism rather than heterosexuality, as Jonathan Goldberg points out when he discusses 'the initial sequence in Shakespeare's sonnets, where the sonneteer urges the young man to marry in order to further solidify bonds between men':[23]

> Make thee another self for love of me,
> That beauty still may live in thine or thee.[24]

Moreover, one of Shakespeare's earliest pieces of poetry, 'The Phoenix and the Turtle', epithalamion though it may be, was written for the wedding of Ursula Stanley, illegitimate daughter of the Earl of Derby, to Sir John Salusbury, whose grandfather, Roland de Velville, was often (erroneously) believed to be the bastard of Henry VII. As such it offers a celebration of marriage sharply tempered by the knowledge that marriage does not offer the only route to the acquisition of a family. (Indeed, in the North Welsh society into which Ursula Stanley was marrying, her bastardy would be no taint, since traditional Welsh law drew no distinction between legitimate and illegitimate offspring.) Recent scholarship has persuasively argued that while it was Ursula Stanley whom Sir John married, it was her sister, Dorothy, whom he loved and who is, in fact, covertly celebrated as the Phoenix, problematising the tone of the epithalamion even further.[25]

Within Shakespeare's personal experience, therefore, marriage seems to have played a less central part than it does in his dramatic work. One obvious explanation of this discrepancy is to be found in the very different demands of daily life and dramatic construction: marriage provided the obvious telos of his comedies. Nevertheless, the emphasis he gives it is striking. No other dramatist of the period so insistently offers us the multiple weddings which habitually make up the ending of Shakespearean comedies; no other dramatist of the period, and none of the classical tragedians whom Shakespeare could have taken as models, so relentlessly uses marriage as the mainspring of tragedy. It seems that this emphasis may well be linked to Shakespeare's fascination with the practical and ideological mechanisms which underpin the structures of his society. It has long been recognised that throughout his dramatic career he submitted the workings of government to a sustained and often comfortless scrutiny, which includes kings, beadles, constables and even dogs. I want to argue that his use of the marriage motif is driven by a similar awareness of both its usefulness as social glue and its arbitrariness and psychological cost, and that he subjects the workings of the microcosm to precisely the same kinds of examination as he does those of the macrocosm. In these days of Tory Party panic over single motherhood, Shakespeare is indeed, it seems, our contemporary, as he lays bare the extent to which marriage can function as a social rather than as a psychological prop.

I shall argue, then, that Shakespeare habitually dramatises marriage as both redemptive and painful, a state which may well be socially indispensable but is not, however hard Puritan (and indeed contemporary) rhetoric may protest to the contrary, 'natural'. In many ways, I would wish to align Shakespeare here more closely with an aristocratic ethos, which minimised the role of love within marriage, and stressed instead compatibility of background.[26] He certainly seems closer to this than to the romanticised perspective of the bourgeoisie, which very often provided Puritanism with its strongest supporters.[27] In practice if not in theory, aristocratic marriages were often strikingly – if perhaps not pleasantly – different from those lower down the social scale: they tended to operate as a much looser tie and to function less in terms of a lifelong bond than of a union whose specific purposes were the cementing of alliances and the production of children. David Lindley, commenting on the irretrievable deterioration of Frances Howard's first marriage to the Earl of Essex, comments that '[t]o many observers marital breakdown in upper-class marriages must have seemed far from unusual',[28] and Marianne Novy observes that 'there seems to have been increased strain on aristocratic marriages just at the time Shakespeare was writing'.[29] Lawrence Stone calculates that between 1595 and 1620 about a third of the old nobility lived separately from their wives,[30] and Alan Macfarlane points to a common view that happiness was not a consideration in the marriages of the aristocracy, which were seen as far more likely to be arranged for financial and kinship considerations.[31]

There were certainly some really spectacular cases of marital breakdown amongst the aristocracy, and it is a telling irony that scholars who suggest particular aristocratic marriages as the probable occasion of *A Midsummer Night's Dream* so consistently point out the extent to which the political rather than the personal predominated in the formation of these alliances; proponents of both the Carey–Berkeley and the Northumberland–Devereux marriages as the stimulus for *Dream* comment on how appropriate the play's presentation of shallow, easily transferred affections would be for these particular weddings.[32] Notably, the Northumberland–Devereux alliance later provided one of the period's most notorious instances of marital collapse, with the Countess, Beatrice-like, threatening to eat the Earl's heart. The Countess of Northumberland's sister, Penelope Devereux, fared little better. Having been carried protesting to the altar, she eventually deserted her husband Robert Rich to live in open, tolerated adultery with Charles Blount, friend of her brother, the Earl of Essex. Another broken aristocratic marriage of which Shakespeare was likely to have been well aware was that of the Earl of Shewsbury and his Countess, better known as Bess of Hardwick. Bess's recent biographer has commented interestingly on the hard-headedness of the business arrangement which united not only the Earl and Countess but four of their respective children from previous marriages.[33] They worked, in that the property proved to be lastingly tied up, but the marriage itself collapsed irrevocably under a welter of mutual accusations including adultery, persecution, financial chicanery and shrewishness – though this latter charge found short shrift with the Bishop of Coventry, who, trying to bring about a reconciliation between the couple, commented acidly that 'if shrewdness and sharpness may be just cause for separation I think that few men in England would keep their wives for long, for it is common jest yet true in some sense, that there is one shrew in all the world and every man hath her'.[34]

The aristocracy, however, can be seen as distinctive not only in their marriage practices, but also in their attachment to certain values and interests, particularly to do with their preservation of their own self-image, their sense of England and the prominence of their own families. If their marriages were arranged with a view to safeguarding family futures, the aristocratic sense of the origin and role of those families was firmly rooted in the past, of which their architecture, their lifestyles and their literary patronage so often displayed a heightened awareness. I shall certainly suggest that in his history plays in particular, but perhaps also elsewhere in his work, Shakespeare seems to expect the more educated sector of his audience to tap into certain unstated but important areas of the past, as they would have known it from the chronicler Holinshed, which would point them towards specific, not always encouraging, readings of the marriages depicted in the plays. Awed though the young Shakespeare doubtless felt by the huge shadow cast by his contemporary Marlowe, who had had the university education which Shakespeare himself had not, it seems to me that he never hesitates in his plays to claim the artistic high ground by identifying himself largely with the aristocratic and the educated rather than with the popular perspective; indeed, the word 'popular' itself is one of his standard insults. It seems ironic that while Marlowe should write plays which were often read as catering to popular prejudices about foreigners and which seem to have been on the lips even of those watching the Bridewell dustcart go by,[35] Shakespeare's plays can frequently be seen as sharing the politics of a much more select group, and this, I shall argue, is particularly the case in his representations of marriage, where the one relationship never tolerated is that of 'disparagement', or the crossing of class barriers. Demetrius may change Hermia for Helena, but for Titania to dote on Bottom is an affront; personal satisfaction takes second place to the preservation of social structures. Even if an Angelo, a Bertram or an Emilia (in *The Two Noble Kinsmen*) is unwilling to marry, authority and their peer group demand that they must. As the Countess of Salisbury reminds the King in *Edward III*, a play occasionally attributed to Shakespeare, marriage in this society is the oldest and the ultimate guarantor of social stability and social identity:

> To be a king is of a younger house
> Than to be married. Your progenitor,
> Sole-reigning Adam, on the universe,
> By God was honoured for a married man,
> But not by him anointed for a king.[36]

Indeed in the dark and turbulent world of the tragedies and, to a lesser extent, the tragi-comedies, one may well feel that the reason marriage may sometimes succeed in restoring social order is because it works to eliminate and eradicate that disturbing emotion, love.

One palliative to the disorder which marriage introduces into the lives of Shakespeare's protagonists is to hedge it about with ritual. This affords the individual a means of reasserting at least some control over events, and allows a safety valve by means of the symbolic acting out of some at least of the confused emotions which the event may generate. It is, therefore, significant that, as the title of Carol Thomas Neely's book *Broken Nuptials in Shakespeare's Plays* suggests, Shakespeare repeatedly dramatises incomplete, improper or interrupted ceremonies which both enact and emblematise the tensions he sees within the institution of marriage. As his young people move towards matrimony they must undergo devastating psychological shifts which reform their social, cultural and personal senses of identity; for his maturer, more fully formed characters it is quite simply fatal. Nevertheless, although I shall be exploring the less positive sides of Shakespeare's depictions of marriage, I do not wish to paint the plays as unredeemedly dark. Although I am unable to subscribe wholeheartedly to the happiness of the marriages of Shakespeare's 'happy comedies', I do see happiness and comfort offered elsewhere in them. This is a dichotomy made explicit in the late romances, where the central relationship is not a marital one but a parent–child bond, with Shakespeare here coming full circle to return to the drive of the first 18 sonnets. It is, too, in these late plays, rather than in the comedies that centre on marriage, that Shakespeare's use of the rhetoric of nature moves into full power, for this, I think, is the one bond that he did see as fully natural. As the primary means for the production of children, marriage is validated in his plays; but he never loses sight of its cost to identity, personal freedom and gender solidarity, nor of the simple fact that it is not only within marriage that procreation can take place.

Nor is it within marriage only that personal fulfilment may be found (I think it would be odd if Shakespeare thought that it was).[37] Extramarital sexuality may be so severely punished in his society that it is not really worth the candle, but Shakespeare's plays register an acute awareness that human energies and desires need not be channelled exclusively into sexuality. Great emotional energy is invested by many of his characters in homosocial friendships and activity, as well as in the conventional arenas of politics, war and business, which are themselves largely dependent on homosocial interchange. I draw here on the work of Eve Kosofsky Sedgwick, but I want to give much greater emphasis than she does to the existence of homosocial elements in female as well as male same-sex relationships[38] – it is, after all, their shared experience of heterosexual marriage which to some extent empowers the strong homosocial bonds of Mistress Ford and Mistress Page, Titania and her 'votaress', and Hermione and Paulina; Linda Woodbridge points out the extent to which 'many Shakespearean women talk about men and sex when they are alone together'.[39] The pleasures of such bonding elements are vigorously conveyed in Shakespeare's plays, and it is here, indeed, that we perhaps most need to historicise, to recover the sense of a society with a far greater investment than our own in social groupings predicated on same-sex relationships. Initially, such links may seem to be threatened by marriage – such a fear is, indeed, expressly articulated by a number of characters, including Benedick in *Much Ado About Nothing*, Hermia in *A Midsummer Night's Dream* and Emilia in *The Two Noble Kinsmen* – but I want to argue that such homosocial bonds can negotiate the marriage tie with a striking degree of success. Homosociality, after all, depends precisely on a strongly drawn distinction between the sexes, and nothing can enforce that so strongly as the polarisation of sexual roles effected by marriage. Following partly from theories about the exchange of women – an element that is particularly pronounced in aristocratic marriages, with their stress on the bringing together of different political and kinship groupings[40] – I have tried to develop an argument that marriages in Shakespeare function not only, and perhaps not even primarily, to regulate relationships between the sexes, but also to regulate and facilitate relationships *within* same-sex groups, and to ensure the maintenance and perpetuation of the structures of civilised society as a whole. If this entails a loss of personal freedom and psychological security, that is a price that must be paid, just as an acute awareness of the tainted, provisional and problematic nature of authority must never be allowed to interfere with the workability of kingship, which is, in the end, consistently imaged as a better state of affairs than its alternatives.

Concomitantly, I shall read from a feminist perspective, not only because that is the result of my own personal positioning, and certainly not from an assumption that women's characters or issues associated with women are inherently more interesting than those to do with men, but because the woman is consistently the underexamined term in the plays' repeated instantiation of the status quo. To open up their workings, to read against the grain, requires a frequent focus on the female characters just as much as an examination of the representations of kingship would demand an equivalent probing of the subaltern figure. Ultimately, too, it is only by unlocking the issue of emotional satisfaction on which the comic structure attempts to foreclose, and which is habitually located in 'feminine' subjectivity, that we can begin to read the realm of the psychological at all. Once it is entered, the male characters too can begin to be read in a new light.

One marked cultural difference between our own society and Shakespeare's appears to be the obsessive Renaissance fear of sexual betrayal and of cuckoldry. Since this is no longer so widespread or so automatic a concern in male–female relationships, it can hardly be a 'natural' one. I shall suggest that it is not only a cultural construction, but one that is consistently perceived as such by Shakespeare. Ostensibly a story of uncontrollable male fear of female sexuality, the cuckold topos seems in his plays to take a very different form: it becomes, indeed, a story of an (ultimately controllable) male fear that women are actually averse to sex, and its comforting corollary, a mechanism for the production of male–male bonds which are stronger than those between men and women. It acts, therefore, as a double reassertion of the depth and ineradicability of gender difference. Apparently a troubling experience for men, sexual jealousy brings with it a psychological pay-off, reasserting the bonds of homosociality and essentially negating the fear that it itself enacts, that male identity can be compromised by female unreliability. Moreover, I shall argue that in his history plays in particular the marriage tie offers a psychologically compelling mechanism for bonding not only with one's contemporaries, but also with the lost, revered figure of the father, the ultimate authoriser of wedlock.

One final element of Shakespeare's representations of marriage is the absence of actresses from his stage. All his maids, widows, wives and whores were written to be played by boys. Various emphases have been given to this fact by recent critics, particularly when it comes to examining the several instances where Shakespeare employs the device of cross-dressing; indeed, it may stand as perhaps the example *par excellence* of the remarkable openness to interpretation of so many aspects of Shakespeare's text. Carol Rutter's study of modern actresses who have played Shakespearean heroines quotes Sinead Cusack as saying that 'any actress will find that whatever choice she makes, Shakespeare will help her to construct that interpretation', and it is notable that all the actresses Rutter interviews 'see Shakespeare's endings as "open", rather than "closed"'.[41] My own historical positioning as a child of the postmodern makes me acutely aware of the provisionality of all my readings of these texts, which can, ultimately, never be anything more than the product of that temporary marriage between my own preoccupations and what my cultural conditioning enables me to see in the plays. Nevertheless, it has been, for me, a happy, and I hope, a fruitful partnership.

1
Marriage as Comic Closure

The most outstanding feature of Shakespearean comedy is its pervading obsession with marriage. In many instances single or multiple marriages are used to provide comic closure, as in *As You Like It* and *Love's Labour's Lost*, in which four couples marry or are expected to marry, *A Midsummer Night's Dream* and *Twelfth Night*, in each of which three couples marry, and *Much Ado About Nothing* and *Two Gentlemen of Verona*, in each of which two couples marry. In other examples the very fact of marriage is used as the mainspring of the comedy, as in *The Merry Wives of Windsor*, where the very title of the play indicates the importance of marriage, or, to a lesser extent, *The Comedy of Errors*, *The Merchant of Venice* and *The Taming of the Shrew*, in each of which a marital relationship plays a central part. Indeed, marriage is so central a topic in Shakespearean comedy that it is the presence of marriages in their plots which has problematised the genre classifications of both the late romances and the two 'dark' comedies, *Measure for Measure* and *All's Well that Ends Well*, and which provides the main justification for whatever claim they are accorded to be treated as comedies.[1] We know, moreover, that many of Shakespeare's comedies bear clear marks of having been written expressly for performance as part of the celebrations surrounding the solemnisation of actual marriages, so that the connection would have been still more obvious to their original audiences.

But for all that the plays can indeed be grouped together with reasonable accuracy into these broad classifications, to do so obscures both some significant and some interesting differences between them, and also the problematic ways in which marriage is generally treated in these plays. For one thing, despite the traditional view that marriage provides comic closure, this is, in fact, very rarely achieved.[2] The idea is of course drawn on – the audience is repeatedly encouraged to expect that the proceedings will be appropriately closed with a wedding – but these expectations are then either disappointed, or gratified in such a way that the spectator will be forced to question both the meaning of the events he or she has witnessed and also the assumptions underlying his or her response to the events.

Marriage is appropriate as a provider of closure for comedy because it focuses primarily on the experience of the group, as opposed to the individualist, isolationist emphasis of tragedy. The tragic hero lives and dies a fundamentally lonely figure, traumatically separated from his God, his society and his surroundings. Marriage both counters this element of separation by showing humans in a relationship which is, in theory at least, one of indissoluble bonding, and also holds out the promise of renewed life in the birth of offspring (referred to both in the words of the marriage ceremony and in Elizabethan wedding customs, and assumed to be the inevitable product of all heterosexual intercourse).[3] The ultimate polar opposite of the tragic closure provided by death would of course be birth itself, which is indeed sometimes used in this symbolic sense (*All's Well that Ends Well* may be taken as an example of this); but birth, too, places primacy on the experience of the isolated individual, and the social ritual of marriage, with its stress on continuity and group survival, therefore provides a more effective counterbalance to the finality implied in the death of the tragic individual.

Such an emphasis on continuity is undoubtedly present in much of Shakespeare's work. It can be traced explicitly through the first 18 of his sonnets, and it can also be detected in Oberon's blessing of the bridal bed in *A Midsummer Night's Dream*, and in Rosalind's reference to Orlando, almost as soon as she sees him, as 'my child's father'.[4] It is also possible to discern in Shakespeare's comedies clear signs of the conservatism which is so often felt to flourish in comedy: the lovers in *A Midsummer Night's Dream* may flee from Athens at the outset of the play in rebellion against the patriarchal order articulated by Theseus and Egeus, but they do so only to find themselves in a wood ruled by a patriarch just as powerful (a point neatly made by the theatrical tradition of using the actor who plays Theseus to double Oberon), and at the end of the play the two couples willingly return to the society from which they had fled to take their allotted parts as leading members of it and, no doubt, to assist in its perpetuation. In similar fashion, Rosalind, Celia, Oliver and Orlando return from the Forest of Arden, where they had so briefly glimpsed a world in which traditional gender roles could be reversed and the patriarchal system of property division overturned by Oliver's renunciation of his patrimony in favour of

Orlando, to take their places in the hierarchy of the court; and in *The Two Gentlemen of Verona* the excursion into the forest of Valentine, Proteus, Silvia and Julia merely enables them to return to the city properly established as clearly defined couples. In *Hamlet* and *King Lear, Othello* and *Macbeth*, worlds may be broken and assumptions overturned; in the comic universe, however, the world not only remains fundamentally the same, but is indeed reinforced by the reaffirmation of that most basic of all props of social and patriarchal order, marriage.

Although these elements of conservatism may doubtless be traced, other factors, far more radical, are also at work. It is noteworthy that although single or multiple marriages are almost invariably the obvious goal of Shakespearean comedy and are clearly signalled from the outset, either by such transparent devices as the King of Navarre's misogyny,[5] which is clearly riding for a fall, or by the even more obvious sign of a crucially placed, slow-paced meeting between the hero and heroine such as that between Rosalind and Orlando, this expected telos is only very rarely attained within the confines of the play itself. The truism that Shakespeare's comedies all end with marriages is not true. There was of course no theoretical prescription that all comedies should end thus – indeed, comedy in general lacked a theory such as that supplied by Aristotle for tragedy – but there was nevertheless a growing tradition which established marriage as the goal at least of romantic comedy. That tradition Shakespeare habitually disrupts.

AS YOU LIKE IT

As You Like It may appear to contradict this assertion immediately, since it closes with not one but four weddings: those of Rosalind and Orlando, Celia and Oliver, Silvius and Phebe and Touchstone and Audrey.[6] But although the audience certainly perceives these couples as having been finally united and receives the appropriate sense of comic closure, the weddings do not take place on stage, or indeed within the timescale of the play at all. Rosalind and Celia are brought on to the stage by what the New Penguin editor terms 'a masquer representing Hymen'.[7] In the theatre this part is usually taken by the actor who plays Corin, one of the few named characters who does not have to appear on stage at this time; but there is some residual ambiguity about whether we are to perceive this as a metatheatrical doubling or one operating and acknowledged within the fictional world of the play – whether we are to see it as one actor doubling two parts which have no necessary connection between them other than the fact that they never appear on stage at the same time, or whether we are to assume that Rosalind and Celia, having no one else to whom they can turn, have taken Corin into their confidence and asked him to represent Hymen in the masque that they wish to stage.[8] Trivial though this point may seem, it may nevertheless be of some interest; if the masquer is obviously Corin in disguise, and is visibly perceived as such by the other characters on stage, then the whole affair is going to seem very much less mysterious than it might otherwise do. The supernatural elements which Rosalind has earlier tried to invoke with her claim to be the nephew of a magician will be at once debunked, and it will even be apparent to the quick-witted where Rosalind has been hiding all this time, and how the whole scene has been stage-managed. (That this *is* apparent to the characters seems clearly suggested by the fact that nobody ever troubles to explain it, and by Phebe's immediate exclamation 'If sight and shape be true, / Why then, my love adieu!') However, to have Corin taking part in a masque will provide a visual blending of country character with courtly form, offering an image of that utopian mingling of classes which Arden may initially have seemed to promise but which it has never, until now, achieved, so that a sense of magic lost in one area may perhaps be miraculously regained in another.

Whoever plays Hymen, however, one thing is certain: he is not competent to perform a marriage. Indeed he explicitly admits as much in his words to the Duke:

> Good Duke receive thy daughter,
> Hymen from heaven brought her,
>   Yea brought her hither,
> That thou mightst join her hand with his
> Whose heart within his bosom is.
>
> (V.IV.110–14)

The god of marriage, then, seems to be transferring his responsibilities to the Duke; but the Duke is no more able than he to conduct the ceremony. It would, of course, be normally expected that he would have to give his consent, but even that seems to be pre-empted when, immediately after Hymen's speech, Rosalind intervenes:

> *Rosalind* [*To the Duke.*] To you I give myself, for I am yours.
> [*To Orl.*] To you I give myself, for I am yours.
>
> (V.IV.115–16)

At the same time as she reinscribes herself within the patriarchal order by investing her rights in herself in her father, she also challenges it by asserting her desire for Orlando; Diane Elizabeth Dreher comments of this moment that 'discovering her animus or inner authority, she performs what has traditionally been the father's function, arranging her marriage and those of the other couples'.[9] Fortunately, the Duke is unlikely to prove a demanding father; he will accede happily to her wish to marry the son of his own old friend, and neither he nor the audience is liable to pick up on any potentially disturbing undercurrents in Rosalind's words. Unlike the story of Cordelia, where the divided selfhood which must attempt to please both father and husband becomes a source of anxiety, the emphasis here is less on the division implied by Rosalind's phrasing than on the reintegration and reconstitution of the family. The potential disharmony of the double promise is left unexplored. But it is there.

More obviously an issue, though, is that no one has come forward who has the authority to sanction and legitimate the weddings. As Celia says when Rosalind entreats her to conduct the mock marriage, 'I cannot say the words' (IV.I.121) – or rather, she can utter them, but in her mouth they have no performative validity. Diane Elizabeth Dreher feels that this exchange 'not only assures Rosalind of Orlando's love, but also approximates a legal marriage';[10] but this seems an odd view to take of it given Celia's own disclaimer of competence in the matter. Only a priest can speak the words of the marriage service, and priests in the forest are few and far between. Indeed clerics in general prove elusive in the play: there is the 'old religious man' who converts Duke Frederick, but his whereabouts are unknown, and there is Sir Oliver Martext, whom Richard Wilson sees as the outlaws' Friar Tuck,[11] but he, as Touchstone and Jaques agree, 'is not like to marry... well' (III.III.82–3). Just as in the mock marriage performed by Celia – which can indeed be read as foreshadowing this difficulty – so here at the time of the real marriage there is no-one who can say the words. Hymen's declaration that ' 'Tis I must make conclusion / Of these most strange events' (V.IV.125–6) has its claim to finality undercut when 170 lines later the Duke pronounces the end of the play proper with a rhyming couplet of his own: 'Proceed, proceed. We will begin these rites, / As we do trust they'll end, in true delights' (V.IV.196–7). Here, closure deconstructs itself with its emphasis on proceeding and beginning; and even this sense of beginning is in turn eroded by Rosalind's immediately following remark that 'It is not the fashion to see the lady the epilogue' (V.IV.198). Into this slippage of time, paradoxically caught between conclusions, beginnings and epilogues, the weddings themselves disappear. They have not been performed by the end of the play; and when Rosalind with her epilogue returns the audience to the real world of time, the play no longer has any future in which they could still take place. So although the marriages may be promised, implicit and assumed, they can never happen.

Moreover, the whole idea of marriage itself becomes an issue in the play. Touchstone has earlier attempted to disrupt the traditional pattern of comedy by having his marriage to Audrey performed in the very middle of the play (III.iii) but in fact his aim in attempting to arrange such a marriage is paradoxically not to achieve closure, but to leave open in his life possibilities which marriage is seen as precluding: Jacques exhorts him not to have his marriage performed by Sir Oliver Martext because 'This fellow will but join you together as they join wainscot; then one of you will prove a shrunk panel, and like green timber, warp, warp' (III.III.77–80). If marriage is traditionally used to achieve closure, then Touchstone's sentiments call into question the very possibility of such closure by his insinuation that marriages are prone to dissolution, and not just by the hand of God removing one of the partners.

Nor is Touchstone's an isolated perspective on his situation: Hymen sings ironically that he and Audrey are 'sure together / As the winter to foul weather' (V.IV.134–5), while Jacques tells him 'thy loving voyage / Is but for two months victuall'd' (V.IV.190–1). Granted that what is envisaged here is not so much divorce as squabbling within marriage (as Rosalind in more playful mood also forecasts for herself and Orlando [IV.I.135–54]), even so Touchstone's earlier resolution to be married by Sir Oliver has explictly addressed the question of termination of marriages, and it is even possible to see it hinted at when Orlando agrees to go through the mock-wedding ceremony with Ganymede 'now, as fast she can marry us' (IV.I.127), where 'fast' can be taken to refer not only to the speed but also to the validity of the ceremony. And of course another form of the dissolution of marriages is figured in the plot not only of this play alone but of virtually all Shakespeare's comedies: while both Rosalind and Celia have living fathers and Orlando has one who was alive recently enough for his memory to be green, no one in the play has a living mother.[12] The male partner, it seems, may survive after marriage, but the female partner has borne her children and then disappeared, her identity so utterly effaced that we do not even know what happened to her.[13] The implication may well be that within their marriages a similar fate may lurk to obliterate the vivacity even of a Rosalind or a Celia. Certainly, it would be possible to cast a sceptical eye over the likely effects on Phebe's health and life expectancy of the perpetual pregnancy and parturition forecast for her in Jacques' valediction to Silvius, 'You to a long and well-deserved bed' (V.IV.189).

But if a constant and life-threatening involvement in the processes of pregnancy and childbirth is the inevitable destiny of the married woman, the married man too has an unpleasant fate which he cannot avoid and which is repeatedly foreshadowed for him in the course of the play: cuckoldry. It forms the standard theme of Rosalind's teasing of Orlando: the snail, she tells him, brings its destiny with it, and when he inquires what that is she replies 'Why horns – which such as you are fain to be beholding to your wives for; but he comes armed in his fortune, and prevents the slander of his wife' (IV.I.56–9) – with perhaps an implication that even where cuckoldry itself is not present in a marriage, the rumour of it is bound to be. It is seen by Touchstone as not only unavoidable, but in some sense even acceptable:

As horns are odious, they are necessary. It is said, many a man knows no end of his goods. Right. Many a man has good horns and knows no end of them. Well, that is the dowry of his wife, 'tis none of his own getting. Horns? Even so. Poor men alone? No, no. The noblest deer hath them as huge as the rascal. Is the single man therefore blessed? No. As a walled town is more worthier than a village, so is the forehead of a married man more honourable than the bare brow of a bachelor; and by how much defence is better than no skill, by so much is a horn more precious than to want.

(III.III.45–57)

Indeed, as Touchstone has earlier pointed out, the very environment of the forest is full of reminders of cuckoldry: contemplating his imminent marriage, he remarks, 'A man may, if he were of a fearful heart, stagger in this attempt; for here we have no temple but the wood, no assembly but horn-beasts' (III.III.42–4).

This is a point raised again in the short and bizarre scene in which Jaques and the Lords celebrate the deer-killer with a song:

> *What shall he have that kill'd the deer?*
> *His leather skin and horns to wear.*
> *Then sing him home. The rest shall bear*
> *This burden.*
> *Take thou no scorn to wear the horn,*
> *It was a crest ere thou wast born.*
>   *Thy father's father wore it,*
>   *And thy father bore it.*
> *The horn, the horn, the lusty horn,*
> *Is not a thing to laugh to scorn.*

(IV.III.10–19)

The scene seems to be introduced solely to allow for the singing of this lyric, which, like Jaques' speech, both affirms and defuses the inevitability of cuckoldry by representing it as natural, figured even in the idyll of the pastoral by the horns of the deer, which become a badge of potency – the sign of the deer-killer – simultaneously with their more normal role as signifiers of shame. This song also, though, addresses one of the most fundamental of all aspects of cuckoldry, the threat it poses to the transmission of land and property from undoubted father to undoubted son. The spectre is raised in the sixth line ('it was a crest ere thou wast born') simultaneously evokes the pride of ancestry symbolised by heraldry, and casts doubt on the line of descent by associating birth and cuckoldry so intimately. However, the threat has no sooner been raised than it is triumphantly defused: the fear of not being able to identify the father is countered with the assurance that in this matter all fathers are alike – all are cuckolds. A kind of collective identity is thus asserted which can take precedence over the ultimately unknowable individual identity of any one father. Male bonding has triumphed over the apparent threat to patriarchal and class power posed by women's sexual infidelity.[14]

As You Like It does, indeed, then, take marriage as a central theme; but just as the structural patterning of the play resists closure, so does the apparent ideological fixity of the meaning of marriage itself break down under the pressure of the meanings imposed on it by the play. Even the play's Edenic overtones work ultimately to undermine the stability of the marital ideal that is apparently held up at its end: for all the return to a prelapsarian state in the duchy (a theme obviously signalled by Adam's name), this is an Eden with a snake, and, moreover, a lioness (interestingly changed from a lion in Shakespeare's source);[15] and if the couples at the end in any sense figure Adam and Eve, they must equally image the collapse of the pastoral ideal and of marital harmony which was to occur in that first of all marriages. Rather than a device to close the play securely, to ensure female subordination to patriarchal power and to secure the transmission of property between members of the elite, marriage is revealed as allowing interference with all three elements. But while the male characters of the play seem able to accept and even to embrace these contradictions within marriage, for the female characters the absence of mothers – the fact that the previous generation of married women have apparently vanished without trace – postulates a less hopeful future.

A MIDSUMMER NIGHT'S DREAM

In *A Midsummer Night's Dream* the difference in the nature of the experiences offered by marriage to men and to women is signalled right at the outset, in the opening dialogue between Theseus and Hippolyta. The couple seem to be united in their eagerness for the approach of their ensuing wedding:

> *The.* Now, fair Hippolyta, our nuptial hour
> Draws on apace; four happy days bring in
> Another moon: but O, methinks, how slow
> This old moon wanes! She lingers my desires,
> Like to a step-dame or a dowager

Long withering out a young man's revenue.
Hip. Four days will quickly steep themselves in night;
Four nights will quickly dream away the time;
And then the moon, like to a silver bow
New bent in heaven, shall behold the night
Of our solemnities.[16]

In fact, Hippolyta's lines are susceptible of a very different interpretation, as was shown by the way that Penny Downie played the role at Stratford-upon-Avon in 1982. Her Hippolyta was a deeply reluctant, indeed sullen, bride: her statements that the time would pass quickly were motivated not by joy but by a disempowered acceptance of the inevitable, and her flat future tenses, without any use of the optative, reflected this sense of despairing entrapment.

Such a reading also serves to highlight the fact that Theseus insistently perceives all the blocking figures to their marriage as female. He alludes, in turn, to the moon (most usually figured in Elizabethan discourse in her classical personae as Cynthia, Diana, Dictynna or Artemis, and as such associated with the Virgin Queen herself), a stepdame and a dowager.[17] Hippolyta, in marked contrast, concurs in imaging the moon as female, but views it as a symbol of empowerment, a representation of the 'bow' (I.I.9) which was once her weapon. Theseus' assumptions are even more remarkable in a play where the blocking figures are in fact uniformly male – Egeus, who objects to his daughter's marriage, and, arguably, Oberon, though, like Theseus, he himself constructs the cause of the quarrel between the fairies as the opposition of Titania – and where the women tend to be unusually powerless for representatives of the comic feminine.[18] But if the plot of the play minimises the power of women, its imagery maximises it, and concomitantly figures men as weakened, clearly suggesting a deep-rooted fear, as in Titania's elegiac comment that 'the green corn / Hath rotted ere his youth attained a beard' (II.I.94–5). Even the play-within-the-play may encode a fearful female. 'Ninny's tomb' may be funny, but it also memorialises Ninus, King of Assyria, whose wife, as Sir David Lindsay of the Mount recorded in his attack on female rulers, was the 'proude and presumptious' Semiramis,[19] who is one of the examples Lindsay cites to prove the innate unfitness of women to occupy posts of power.

The idea briefly indicated in Hippolyta's speech that women may be unwilling to marry recurs throughout the play.[20] In many of Shakespeare's romantic comedies, the women are seen as being very actively in search of a husband: Viola has barely landed in Illyria before she is enquiring about Orsino's marital status, Olivia rapidly proposes marriage to the supposed Cesario, and Feste is able to tease Maria by alluding to the possibility of Sir Toby marrying her; both Julia and Silvia in *The Two Gentlemen of Verona* actively seek their lovers out, and Rosalind in *As You Like It* effectively engineers her own marriage when Orlando, blinded by her male disguise, does not take the initiative. In *A Midsummer Night's Dream*, Helena does indeed actively pursue Demetrius, but whereas the other heroines who do this are presented as spirited and determined, and invariably preserve their dignity and their self-respect, she is seen as merely ridiculous:

> I am your spaniel; and, Demetrius,
> The more you beat me, I will fawn on you.
> Use me but as your spaniel, spurn me, strike me,
> Neglect me, lose me; only give me leave,
> Unworthy as I am, to follow you.
> What worser place can I beg in your love –
> And yet a place of high respect with me –
> Than to be used as you use your dog?
>
> (II.I.203–10)

Titania, who (although for very different reasons) similarly pays court to the man of her choice, is equally seen as a butt of jokes. Far more popular, both with the men of the play and generally with audiences and critics, is Hermia, who, unlike the majority of Shakespeare's heroines, shows a distinct concern for propriety – 'Nay, good Lysander; for my sake, my dear, / Lie further off yet; do not lie so near' (II.II.42–3). In fact, if Hermia and Lysander had decided to perform a contract of *per verba de futuro* in front of a witness such as Helena and had then consummated their marriage in the woods, it would have become immediately legal; but that is never suggested, and Hermia's behaviour is presented instead as the polar opposite to Helena's. When attitudes such as this are highlighted, the decision to set the opening scene of the 1982 Stratford-upon-Avon production in the Victorian period becomes a highly suitable one.

Hermia's concern to protect her virginity has previously gone even further, when, unamazed by the choice she is offered between enforced marriage, execution, and the cloister, she unhesitatingly chooses the lifelong chastity of sisterhood rather than marriage with Demetrius.[21] Here, of course, her decision is perfectly understandable, since the partner offered her is one she has no liking for; but taken along with other instances of women not wishing to marry or to live within marital relationships in the play, it may nevertheless be seen as significant. Titania may be eager enough for Bottom, but she is undergoing what seems to be an effective separation from her 'lord' Oberon; and whatever Hippolyta's feelings for Theseus may be now, we are told clearly enough what they must have been initially when Theseus reminds her 'Hippolyta, I woo'd thee with my sword, / And won thy love doing thee injuries' (I.I.16–17). Moreover, the play even includes more or less direct reference to that ultimate refuser of marriage, 'the imperial votress' (II.I.163) herself, Elizabeth I, whose decision to remain single had given rise to the cult of the Virgin Queen.[22]

As if this were not enough, the play clearly warns of the possible dangers of marriage: a wife risks quarrels and the curbing of her will, such as occurs in the relationship of Titania and Oberon, and death in childbirth, as happens to the mother of the changeling boy; or her children may be deformed – although the fairies promise that this will not happen to any of the couples in the play, their mere mention of deformity nevertheless serves to confirm it as a real possibility.[23] This last is an issue that would affect the husband too, and the death of both Pyramus and Thisbe in the mechanicals' playlet could perhaps serve as a reminder that love offers perils for both sexes. Nevertheless, neither Demetrius nor Lysander is threatened with anything like the dreadful choice that is offered to Hermia, and both Theseus and Oberon end the play with very much the upper hand in their relationships: Titania has been thoroughly humiliated by the discovery of her love for an ass (an ironic and radically reductive rewriting of Theseus' much more heroic adventures with the Minotaur), and Theseus at the banquet firmly overrules Hippolyta's distaste for the mechanicals' play with her first lesson in theatre criticism and public behaviour (V.I.89–105).

Moreover, in this play too the marriages do not provide closure by occurring at the end of the play.[24] Almost all the plot material has been used up by the opening of Act V: Titania and Oberon are reconciled, the lovers have come together in mutually agreeable couples, returned to the city and been reconciled with Theseus and

Egeus, Bottom has been transformed back to his normal shape, and all that remains is for the mechanicals to perform their play. We may perhaps wonder to what extent the fairies Titania and Oberon can be considered bound by the human rite of marriage at all – especially since each accuses the other of having effectively conducted an open relationship. As for the marriages of the mortals, they appear to have taken place between IV.I and V.I: in the first of these scenes Theseus announces that 'in the temple by and by with us / These couples shall eternally be knit', and in the second all are looking forward to the advent of the evening which will allow them to consummate the marriages. It would in fact be perfectly possible in narrative terms to end the play after Act IV.I.

What comes after that point is obviously important in terms of providing a suitably celebratory finale, but it offers too a comment on what has occurred. The tragic story of Pyramus and Thisbe may serve to remind us how very easily the events of the play could have developed along the lines of *Romeo and Juliet*; the fairies' final benediction can be seen as indicating how much such a blessing may be needed. Marriage then is not seen as some sort of transcendental signifier which automatically confers meaning on events: its own meaning is open to probing and exploration. Even when closure does finally occur, its meaning is unmade even as it is made:

> If we shadows have offended,
> Think but this, and all is mended,
> That you have but slumber'd here
> While these visions did appear.
> And this weak and idle theme,
> No more yielding but a dream,
> Gentles, do not reprehend:
> If you pardon, we will mend.
> And, as I am an honest Puck,
> If we have unearned luck
> Now to 'scape the serpent's tongue,
> We will make amends ere long;
> Else the Puck a liar call.
> So, goodnight unto you all.
> Give me your hands, if we be friends,
> And Robin shall restore amends.
>
> (V.I.409–24)

Puck's paradoxes both return the play to the real world and, at the same time as they offer a final comment on the play, they deny the possibility of making any such comment at all, since the making of meaning must finally be in our hands. In offering itself for approval the play finally abdicates control over its own authority; and thus, although it has been careful to present itself as an ostensible celebration of marriage, the diametrical antithesis of the 'some satire, keen and critical, / Not sorting with a nuptial ceremony' (V.I.54–5) which Theseus fears, it ultimately acknowledges that the meaning-making audience is equally free to construct out of it as potentially subversive a critique as it wishes of contemporary marriage, and, above all, of the role of women within it. As Christopher Brooke, in his history of marriage, observes of the idea that *A Midsummer Night's Dream* was an occasional play feting an actual wedding, 'I am glad it was not my wedding it celebrated, for it proceeds by showing us the lowest view of human marriage we have so far encountered'.[25]

If both *As You Like It* and *A Midsummer Night's Dream* seem to offer sympathy for the position of women within marriage, it must not be forgotten that the issue of men's role within marriage has, even if only marginally, also been addressed in them.[26] In *The Two Gentlemen of Verona*, as later in *The Merry Wives of Windsor* where Herne the Hunter functions as a recuperative figure in exactly the same way as the horn song does, this becomes of far greater importance.

THE TWO GENTLEMEN OF VERONA

In *The Two Gentlemen of Verona*, the character who in many ways appears the most vulnerable is not Valentine, whose good faith leads him into banishment, nor Silvia, distressed and frightened though she undoubtedly is by the attempted rape, nor even Julia, forced to witness the faithlessness and villainy of her lover, but Proteus himself, the man who causes the suffering of all of them. Proteus says of himself, 'I do as truly suffer, / As e'er I did commit'.[27] These lines, and Proteus' part in general in this scene, have often been considered badly underwritten, but Barry Lynch's moving delivery in the 1991 Swan Theatre production by David Thacker at Stratford-upon-Avon showed that they can in fact be seen as more than adequate to the situation, since what they suggest is that Proteus' own suffering is directly proportional to that experienced by all the other three lovers in combination. Indeed, it could even be argued that he has undergone more than they have had to do: for whereas they have throughout the play been firmly locked into stable, unshakeable identities, Proteus has undergone a most violent and radical attack on his very sense of selfhood, bordering almost on what might now be termed a form of schizophrenia.

This is seen clearly in II, VI, where, like Richard III before Bosworth, Proteus effectively falls apart. Given, in modern editions, the whole scene to himself, he soliloquises:

> I cannot leave to love; and yet I do;
> But there I leave to love, where I should love.
> Julia I lose, and Valentine I lose;
> If I keep them, I needs must lose myself;
> If I lose them, thus find I by their loss:
> For Valentine, myself; for Julia, Silvia.
> I to myself am dearer than a friend,
> For love is still most precious in itself,
> And Silvia (witness heaven, that made her fair)
> Shows Julia but a swarthy Ethiope.
>
> (II.VI.17–26)

Underlying the apparent arrival at a decision here is a terrifying sense of the dizzying relativity of all available senses of identity. The first line sets up a logical impossibility which the balanced syntax can do no more than leave as paradox. It may be glossed over by the sophistry of the second, but that also introduces another, equally worrying, idea: 'I' is no longer absolute, standing unbounded as subject of the sentence, but modified and compromised by its physical location – 'there', 'where'.

'I' finds itself even further destabilised in the third line when both Julia and Valentine successively usurp the apparent subject position of their respective phrases, and in the fourth line the issue is explicitly addressed when Proteus admits to himself the awful possibility that he may 'lose myself'. This is hastily dismissed when a swift change of object alters the situation to losing not himself but 'them' – a safely demonised, externalised group which leaves his own sense of identity apparently unthreatened and intact. But

Proteus, as his Protean name suggests, has exposed a far more radical possibility than that of simple self-loss: lurking behind the exchange of persons which he now proposes is the spectre that he may have no self to lose. If Julia can replace Silvia and Proteus Valentine, and if Julia's former self is indeed modified and devalued by the mere existence of Silvia, as suggested in the two closing lines, then in what sense can any of these people be presented as a 'self'? In this sense Proteus' 'I do as truly suffer / As e'er I did commit' is a statement which is both admirably expressive and a profound psychological restorative, for in it he has finally achieved an assertion of the coherence of the two parts of his previously shattered self: what 'I' has done, 'I' is also paying for, and the payment is small price for the reintegration of self which the language enables him to assert. Looked at in this light, the 'marriage' which seals the end of the play is less one between Proteus and Julia than between Proteus and his estranged selfhood, or perhaps with Julia as a manifestation of that former, regretted state of psychological unity.

The play does end with the promise of other, more conventional marriages. Valentine assures his regained friend:

> Come, Proteus, 'tis your penance but to hear
> The story of your loves discovered.
> That done, our day of marriage shall be yours,
> One feast, one house, one mutual happiness.

(V.IV.168–71)

All is apparently well that ends well, and Valentine's extraordinary offer of his own interest in Silvia to Proteus could also be read as indicating that the friendship of the two gentlemen will, despite all the strains to which it has been subject, survive and even prosper. Nevertheless the darker notes are there. The ring which Julia produces as a token both of her own identity and of Proteus' former affection for her may serve to remind us that bonds sealed by rings have been broken before and could be again. Moreover, while the two women have shown themselves eager for marriage throughout the play, the behaviour of both Proteus and Valentine can be seen as registering a rather more ambivalent attitude. When we first meet them, in I.I, love is already a force which threatens to pull their friendship apart: Proteus will stay at home because of it, losing the chance of adventures and finding himself separated from his friend. And it remains throughout the play the single greatest threat to male bonding, not only disrupting the relationship of Proteus and Valentine but also falsifying and eventually undermining their interactions with the male authority figure, the Duke.

It would be plausible to see Proteus' sudden switch to Silvia as operating effectively as a continuation of that movement away from love which has already been inaugurated by his decision to leave Julia: subconsciously, he has chosen the most inaccessible of all possible females, the beloved of his friend. It is a move guaranteed to precipitate the crisis which has until now been only latent, to force a radical choice between the two parts of his fissured identity. As in *The Two Noble Kinsmen*, so much later in Shakespeare's career, what we see here is the crippling psychological cost in terms of the loss of personal and social selfhood which men may fear will be the price of marriage.[28]

Another fear, too, can be seen as lying behind both this play and others of Shakespeare's apparently 'happy' comedies. Finding himself unable to persuade Silvia to yield to his advances, Proteus decides to rape her. This is not only his own lowest psychological point; it is also devastatingly revealing about his attitude to marriage. Obviously no modern feminist can admit any sort of defence of his act, but it may be possible to look at in a light rather different from that in which it is customarily considered. If Proteus himself regards marriage as a threatening, dangerous state, he might well project such feelings of reluctance onto his female partner – and this could lead him to regard not only Silvia but *all* women as quite simply needing to be raped in order to make marriage possible at all. We can read his action less as an individual, isolated act of violation than as the emblem of his views of all relationships, in which either others or the self must always be lost; in one sense, it is himself that he tries to rape. The idea of female reluctance to marry, which had figured so threateningly in *A Midsummer Night's Dream*, thus recurs here, raising the question of whether it could be that the universal assumption of women's desire to cuckold their husbands by incessant sex actually masks in general the repression of a deeper fear too threatening even to voice – that female participation in sex is reluctant.

Frigid women, who are at the same time impossible to keep chaste; fragmented men in danger of losing their selves, their honour and their friends; incompetent or unavailable priests and defective ceremonies; savage uncivilised settings in which wild beasts roam as the fitting emblem of the human condition – the makings of marriage in Shakespearean comedy are not promising ones. But it is, of course, precisely the innate instability of its personnel and character that make the institution such a vital one. The radical fissuring that splits selves and societies can be kept from cracking only by the constant repetition and reduplication of social and ideological bonds that marriage alone is seen as capable of providing, forming as it does the one framework in which the behaviour of each partner is constantly visible, constantly subject to policing by the other. The Shakespearean 'happy' comedies do not celebrate marriage: they reveal its crucial functioning in the maintenance of society and also the internal stresses and contradictions to which it is constantly subject – an instability instanced by the repeated structural decentring of marriage from its supposed position of comic closure. And contrary to so much of the misogyny and the marital ideology of the time, they powerfully reveal that outside the institution of marriage both men and women are adrift, while inside it both must pay a high price for their security.

2
Marriage in the Middle

If some of Shakespeare's romantic comedies ostensibly hold out marriage as a comic closure and then in fact fail to provide it, others of them more seriously disrupt the expected pattern by having it take place too long before the end to provide a proper termination of events. Very early marriages can be found in *All's Well that Ends Well*, *The Taming of the Shrew*, *The Merchant of Venice* and in *Twelfth Night* (Olivia and Sebastian, and, although we are not aware of it, Maria and Sir Toby too are married well before the end); and in each case, form is tied closely to content as Shakespeare uses the unconventional structure of the play to mirror the unconventionality of the relationships he depicts in them. In two further plays, *The Merry Wives of Windsor* and *The Comedy of Errors*, marriage can be said to provide formal closure without being the main focus of emotional release, since in each case it is a subsidiary couple who marry at the end rather than one of the character-groupings on whom our main interest has been focused.

TWELFTH NIGHT

Formal unconventionality is perhaps most blatantly apparent in *Twelfth Night*. When Olivia proposes to Sebastian she not only inverts the normal gender roles which, as Helena reminds Demetrius in *A Midsummer Night's Dream*, require female passivity and male initiative; she also makes a nonsense of the whole issue of consent, so crucial in sixteenth-century marriage theory, when she marries a man about whose identity she is mistaken. When we first see Olivia, on Viola's initial visit to her, she is veiled; now it is Sebastian who is, metaphorically, veiled, concealed behind the fictive, sketchily developed (in Olivia's eyes, at least) persona of Cesario. The legality of the ceremony is stressed – Olivia, unlike Rosalind, provides a priest and a chantry (Juliet Dusinberre suggests that 'Shakespeare smiles at Olivia, wedding in the chapel she used for mourning'),[1] and the priest is careful to point out the unquestionable legitimacy of the proceedings:

> A contract of eternal bond of love,
> Confirm'd by mutual joinder of your hands,
> Attested by the holy close of lips,
> Strengthen'd by interchangement of your rings,
> And all the ceremony of this compact
> Seal'd in my function, by my testimony...[2]

Nevertheless, this, perhaps the most pointedly proper and complete marriage ceremony in the Shakespearean canon, sits oddly alongside the confusions and uncertainties surrounding the actual identities of the participants, never mind their motivations and the extent of their commitment.

Olivia, already anomalous in exercising sole rule over a household containing men who are awkwardly and unhappily dependent on her, becomes doubly so when she explicitly defines Orsino as the ideal of Renaissance manhood but enfolds her very eulogy within a double rejection of this paragon:

> Your lord does know my mind, I cannot love him.
> Yet I suppose him virtuous, know him noble,
> Of great estate, of fresh and stainless youth;
> In voices well divulg'd, free, learn'd, and valiant,
> And in dimension, and the shape of nature,
> A gracious person. But yet I cannot love him.
>
> (I.V.261–6)

She finds herself, instead, attracted to the androgynous figure of Viola-as-Cesario, of whom Orsino has so recently offered a word-picture of his own:

> For they shall yet belie thy happy years,
> That say thou art a man; Diana's lip
> Is not more smooth and rubious: thy small pipe
> Is as the maiden's organ, shrill and sound,
> And all is semblative a woman's part.
>
> (I. IV.30–4)

Stephen Greenblatt comments tellingly of the androgyny of both twins that '[w]ith a change of a few conventional signals, the exquisitely feminine Viola and the manly Sebastian are indistinguishable',[3] and Olivia's choice of Cesario over the fully manly Orsino must surely raise questions about both her sexuality and the extent to which she proposes to play the properly subordinate role of a wife, especially given the conclusion of her initial exchange with Sebastian:

> Olivia. Nay, come, I prithee; would thou'dst be ruled by me!
> Seb. Madam, I will.
> Olivia.   O, say so, and so be.
> (IV.II.64–6)

The word 'rule', Sebastian's use of 'Madam' and Olivia's final double imperative all serve to underline the inequality of power which structures this relationship.

A similar issue of status is raised by the marriage between Sir Toby Belch and Maria. The question of hypergamy – marrying above one's class – is comparatively rare in Shakespeare's plays, but *Twelfth Night* is steeped in it.[4] It is, however briefly, Olivia's first concern on finding herself in love with Cesario – 'Unless the master were the man' (I.V.298). It is the entire point of the trick played on Malvolio, as well as of the obscure episode of 'the Lady of the Strachy' and 'the yeoman of the wardrobe' (II.V.39–40). Indeed it is Maria's success in engineering the humbling of Malvolio's pretensions in this respect that proves, ironically, to be directly responsible for her own social elevation: as Fabian explains,

> Maria writ
> The letter, at Sir Toby's great importance,
> In recompense whereof he hath married her.
> (V.I.361–3)

'Importance' here means 'importunity'; but it also carries an echo of the superior social status which is what makes marriage to an impoverished sot a reward for a clever woman like Maria. It is the social, rather than the affective, importance of marriage which is here given sharp prominence.

Both of these elements are present in the strangely protracted proposal of Orsino to Viola. Its probable imminence is first signalled immediately after the revelation of her true identity:

> *Duke.* Boy, thou hast said to me a thousand times
> Thou never should'st love woman like to me.
> *Viola.* And all those sayings will I over-swear
> And all those swearings keep as true in soul
> As doth that orbed continent the fire
> That severs day from night.
> *Duke.*   Give me thy hand,
> And let me see thee in thy woman's weeds.
>
> (V. I.264–71)

It is perhaps a mark of Orsino's residual confusion over Viola's gender that it is she who is required to reaffirm her affection by producing the discourse of Petrarchan love. She does so rather weakly: her principal tool is repetition, and she is then driven to a rather jarring image of perpetual polarisation rather than of unity or harmony. Orsino also strikes a tentative note: 'Give me thy hand' seems to presage a betrothal, but he follows it merely with a request to see her in her female clothing. This perhaps suggests an indication that it is taking him time to adjust; equally, it could be read as implying a desire to be sure that he will find her sexually attractive, as when Othello reads the state of Desdemona's hand as an index of her sexuality.

Orsino's uncertainty also seems signalled by the fact that, although socially the most important person in the company, he does not speak again for 41 lines, and when he finally does, it is only to offer a one-line comment on Malvolio's letter. Soon after that, however, he finds his tongue again, when he responds to Olivia's proffered hospitality with:

> Madam, I am most apt t'embrace your offer.
> [*To Viola*] Your master quits you; and for your service done him,
> So much against the mettle of your sex,
> So far beneath your soft and tender breeding,
> And since you call'd me master for so long,
> Here is my hand; you shall from this time be
> Your master's mistress.
>
> (V.I.319–25)

If the language of sexuality was perhaps discernible behind Orsino's desire to see Viola dressed as a woman, it is clearly audible here, in 'sex', 'soft' and 'tender'. Equally clearly present, though, is the language of status. The last word of Olivia's speech, which immediately preceded this one, was 'cost'; and it is at this formal level of settlements and practicalities that Orsino is operating here. Olivia is 'madam'; Viola, for the first time, is 'you' throughout the speech, rather than 'thou', and the emphasis is on the repeated status denotations of 'master' and 'mistress'. And after that come nearly 60 lines more of silence from Orsino (as well as Viola and Sebastian), while Olivia attends to questions of practicalities and arbitration, before he departs with his closing couplet, 'But when in other habits you are seen, / Orsino's mistress, and his fancy's queen' (V.I.386–7). 'Fancy' may speak of an emotional response, but both 'mistress' and 'queen' remind us of the social structures within which it is contained. Here, as with Maria and Sir Toby, it is the social and not the personal aspect of marriage which is uppermost in Orsino's mind.

There can, however, be no doubt that there does exist a profoundly important personal relationship between himself and Viola. However stilted their expressions of emotion may be in the final scene, they have in the past both talked the language of love in each other's presence with impressive eloquence:

> *Duke.* There is no woman's sides
> Can bide the beating of so strong a passion
> As love doth give my heart; no woman's heart
> So big to hold so much: they lack retention...
>
> (II.IV.94–7)
>
> *Viola.* A blank, my lord: she never told her love,
> But let concealment like a worm i'the bud
> Feed on her damask cheek.
>
> (II.IV.111–13)

In these moments of (apparently) homosocial companionship, unfettered by external constraints, their relationship has flowered. Marriage may provide a socially and dramatically acceptable framework for what lies between them, but it will also impose new constraints on them. By the same token, however, marriage may provide an acceptable veil for Olivia's dominance, but her volubility in the final scene, in strong contrast to the virtual silence of both Orsino and Sebastian, suggests that whatever the public expectations of the relationship, the private dynamic will remain largely unaltered. Eric Mallin notes that 'in *Twelfth Night* women are, for once in Shakespeare, portrayed not as trivial, enervated, or emasculating figures but as pleasurably forceful practitioners of their complicated wills', and this certainly aptly characterises the probable attitude of Olivia and indeed of Maria, even within marriage.[5] Those of us with romantic inclinations can only hope that the same will hold true for Viola and Orsino, and that what the structural dislocation of Olivia's and Sebastian's marriage to an earlier part of the play has enabled us to judge is precisely the effect of time (albeit brief) and publicity on personal interplay. Certainly the surprise announcement of Sir Toby's marriage to Maria points out the often oblique connection between private dynamic and public perception of it; and it also suggests the accommodating nature of marriage in this play – with that unusual emphasis on hypergamy – where so many kinds of relationship can be successfully accepted by the community even when it has neither engineered nor even predicted them.[6]

In that sense, then, marriage in *Twelfth Night* provides not a sense of closure in terms of the development of a relationship, but more of an indication of points at which personal investments and achievements can be rendered publicly known and accepted. Indeed, the play in general repeatedly eschews and deconstructs the very concept of closure. Ejner Jensen points out that 'Viola recounts the history of her father's daughter, who "never told her love", but breaks off her account rather than respond to Orsino's desire to learn the story's closure'.[7] Moreover, the story itself gestures towards the possibilities of both death and marriage as available resolutions, and in the play as a whole the ostensible teleology of marriage in insistently shadowed by an almost equal emphasis on mortality. Even death proves not to provide an absolute ending when we are reminded of the bewildering possibility of potential afterlives – Olivia's brother may have gone to heaven, but Feste demands that Malvolio subscribe to the theory of transmigration of souls. What is created here is a sense that marriage need not be the only thinkable ending even of comedy, and that may pose not so much a threat as a sense of potential, of a genuine fluidity and capacity for variation in human destiny.

Most notable of all, perhaps, is the fact that here, unlike *As You Like It* or the problem plays, no cloud of prophecy or punishment hangs over any of the marriages (Sir Toby's feelings are not related, but we know that his act was voluntary), and the fact that Malvolio departs both unmarried (contrary to his hopes) and unreconciled may well encourage us to think that in *Twelfth Night* to achieve a marriage is, above all, to find a means of full and successful integration into the community. Such will certainly be the case for both Viola and Sebastian: landless aliens, each has used marriage as a direct route to participation in Illyrian society. Indeed, we may pehaps read such a motive as the most likely explanation for Sebastian's eager accession to Olivia's wishes, since his name and Antonio's had homosexual connotations and the strongly homoerotic nature of Antonio's language to him might initially seem to imply that there are some relationships which must always lie outside the social sanction and protection offered by marriage. And yet even there, the suggestion of perversity in the relationships between mannish Olivia and homoeroticised Sebastian, and between cross-dressed Viola and passive Orsino, may imply, once again, how much of diversity can, in this play at least, be happily allowed for within the accommodating framework of marriage, which can function as structure of enablement as well as of schematisation.

THE TAMING OF THE SHREW

There is far less sense of tolerance in the play which, at first sight, seems to be the polar opposite of *Twelfth Night*, *The Taming of the Shrew*. Here, too, the marriage takes place unusually early – in III. II – but there the similarities seem to end: driven by social and financial imperatives rather than erotic or affective ones, the inhabitants of Padua and the numerous visitors to it may initially seem to show little trace of personal feeling of any kind. Nevertheless, there have been insistent critical moves to read the play in the light of a theory of significantly differentiated public and private codes of behaviour: Kate is not really crushed, but has learned the code of public conformity, though it will actually be largely irrelevant in what Marianne Novy, for one, sees as the unusual privacy of her marriage.[8] Marriage would be an accommodating institution indeed according to this reading, since it would in effect be functioning as a site of opposition to patriarchal ideology while masquerading as its mainstay; alternatively, of course, to adopt a kind of New Historicist approach, one could more cynically argue that the ending reveals a telling contrast between the enormous change required of Kate and the relatively tiny size of the concession that the patriarchy has made in order to ensure its untroubled continuation. Other readers and audiences have found the play less easy to recuperate even within these strictly limited terms: a famous production had its Kate prostrate in a nervous breakdown at the end of her final speech, while the male spectators looked on in horror at the devastation they had wrought.

However one wishes to read the reasons for the changes in the behaviour of Katherine, the play makes it quite clear that, whatever her own intentions, her submission to Petruchio must of its very nature be a qualified one. The turning-point in her attitude is often traced to IV. I, when she drops her resistance to calling the moon the sun:

> Then, God be blest, it is the blessed sun.
> But sun it is not, when you say it is not,
> And the moon changes even as your mind.
> What you will have it nam'd, even that it is,
> And so it shall be so for Katherine.
> *Hor.* Petruchio, go thy ways, the field is won.[9]

The victory, however, is a Pyrrhic one. It is often suggested that Petruchio teaches Katherine to perceive his own centrality by recognising an equation between the sun and his mother's son,[10] but his lesson may equally be taken as not only the essential interchangeability of moon and sun, but also, by analogy, the male and female genders of which they are the prime symbols, and the extent to which gender difference is constructed by language, whose operations are here exposed as arbitrary. The point is made more acutely when Petruchio follows this initial triumph by making Katherine call Vincentio 'woman' and 'man' by turns, suggesting even more strongly the absence of that absolute distinction on which the subordination of women is predicated. It is an odd way for a patriarch to proceed. It is worth noting, too, that though many male-dominated societies are often said to be structured on a pattern of bonds created through an exchange of women, social life in Padua, despite its conformity to this pattern in some respects, is also notably underpinned by a system of exchange of *men*. Petruchio's gift to Baptista to inaugurate his courtship is Hortensio, in disguise as Licio; the supposed Lucentio's offering is the real Lucentio, disguised as Cambio, meaning essentially 'Change', and still used today for the Italian equivalent of a *bureau de change* – a name which makes quite obvious his status as token of exchange as well as concealed wooer. There is even a similar tone in Petruchio's bald statement that 'You knew my father well, and in him me' (II.I.116).

Similarly, the effect of Kate's final speech is fissured by a sharp tension between content and form. *What* she says is irreproachable; but the very fact that she *does* say it, at such length, and in public too, is, however licensed by her husband, at one level at least, subversive.[11] Cordelia in the same situation chose silence; Kate – typically perhaps – proselytises. Even in her meekness, she is not meek. Katherine may have been tamed, but she has, very pointedly, not been silenced; indeed she has just been given the longest speech in the play. It may seem a particularly savage irony that her reward for her obedience should be sex – 'Come, Kate, we'll to bed' (V.II.185) – but it would be worth remembering that, in terms of Elizabethan ideologies, she is being offered first, sexual pleasure, second, the indisputable, public affirmation of her marriage (and hence her status) as a married woman, and third, in terms of the persistent Elizabethan equation of sexual activity and conception, motherhood, which will function as an independent extension and development of her identity. Since she has, additionally, just been listing the material benefits of being a wife, it might seem, pragmatically speaking, that it is not a bad bargain in exchange for a few words – though for me, with my modern feminist sensibilities, it is one I could never make.[12]

However uncertain the precise tenor of the ending, Shakespeare seems to be much less equivocal about one aspect of the play: the nature of the arrangement of and preparations for marriage. From the outset, we are made aware of the strict conventions governing this, as Baptista is adamant that he will not 'bestow my youngest daughter / Before I have a husband for the elder' (I.I.50–1), and the emphasis on proper procedure is maintained as Petruchio and Baptista clarify the details of Katherine's dowry and (exceptionally generous) jointure (II.I.120–7), and Tranio and Gremio bid for Bianca's (II.I.335–90).[13] There seems even to be a reference (unusual in Shakespeare) to the necessity for being married within the canonical hours in Petruchio's warning, 'The morning wears, 'tis time we were at church' (III.II.109).

Within this context, we are made sharply aware of the very marked contrast not only between the personalities of Katherine and her sister Bianca, but between the way they approach the question of matrimony. Though – or indeed perhaps partly because – Petruchio's motives are avowedly mercenary, he works very much within the patriarchal system: 'I know her father, though I know not her, / And he knew my deceased father well' (I.II.100–1). Moreover, his determination to valorise Baptista and his will pays immediate dividends, since it procures him for a position of quasi-heroism within a group of men to whom he would otherwise be utterly unknown:

> *Tra.* If it be so, sir, that you are the man
> Must stead us all and me amongst the rest,
> And if you break the ice and do this feat,
> Achieve the elder, set the younger free
> For our access, whose hap shall be to have her
> Will not so graceless be to be ingrate.
> *Hor.* Sir, you say well, and well you do conceive.
> And since you do profess to be a suitor,
> You must, as we do, gratify this gentleman,
> To whom we all rest generally beholding.
>
> (I.II.263–72)

Entering into a community characterised chiefly by rivalry amongst its males, Petruchio has, almost instinctively, it seems, adopted the one position that both secures him an *entrée* and also offers him a relationship of gratitude, empowerment and anteriority, rather than competition, with every other contemporary male. Thus his pursuit of Katherine, improbable though it may seem, has already begun to offer him substantial rewards of status and recognition even before it is successful. Shakespeare in fact makes much game of the schematic nature of Petruchio's manoeuvre here:

> Petruchio is my name, Antonio's son,
> A man well known throughout all Italy.
> *Bap.* I know him well. You are welcome for his sake.
>
> (II.I.68–70)

'Antonio' is of course a laughably common name – Shakespeare himself was to use it in *Twelfth Night*, *The Merchant of Venice* and *The Tempest* – and the idea that Petruchio's father could be identified by that name alone becomes one of the play's series of jokes about language and its referents, as when Grumio fails to recognise an ethic dative (I.II.8–10) or misidentifies his presumably native Italian as Latin (I.II.28). Perhaps, though, it is the very hackneyed quality of this overtly stylised exchange of patronymics which calls attention to the fact that Petruchio's courtship of Katherine, apparently so aberrant and individual, actually serves to situate him more firmly within the established order of patriarchy which prevails in Padua.

For Kate too, courtship brings compensations. Whatever reservations one may feel about the extent of the submission required of her, it is impossible not to recognise that, within the terms of her own culture, Petruchio's accepted suit interpellates her within a position of power from which she has previously been radically disenfranchised. That Kate herself is aware of this is clearly indicated by the fact that she never objects to Petruchio's courtship in itself, however much she may deplore the management of it; moreover, though the final scene may be predicated on the submission of man to woman, this is itself achieved by a clear establishment of a hierarchy *within* women in which Kate is clearly at the top of the pecking order.

Her ability to maintain this position is secured primarily by the fact that however conventional they may have appeared to be, Bianca and the Widow have actually both acted in seriously unconventional ways in the arrangement of their marriages. This is most obviously true of Bianca. In marked contrast to the invocation of the name-of-the-father which has validated her sister's betrothal, Bianca marries a man about whose literal identity she is, initially at any rate, deceived, and whose entire plan must depend on the repeated denial of his own father, and a disregard for convention so absolute that he is prepared to fake the assurances for the dowry and jointure and to opine that:

> 'Twere good methinks to steal our marriage,
> Which once perform'd, let all the world say no,
> I'll keep mine own despite of all the world.
>
> (III.II.138–40)

As Biondello reminds him, 'I knew a wench married in an afternoon as she went to the garden for parsley to stuff a rabbit. And so may you, sir' (IV.IV.95–7). Here the motif of the stolen marriage seems not so much romantic as a wanton, and quite unnecessary, disruption of legitimate household routine. Such clandestine ceremonies, as we see in *Measure for Measure* and *Romeo and Juliet*, cause great disruption, and were precisely the kind of thing which the Tudor state was so anxious to exorcise and control. It is hard not to agree with G.R. Hibbard that of the play's two dramatised modes of marriage, '[t]he road followed by Bianca and Lucentio, though it seems romantic and exciting at first glance, is in fact unreliable',[14] and was meant by Shakespeare to be seen as such.

Hortensio, meanwhile, has doubly wasted his time, first, in courting Bianca when it is the Widow whom he eventually decides to marry, and second, by shadowing Petruchio's taming without, apparently, having much insight into the strategies underlying it. The presence of Hortensio is always prominently signalled at crucial moments in the taming programme – at IV.III.35 s.d. we read '*Enter* PETRUCHIO *and* HORTENSIO, *with meat*', and Hortensio rather lamely echoes Petruchio's 'How fares my Kate? What, sweeting, all amort?' (IV.III.36) with 'Mistress, what cheer?' (IV.III.37). With similar heavy-footedness, he offers summaries of the action in the form of asides to the audience – 'I see she's like to have neither cap nor gown' (IV.III.93) – in a technique which further draws attention to his presence and to the quality of his response. It is he who eventually declares that the taming is over – 'Petruchio, go thy ways, the field is won' (IV.V.23) – and he also resolves to use the same processes as Petruchio has done with his own wife, if necessary. The same decision is reached by Slie, the Sly-figure in *The Taming of a Shrew*, the 'bad quarto' play which may represent either an alternative version or a source of Shakespeare's own,[15] but there is little evidence that the unsophisticated Slie will be able to do any such thing, and *The Taming of the Shrew* makes it quite obvious that Hortensio will be completely unable to apply or reproduce what he has witnessed. When Katherine goes to fetch in the other wives, he demonstrates his failure to grasp the situation by musing, 'I wonder what it bodes' (V.II.108); he has only one line more, the penultimate one of the play – 'Now go thy ways, thou hast tam'd a curst shrew' (V.II.189) – where he unoriginally repeats his own earlier conclusion, suggesting that he is no further forward than he was in IV.V.

I have dwelt at some length on Hortensio because he is a character who has traditionally received little critical attention, but whom Shakespeare seems to have been careful to foreground in ways that suggest that he, and in particular his responses to events, ought to be considered important. Indeed, Hortensio may well be a useful character for feminist critics who wish to find a recuperative reading of the play, since his inability to imitate Petruchio even after he has occupied the privileged position of eye-witness and confidant to him may well suggest that, despite the generalising tone of Kate's last speech, *The Taming of the Shrew* has, pointedly, no didactic import. This is a conclusion which would be supported by the pointed meta-theatricality of much of the play,[16] with its emphasis on the costuming of the page Bartholomew as a woman and its play with the lack of realism involved in Grumio's failure to recognise Italian, and by the obviously fairytale structure of the final scene, with the two bad women and the one good one. If we are invited to perceive Kate's final speech as inserted firmly within this fictive framework, its treatment of sexual politics takes on the playfulness of the gaming motif which structures the scene. In short, Hortensio's ineptitude as a pupil may be one way of reminding us that this play is a comedy, which, as the Lord tells Christopher Sly, is intended primarily to 'frame your mind to mirth and merriment, / Which bars a thousand harms and lengthens life' (Induction Scene II, 135–6).

But if Hortensio has something to offer to the feminist reader, it is also worth noting that he may have very considerable uses for Petruchio too. In many of Shakespeare's comedies, the young man or young woman must move away from the company of same-sex friends to form a heterosexual union; but for Petruchio, this process is reversed. He may initially be at odds with Katherine, but he has acquired Hortensio as a willing and admiring companion, and he is also surrounded by an astonishingly large company of male servants, with Curtis, Philip, Joseph, Nathaniel, Nicholas, Gregory, Gabriel, Peter, Walter, Adam and Rafe all named (IV.I.79–80, 109, 119–23). Indeed, one of the most striking elements of Petruchio's decision to court Katherine is the extent to which it gives him, initially a solitary figure, access to group rituals and common cultural practices. Taming her, he draws on social interactions with other men, like Hortensio himself, the tailor and Vincentio, and he also uses the frameworks of falcon-taming, thus aligning himself with the group of hunters of the Induction.[17] Even his apparently egregiously outlandish appearance at his own wedding is easily recognisable as a deliberately parodic mode with links to other forms of inversion such as the feast of fools and the charivari. It is suggestive that Karen Newman, in her analysis of the play, links it with the events of Plough Monday 1604,[18] for *The Taming of the Shrew*, with its highly localised and particularised Warwickshire setting in the Induction, has deep roots in the agricultural world of common experience and culture – a world implicitly evoked as Petruchio and Katherina, like the couples of *A Midsummer Night's Dream*, leave the stage at the end to make their marriages fruitful.

THE MERCHANT OF VENICE

Another play which features a notably early marriage, but which is far less closely in touch with the rhythms of rural and community life, is *The Merchant of Venice*. The extent to which the society of Venice is divorced from the ritual, agricultural world evoked in *A Midsummer Night's Dream* and *The Taming of the Shrew* is tellingly imaged when Antonio asks Shylock, 'Or is your gold and silver ewes and rams?' and Shylock cheerfully replies, 'I cannot tell, I make it breed as fast'.[19] This is the closest we come in the play to the natural or pastoral, and it serves to register how greatly the Venetians as a group are imbricated in the commercial and the mercantile; James Shapiro points out 'the commercial conditions in the play upon which the green world of Belmont is founded',[20] and Peter Smith sees an even closer relationship contained in a pun on ewes / use / Iews,[21] while Barbara Everett calls the play as a whole 'a very original legend of the rich, for whom Love and Money are terms of each other'.[22] This orientation towards financial productivity rather than actual reproduction colours the whole image of marriage in the play. It is a world of only children – Jessica and Portia are declaredly so, and no other character gives any sign of having a sibling – either in search of fortune or in possession of one; Bassanio, notoriously, introduces the subject of Portia with the words, 'In Belmont is a lady richly left' (I.I.161).

The keynote in the representation of marriage is struck early in the play. When Antonio denies that it is anxiety over his merchandise which is causing his inexplicable sadness, Solanio at once responds, 'Why then you are in love' (I.I.46). Antonio denies this too, and for once in a Shakespearean comedy he is neither lying nor about to be made a fool of by fate: unlike the Duke in *Measure for Measure*, he will not find himself forced to recant his easy dismissal, and unusually in the Shakespearean comic or tragi-comic canon he will remain single at the end. However, although Solanio's guess may thus not prove to have prophetic force in one sense, it may alert us to the unusually high degree of distress surrounding the marriages in the play. Jessica's elopement does not only, in Shylock's eyes, rob him of his child, it also reaches backwards to perpetrate a desecration of the memory of his own marriage: 'Out upon her! – thou torturest me Tubal, – it was my turquoise, I had it of Leah when I was a bachelor: I would not have given it for a wilderness of monkeys' (III.I.110–13). The ring which was given as a token of faith has had its meaning twisted and now stands instead as a symbol of loss and betrayal.

Precisely the same connotations are also attached to two other rings, those which Portia and Nerissa bestow on their husbands and which they themselves, in disguise, later beg back again. The easily invoked innuendo surrounding rings and the fingers that thrust through them makes the two rings highly suggestive foci for a cluster of associations to do with cuckoldry, wrongful possession and betrayal of the very marriage bond which the rings themselves ostensibly symbolise and confirm. They thus represent both security and danger, identity and difference.

These sets of oppositions have in fact been associated from the outset with the question of Portia's marriage. Everything associated with it is radically fissured by ambivalence. Even before we hear the name of Portia, an air of unease is created by the terms in which Antonio and Bassanio discuss her. When Bassanio makes his initial request for assistance, Antonio responds:

> I pray you good Bassanio let me know it,
> And if it stand as you yourself still do,
> Within the eye of honour, be assur'd
> My purse, person, my extremest means
> Lie all unlock'd to your occasions.
>
> (I.I.135–9)

This may be simply the enthusiastic eagerness of friendship or, perhaps, of a naturally generous person, as Antonio does indeed seem to be. Nevertheless, there was a fairly well-established

Renaissance tradition of associating the name 'Antonio' with homosexuality, an idea that is perhaps played with in Shakespeare's portrayal of the strong affection between Antonio and Sebastian in *Twelfth Night*, and we may be tempted to read an unusual warmth in the extent of Antonio's willingness to help Bassanio. This is certainly an element often explored in production; in Jude Kelly's 1994 West Yorkshire Playhouse version, Antonio and Bassanio were conducting a virtually open affair, which a world-weary and cynical Portia was perfectly happy to tolerate.

If the relationship between Antonio and Bassanio seems to admit of more than one interpretation, that between Bassanio and Portia is even more ambiguously figured. His initial description of her is many-faceted:

> In Belmont is a lady richly left,
> And she is fair, and (fairer than that word),
> Of wondrous virtues, – sometimes from her eyes
> I did receive fair speechless messages:
> Her name is Portia, nothing undervalu'd
> To Cato's daughter, Brutus' Portia,
> Nor is the wide world ignorant of her worth,
> For the four winds blow in from every coast
> Renowned suitors, and her sunny locks
> Hang on her temples like a golden fleece,
> Which makes her seat of Belmont Colchos' strond,
> And many Jasons come in quest of her.
>
> (I.I.161–72)

What is striking here is the variety of discourses deployed by Bassanio in relation to Portia. He speaks of her in terms of 'rich'ness, 'value' and 'worth', and he is, after all, making this speech in the first place essentially as a means of persuading Antonio that wooing Portia would be a sound investment; but he also decorates his description with both borrowings from the classical mythology which identifies him as the recipient of a humanist education, referring to 'Cato's daughter' and 'Colchos' strand', and with the language of love – though one might well feel that it is in this area that he is at his least engaged and inventive, falling back rather lamely on the iterative 'fair', 'fairer' and 'fair'. Perhaps, though, this poverty of language is appropriate to the relationship he sketches, since it has so far been predominantly non-verbal: 'Sometimes from her eyes / I did receive fair speechless messages.' Perhaps, then, Bassanio is not as mercenary as his first line indicates; perhaps he is indeed making the proper noises about affection and virtue – but he is making them very quietly. There is no unbridled passion here such as that which drives Romeo and Juliet to suicide, or the lovers of *A Midsummer Night's Dream* to the woods, though the prudence which insists that wealth is as necessary to marriage as personal desire might well have met with greater approval amongst certain sections at least of the play's original audience.

The audience's opinion on the matter is openly solicited by Portia in her sharply-worded statement of her predicament:

> I may neither choose who I would, nor refuse who I dislike, so is the will of a living daughter curb'd by the will of a dead father: is it not hard, Nerissa, that I cannot choose one, nor refuse none?
> (I.II.22–6)

The question 'Is it not hard?' cries out for an answer, and certainly the situation which Portia so pithily sketches here is one which would run counter to virtually every tenet of Renaissance marriage theory, with its fundamental emphasis on the paramountcy of consent and the absolute necessity of allowing a child at the very least a right of refusal in a case of utter repugnance. The overtones of Portia's statement may, however, work to make us aware of the logic underlying her father's decision, for the word 'will' was, as Shakespeare's own sonnets show, primed with strongly sexual connotations. In the celebrated sonnet beginning 'Whoever hath her wish, thou hast thy will', 'will' simultaneously connotes sexual desire and both the male and female sexual organs, as well as the clear meaning (obviously appropriate here) of testamentary deposition (itself etymologically connected with 'testicle', and so radically encoding the primacy of male authority). The formal grammatical structure of Portia's notably lucid argument may therefore seem to assert equal status for the male and female wills, but the resonance of the words undercuts that by insistently reminding us of the dynamic of the underlying structure of the sexual politics. A Renaissance audience might well be more inclined than we are to think that female sexuality should indeed be curbed by legitimised male authority; they might even be inclined to snicker at the possible *double entendre* of Portia's 'Is it not hard?'.

Certainly Nerissa does not encourage Portia to repine. She asserts confidently that 'The lott'ry that he hath devised... will no doubt never be chosen by any rightly, but one who you shall rightly love' (I.II.28–32). Nerissa subscribes to a benign providentialism which sees the will of the dead father as moving inextricably in parallel with the miraculously combined forces of both 'right' and 'love'; she thus reconciles the potential ambiguities of both Bassanio's courtship and Portia's position, and she performs a similar marrying of opposites when she praises Bassanio as both 'a scholar and a soldier' (I.II.109). Nerissa, indeed, interpellates Bassanio firmly as transcendental signifier in the psychic economy of love, classifying him by means of the very language of affection which he himself deployed so ineptly, and, in a suggestive syntactic slippage, eliding him with Love itself – 'Bassanio Lord, love if thy will it be!' (II.9.102) is the New Penguin version, but the Arden reads 'Bassanio, Lord Love, if thy will it be', and there are no clear dividing lines between the two. Nerissa will later echo her first statement of trust in providence and acceptance of received wisdom when she asserts that 'The ancient saying is no heresy: / Hanging and wiving goes by destiny' (II.IX.82–3). If Hortensio in *The Taming of the Shrew* illuminates Petruchio's inventiveness by the shadowiness of his imitation of him, Nerissa's parallel duplication of Portia's actions works rather to soften their assertive individuality by inserting them within the frame of comedic repetition, and to articulate a romantic perspective on events which interprets as copiousness and fortune what in the mouths of the lovers themselves is always threatening to sound like calculation and transaction.

Portia unequivocally speaks the language of reckoning and acquisitiveness in her dealings with the Prince of Morocco:

> But if my father had not scanted me,
> And hedg'd me by his wit to yield myself
> His wife who wins me by that means I told you,
> Yourself (renowned prince) then stood as fair
> As any comer I have look'd on yet
> For my affection.
>
> (II.I.17–22)

'Scanted' is bitter indeed; Portia speaks of her father not, as Nerissa does, as someone who has exercised proper and loving care over her, but as a niggardly and restrictive figure. Indeed, it is notable that Portia, unlike the rather similarly situated Olivia, never once expresses grief for the loss of her male protector, although her bereavement may, perhaps, be of rather older date.

Perhaps more disturbing than this open resentment is the simple fact that Portia is lying here.[23] We know that she loathes the Prince of Morocco and dreads the possibility of having to marry him; to call him 'fair' is a scarcely veiled insult to his race which may even reflect worryingly on Bassanio's choice of a threefold repetition of that very epithet for Portia herself. But, even here, there may be ambiguity, for she might conceivably be taken to mean that she dislikes Morocco no more than she has disliked the other suitors. This would not necessarily contradict Bassanio's and Nerissa's assertions that she has already favoured Bassanio, since he did not, technically, approach her as a suitor. To excuse Portia thus is to say that she is guilty merely of equivocation, which is, after all, the very tool she will later deploy so successfully in the courtroom scene; but although this is a much less serious offence than deliberate mendacity, it still suggests a littleness of spirit in her not so far distant from that at which she hints in her father.

However, this exchange also elaborates on a further refinement of her father's scheme. Portia reminds Morocco that by the terms of the 'lottery', if he chooses wrongly he must swear 'Never to speak to lady afterward / In way of marriage, – therefore be advis'd' (II.I.41–2). Portia's father sought to extend his 'will' to arrange not only the affairs of his own daughter but, it seems, of other women as well, since the reason for this prohibition is presumably an assumption that any man so foolish as to make the wrong choice does not deserve to have a wife at all. Suggestively, though, this logic is never actually articulated, and the adoption of perpetual bachelorhood will also have another consequence for men like Morocco and Aragon: it will mean they will have no legitimate children. The caskets sub-plot may seem to reverse the logic of the Antonio–Shylock world in privileging the spiritual values encoded in the choice of lead over the more obviously materialistic ones represented by gold and silver, but it actually subscribes to the same drive towards sterility and the reduction of opportunities for reproduction: the enforced singleness of Morocco and Aragon mirrors the voluntary celibacy of Antonio. Portia's father's precautions may in one sense seem to protect and elevate women by protecting them from shallow men, but their ultimate logic works towards the overall barrenness of a world in which it is only coins, not sheep and rams, that breed, and in which sterility in both areas is metaphorically implied as a daughter robs her father of the 'stones' that symbolise his testicles as well as his wealth.

As the plot leaves Belmont and moves back to Venice, allusions to marriage begin to cluster more thickly, in thematic preparation for the anticipated union of Portia and Bassanio. Old Gobbo and Launcelot play a brief variation on a classic cuckoldry joke when the father says mournfully, 'I cannot think you are my son' and the son ripostes, 'I know not what I shall think of that: but...I am sure Margery your wife is my mother' (II.II.83–6). A secondary marriage intrigue is introduced when Jessica apostrophises Lorenzo, 'If thou keep promise I shall end this strife, / Become a Christian and thy loving wife!' (II.III.20–1) – a phrase which will be ominously echoed when Shylock bitterly comments, 'These be the Christian husbands!' (IV.I.291) as Bassanio and Gratiano both declare they wish their wives were dead so that they could intercede in heaven for Antonio. Lorenzo himself seems to imply a disturbing view of marital practices regularly escaping patriarchal supervision when he promises Gratiano and Salerio, 'When you shall please to play the thieves for wives / I'll watch as long for you then' (II.VI.23–4); however, it is also Lorenzo who offers a fluent articulation of the discourse of romance which had so eluded Bassanio:

> Beshrew me but I love her heartily,
> For she is wise, if I can judge of her,
> And fair she is, if that mine eyes be true,
> And true she is, as she hath prov'd herself:
> And therefore like herself, wise, fair, and true,
> Shall she be placed in my constant soul.
>
> (II.VI.52–7)

It is immediately noticeable how much better provided with categories for describing his mistress Lorenzo is than Bassanio – he itemises wisdom and truth as well as fairness – and also that worldly wealth is never mentioned in his listing of Jessica's qualities. In this, as well as in the issue of obedience to the will of the father, the Lorenzo/Jessica relationship may well seem to be designed to function as a deliberate contrast to the Bassanio/Portia one.

There is certainly no shortage of uneasy notes struck as we follow through the processes of Bassanio's choice and its aftermath. When Bassanio declares that in his impatience for the trial he is 'upon the rack', Portia responds, 'Upon the rack Bassanio? Then confess / What treason there is mingled with your love' (III.II.24–7). The image may be a witty, but it is not a pretty one, as is confirmed when Bassanio replies, 'None but that ugly treason of mistrust, / Which makes me fear th'enjoying of my love' (III.II.28–9). The words may well seem to be meant lightly enough, but potential areas for mistrust will occur again in the scene. Why, for instance, does Portia say to Bassanio, 'First go with me to church, and call me wife, / And then away to Venice to your friend!' (III.II.302–3)? Divorcing the ceremony of marriage from its consummation, she plunges both herself and her husband into an ill-defined relationship which immediately disallows the possibility of the normal comic conclusion and which will be characterised by disguise, mistaken identity, emotional blackmail and threats of cuckoldry. For none of this is her motivation clear. The idea of a period of trial and confusion before the happy marriage can occur is common enough in Shakespeare's usual comic structures, but it is rare indeed for the wedding to take place so long before physical union and emotional harmony are achieved. The result seems almost to sideline the wedding itself as an irrelevance – not staged, hastily despatched and noticeably failing to mark any major development in the couple's relationship; and one might also speculate whether Portia's insistence on the enactment of a legal bond is not perhaps evidence of a kind of mistrust on her part – and, indeed, of a sensibility not so radically different from that of Shylock himself, whom she is so soon to castigate for that very failing.

Another potential area of mistrust has come from critics, and has centred on the question of Portia's good faith in the build-up to Bassanio's choice. Diane Elizabeth Dreher argues that Portia actually jumps the gun when she tells Bassanio *before* the test 'One half of me is yours, the other half yours, – / Mine own I would say' (III.II.16–17): '[t]hese words, spoken in the present tense before witnesses, constitute at the very least a proposal, at most, part of a formal spousal'. Dreher goes on to suggest that Portia also plays the groom's rather than the bride's role, and that Antonio performs for Bassanio the rituals normally undertaken by the father of the bride.[24] There is also the question of the song which Portia chooses to have played to Bassanio while he is making his decision. The audience has by now watched Portia as both the gold and the silver caskets were opened; we know, therefore, that she knows that it is the lead one which contains the miniature. Is it, then, a coincidence that the song begins with three lines which conclude with rhymes for 'lead' – 'bred', 'head' and 'nourished' – and that closing lines should include the phrases 'ring fancy's knell' and the twice-uttered 'Ding, dong, bell' (III.II.63–72)?[25] Certainly in performance these elements of the song can be emphasised in such a way as to suggest that any reasonably intelligent person can take a hint from them. Bell-metal, it is true, is not the same as lead, but it is considerably closer to it than either silver or gold, and the triple rhyme-sound may well seem insistent. Immediately the song has concluded, Bassanio comments, 'So may the outward shows be least themselves' (III.II.73). Has Portia ensured that the ceremony of her father's will has been overtly complied with, while secretly attempting to subvert his posthumous control over it?[26] We can only speculate, and perhaps remember that it is precisely by a stickling for the letter of the law that she succeeds in derailing the court case.

We can, however, notice that other aspects of the play's central relationships are unequivocally troubling. When Lorenzo and Jessica walk through the night at Belmont their poetry may be beautiful, but the examples of lovers that they choose are each more ominous than the last: first Lorenzo cites Troilus and Cressida (V.I.4–6), confirmed in Shakespeare's own eponymous play as virtually synonymous with betrayal and disappointment; then Jessica mentions Thisbe, again treated by Shakespeare himself, who killed herself after the error-driven suicide of her lover Pyramus. Lorenzo counters with Dido, deserted by Aeneas, and Jessica offers Medea, who killed her own children in revenge for her repudiation by her husband, Jason. When Lorenzo offers Jessica herself as the fifth in this list of women, it can hardly be thought to bode well. Equally, we might conclude that the ring-trick played by Portia on Bassanio is a pointless and unmotivated piece of mischief, and more importantly – and in marked contrast to the test devised by her father – one which actually engineers a no-win situation, since Bassanio stands to be scorned and derided by Portia in one guise or another whether he succumbs or resists. Though the close of the play brings formal resolution, it is all too easy to see why modern productions have frequently tended to see *The Merchant of Venice* as coming far closer to the joylessness and emotional unease of the problem plays than to the energy and abundance of *As You Like It* or *Twelfth Night*. The problematic character of Shylock may provide one obvious source of empathy against the grain, but the premises and progress of the central love-interest may well work towards an equal derailment of sympathetic response.

ALL'S WELL THAT ENDS WELL

If *The Merchant of Venice* splits the actuality of the wedding from the celebration of it, so to an even more marked extent does the problem play *All's Well that Ends Well*. Disjointed relationships are, as in *Hamlet*, strongly signalled from the very outset of the play by confusions of terminology. The first line is the Countess's: 'In delivering my son from me, I bury a second husband'.[27] Soon afterwards, Lafew assures her, 'You shall find of the king a husband, madam; you, sir, a father' (I.I.6–7). This might articulate the most benevolent of paternalisms, or it might sound a warning note about inappropriate models; in either case, it is soon echoed when the king, noting that the Florentines and Siennese are at war, comments on the advice given him on the subject by his 'cousin Austria' (I.II.5), which reinforces the sense that, from the king's perspective, the world is a small one, comfortably structured by familial or quasi-familial relationships. It will indeed be appropriate that the gift Helena will seek from him will be a husband, for there could be none that he would be more inclined to give. It is he, after all, who adjures the young men of his court to let the world see that they come 'Not to woo honour, but to wed it' (II.I.15), and who will later insist upon proper celebration and solemnity for the marriage of Bertram and Helena, warning his young ward that 'As thou lov'st her / Thy love's to me religious; else, does err' (II.III.182–3).

Just as the king's speech yokes together cousinhood and war, so the play's early description of relationships tend to focus on states markedly less than the ideal. When the Countess asks the Clown, 'Tell me the reason why thou wilt marry' (I.III.25) he responds matter-of-factly, 'My poor body, madam, requires it' (I.III.26); he then offers the alternative response, 'I have been, madam, a wicked creature... and indeed I do marry that I may repent' (I.III.33–5), and finally claims that he wants to increase his stock of friends out of the lovers which his wife will take – a classic schematisation of the homosocial bonding effected by the exchange of women. At least, though, his perspective on marriage is a celebratory one – 'Your marriage comes by destiny, / Your cuckoo sings by kind' (I.III.61–2) – and the same determination to salvage acceptability from despair structures his ironic acclamation of Helena:

> *Was this fair face the cause, quoth she,*
>   *Why the Grecians sacked Troy?*
>   ...
> *With that she sighed as she stood,*
>   *And gave this sentence then:*
> *Among nine bad if one be good,*
> *Among nine bad if one be good,*
> *There's yet one good in ten.*
>
> (I.III.67–76)

To the Clown, Helena bears primarily not the marks of an individual identity but of a link, cemented both by the general fact of her gender and the particular one of her name, with the adulterous Helen, whose actions precipitated the ten years of the Trojan War, and whose presence may be invoked again when Helena's journey to the French capital recalls the name of her lover, Paris.[28] It is an ominous avatar, and one that becomes more so when Helena's offer to cure the king becomes abruptly and unexpectedly interwoven with a discussion about her own chastity. When he enquires of her 'Upon thy certainty and confidence/What dar'st thou venture?' (II.I.168–9), she replies:

> Tax of impudence,
> A strumpet's boldness, a divulged shame,
> Traduced by odious ballads; my maiden's name
> Sear'd otherwise
>
> (II.I.169–72)

There seems no obvious reason why Helena should make her own sexual reputation the price of her medical venture, except that the two are perhaps associated in her own mind because her motivation is to win the king's endorsement of her dream of marriage with Bertram.

An alternative explanation for the link may perhaps lie in the nature of the king's ailment. This is hinted at rather than explicated, but some suggestive comments on it come from Lafew (whose instinct for straight talking leads to the exposure of Parolles): he first tells the king, 'I have seen a medicine / That's able to breathe life into a stone' (II.I.71–2), and then later reports, 'Why, your dolphin is not lustier' (II.III.26). The word 'stone', commonly connoting a testicle, and the allusions to 'lustiness' and to the proverbially vigorous dolphin may all work together to support a strong suggestion that the king's affliction – already placed within the lower body stratum by being termed a 'fistula' – should be read primarily as a sexual disability. This, given the marked concern evinced elsewhere by the king for legitimate and proper relations, may reflect less on his personal morality than on his clear structural parallels with the mythological figure of the Fisher King, whose thigh-wound compromises the fertility of his whole kingdom. Thus, while Helena's willingness to submit to accusations of sexual depravity may seem to introduce a troubling note, the strongly developed hints of sexual transmission of the king's disease paradoxically allows for expectation of a traditionally comedic teleology by evoking the images of the restoration of fruition and fertility (figured in the visual emblem of Helena, alone of the heroines, appearing heavily pregnant at the end). Some critics have seen the king, like Claudius in *Hamlet*, as a source of taint to the whole community of the play – Peter Erickson, for instance, argues that 'the image of male order is vulnerable not simply because Bertram is a weak link in an otherwise solid chain but also because there is no convincing, living embodiment of the ancestral "first father" (3.7.25) elsewhere in the play as the king himself conspicuously demonstrates'.[29] What we have instead though is, uniquely in the world of Shakespearean comedy, a demonstration of continuity of motherhood, with the first line spoken by the Countess and the ending centring on Helena's pregnancy to lay marked emphasis on the unmistakable chain of matrilineal fecundity.

The nature of the king's affliction seems again alluded to in Bertram's furious protest, 'But follows it, my lord, to bring me down / Must answer for your raising? I know her well'

(II.III.112–13). The lines ring with sexual scorn: 'your raising' clearly implies that the king has, metaphorically at least, been sexually stimulated by Helena, while 'I know her well' draws on the standard phrase 'carnal knowledge' to slur Helena yet further. Bertram does not assert that either he or the king has actually slept with Helena, but his language stales her, casting her first as a sexual stimulant and then as a creature whom he has already mentally categorised and who can hold no mystery or excitement for him. Moreover, 'to bring me down' figures her as a sexual aggressor as well as a radical disrupter of the social order. Bertram images himself here as a figure of disturbing passivity, victimised by both the king and Helena, and his actions henceforward are largely dictated by a desperate urge to regain some at least of the initiative and agency.

Unfortunately, his attempts to do so are unremittingly gauche and are also fissured by tensions and contradictions of which he does not even seem to be aware. Even his initial protest has only aped the language of order and responsibility which he attempts to deploy:

> My wife, my liege! I shall beseech your highness,
> In such a business give me leave to use
> The help of mine own eyes.
>
> (II.III.106–8)

He is proper in his use of titles – 'my liege', 'your highness' – and he refers to marriage gravely as 'a business', but the extended construction of 'give me leave to use / The help' can only point up the bathos of the value-judgements encoded in 'mine own *eyes*'. Bertram is not a man among men, making sensible decisions about his future based on knowledge of his wife's family and background; he seeks beauty, like the young lovers in *A Midsummer Night's Dream* for whom love is figured essentially as an attribute of the ocular nerve, dangerously susceptible to external manipulation. A similar mixture of the stately and the petulant informs his later resolve that 'Although before the solemn priest I have sworn, / I will not bed her' (II.III.265–6).

Instead, he flees to a world of male camaraderie, where language does not need to be carefully chosen in crucial, public situations but where it is, ostensibly at least, free-floating, a vehicle for the nonsense and merriment involved in the baiting of Parolles. Punning and word-games have already underlain the opposition of 'to bring me down...your raising'; now they proliferate in a homosocial culture of the aphorism. 'Wars is no strife / To the dark house and the detested wife' (II.III.287–8) opines Bertram, while Parolles declares, 'A young man married is a man that's marr'd' (II.III.294), and the Clown jokes, 'The danger is in standing to't; that's the loss of men, though it be the getting of children' (III.II.40–1). It is in this culture of misogyny mediated through verbal refusal of anchorage to specific moorings that Bertram comes up with his ultimatum: '*When thou canst get the ring upon my finger, which never shall come off, and show me a child begotten of thy body that I am father to, then call me husband; but in such a "then" I write a "never"*' (III.II.56–9). Here, though, Bertram overreaches himself. He may think he has played a clever game with juggled and destabilised language, but he has, ironically, committed these ludic terms to the fixity of a letter, which can be read out and glossed by Helena, who operates within a very different mode.

If Bertram manoeuvres to arrogate authority to himself, Helena, ironically, fears that she may possess too much of it. Apparently quite confident in her power to cure the king, she consistently envisages herself as a radically empowered agent. Her reflections on Bertram's departure indeed present her as precisely the kind of aggressively dominant figure that Bertram had apparently feared when he claimed to have been 'brought down':

> Poor lord, is't I
> That chase thee from thy country, and expose
> Those tender limbs of thine to the event
> Of the none-sparing war?
>
> (III.II.102–5)

Mentally undressing him down to his 'tender limbs', Helena both infantilises and ogles Bertram. At the same time there is, paradoxically, a hint of her as not only sexually predatory but as a prohibitive figure, as she chases him from the 'country' which, in *Hamlet* at least, so unequivocally puns on 'cunt'. She continues to imagine him as unmanned and defencelessly available:

> Whoever charges on his forward breast,
> I am the caitiff that do hold him to't;

> And though I kill him not, I am the cause
> His death was so effected. Better 'twere
> I met the ravin lion when he roar'd
> With sharp constraint of hunger; better 'twere
> That all the miseries which nature owes
> Were mine at once.
>
> (III.II.113–20)

Bertram here becomes a nonentity, a mere object of struggle, while Helena unfalteringly envisages for herself a fearless confrontation with precisely the kind of perils which, in *The Taming of the Shrew*, authorised male superiority. So that Bertram may live in safety, she will cast herself loose to providence.

What she does in fact is to imitate male actions in a rather different way. She too plays games of slippage and substitution, but her tools are not words but things: operating consistently within the deep structures of the mythological and the symbolic, she uses the bed-trick to destabilise signifieds rather than siginifiers in ways which make sense out of the nonsense of Bertram's conditions. The profound difference of their approaches is made very clear when they meet, for what Bertram has acquired in glibness, he has certainly forfeited in veracity. He lies about his alleged affection for Maudlin (V.III.44–6), he lies about Diana and the ring (V.III.93ff), while now it is the women who riddle, pun, and play with language:

> No, my good lord;
> 'Tis but the shadow of a wife you see;
> The name and not the thing.
>
> (V.III.300–2)

What moves Bertram to his response to this? He ends Helena's half-line with 'Both, both. O pardon!', and soon afterwards promises, 'If she, my liege, can make me know this clearly / I'll love her dearly, ever, ever dearly' (V.III.309–10). These are not eloquent assertions – perhaps their most obvious feature is their heavy reliance on simple repetition – but they are, at least, unequivocal, and provide at any rate the nominal promise of a happy ending.

Obviously, the necessity for a 'happy ending' is in one sense reason enough for Bertram's abrupt recantation, not to mention his extreme relief at this miraculous extrication from the distinctly hot water he had so recently been in: acceptance of Helena is a very different proposition now from what it would have represented for him earlier in the play. Our strong awareness of these constraints may well make us feel that the ending of the play is unusually muted and joyless – indeed, Janet Adelman argues that both here and in *Measure for Measure*, '[t]he marriages that end these comedies fail to satisfy the desires of either the characters or the audience; and their failure marks the extent to which Hamlet's prohibition remains in force and hence the extent to which comedy is no longer a viable genre for Shakespeare'.[30] Nevertheless, there does seem to be at least the ghost of a genuine change of heart in Bertram. Helena has beaten him at his own game of riddling, and has indeed precipitated an exhibition of his relative linguistic poverty; is there in fact a recognition of this in his phrase 'If she... can make me know this clearly'? Initially, he crudely dismissed Helena on the grounds that 'I know her well'; now, learning that he does not in fact know whom he has known, he may be seen as recognising an educative ability in Helena which will finally give him access to the discourses of power and authority which he has previously found it so problematic to attempt to exercise. In Sir Philip Sidney's *Astrophel and Stella*, knowledge is figured as a key step on the road to love; perhaps it functions similarly for Bertram, who may indeed be offering a genuine exchange of his love for the knowledge which he now takes Helena to possess.[31]

THE COMEDY OF ERRORS

Two rather different cases are provided by *The Comedy of Errors* and *The Merry Wives of Windsor*. In the very early *Comedy of Errors*, both emotional and narrative satisfaction are sought for primarily through the construction of family relationships other than marriage. Egeon does refer to the 'divorce'[32] enforced upon his wife and him, but it is his son whom he has come to seek; and that son, in turn, set out to find his brother as much as his mother. Throughout the play, the persistent confusions caused by the twins' similarity mean that resolution can be achieved only by final clarification of this part of the plot, and the disclosure of the Abbess's identity as Emilia is very much secondary. Moreover, we already know that marriage is available for the provision only of partial closure, since Antipholus of Ephesus is already married to Adriana. It is, visibly, not a particularly intense or passionate relationship, but then no one seems particularly to expect that it should be; even Luciana, who opposes her sister's views on the duties of a wife and argues for greater subservience, views the marriage-bed as a site of 'troubles' (II.I.27) and is prepared to condone a husband's infidelity as long as it is not blatant (III.II.5–7, 23). However, liking at least clearly is expected – neither Dromio of Syracuse nor Antipholus of Syracuse could contemplate marriage with a woman they dislike on sight (III.II.153–8), and such a right of veto in cases of instant or insuperable repugnance lies at the heart of all Renaissance marriage theory.

What is also very clear is that both Antipholus of Ephesus and Adriana regard the relationship as an indissoluble one: Adriana uses the same image of a water-drop to characterise their unity as Antipholus of Syracuse had earlier used of his search for his brother and mother (I.II.36, II.II.126), suggesting that the social tie is seen as being as binding as the natural one; she reinforces the idea when she uses the natural imagery of plants to describe the nature of their bond (II.II.174–80). Moroever, both parties have gained by the marriage. Adriana was given to Antipholus by the Duke as a reward, since she was rich; she has, notably, retained control of some of that money – indeed, the play is full of references to her financial empowerment (IV.I.36–8, IV.II.48–50, IV.IV.47, IV.IV.117–19).[33] And though Shakespeare needs a courtesan for his plot, he is careful to allow Antipholus to dissociate himself from any actual guilt with her (III.I.111–13). There is an undercurrent of misogyny in the play – Antipholus of Syracuse, who expects all the women he meets to be witches, terms Luciana a mermaid even though he loves her, and fears that she will tempt him to 'self-wrong' (III.II.162–3), Antipholus of Ephesus calls for a rope's end to beat Adriana (IV.I.15–18), and the exchanges between Adriana and the Abbess do little more than pander to the mentality that relishes the mother-in-law joke.[34] Nevertheless, it also dramatises, in Adriana and Antipholus of Ephesus, the comforts, the social position and the empowerment that can accrue to both sexes in marriage, even when it does not provide either the characters or the audience with their primary arena of emotional investment.

THE MERRY WIVES OF WINDSOR

In *The Merry Wives of Windsor*, the two main female characters are, as the title makes obvious, already married, and therefore not available as providers of comic closure, which is deputed instead to Anne Page. Ominously, perhaps, the first time we hear the word 'marrying' in this play is in a pun on 'marring',[35] and the estate of matrimony itself is sadly troubled by Ford's obsessive jealousy; Slender may well ring true when he says of Anne Page, 'if there be no great love in the beginning, yet heaven may decrease it upon better acquaintance when we are married and have more occasion to know one another' (I.1.229–332).

Nevertheless, the play may well be said to celebrate marriage as much as it interrogates it. Mistress Page, like Adriana, 'bears the purse' (I.3.63), and the course of events not only illustrates the women's firm friendship but shows, as Mistress Page says, that 'Wives may be merry, and yet honest too' (IV.2.99), and that husbands can be taught. Unusually, *Merry Wives* also celebrates motherhood, showing that though she has a nubile daughter, Mistress Page is still sexually attractive to Falstaff, and that Mistress Ford, who seems to be about the same age, continues to obsess her husband; and in its final episode of Herne the Hunter it offers the same glorification of the horn as facilitated the male bonding of *As You Like It*. Though neither the Ford nor the Page marriage can in any sense be said to represent a grand passion, consent and liking in marriage are again insisted on: Evans will not promote Slender's interest in Anne Page unless he can 'affection' her (I.1.209–12), and though Fenton first wooed for money, he has found, in one of the classic value-systems of Shakespearean comedy, that where money is, his heart follows (III.4.13–18). Even Falstaff appeals to the idea of mutual 'sympathy' in his letter to Mistress Page (II.1.6–9), but Falstaff is unmarried, and the wives of Windsor have so internalised the values of their society that sympathy and sexual release are available only within marriage. Unusually in Shakespeare, there are, in this play, no whores; moreover, Falstaff's failure to take a wife not only cuts him off from women, but actually forces him parodically to become one, as he is dressed in the clothes of the old woman. In *The Merry Wives of Windsor*, then, marriage and its values continue to lie at the heart both of the play and of the community it represents, but Shakespeare seems interested in it less as the telos of the romance relationship than as a social structure in its own right transcending those involved in it, and the marginality of the Anne Page plot reflects that.

3
What Makes a Marriage?

In three largely dissimilar plays, and in very different ways, Shakespeare introduces an element of dubiety or disruption into the completion of a marriage – the phenomenon that Carol Thomas Neely identified in her seminal study of *Broken Nuptials in Shakespeare's Plays*. Postponement and improper performance of ritual, analogous to the motif of subversion of courtly entertainment so widespread in drama of the period, occur elsewhere in the canon, but they are most prominent in *Love's Labour's Lost, Much Ado About Nothing* and the problem play, *Measure for Measure*.

The simplest case is that of *Love's Labour's Lost*, where marriage is repeatedly invoked as the expected comic conclusion only to be abruptly displaced by the death of the King of France and the women's demand that the men should demonstrate full emotional maturity before they are ready for commitment. To some extent, this play breaks the ground for the later psychological dynamic of *All's Well that Ends Well*, especially since both plays are so firmly and overtly grounded in the turbulent world of French politics, where marriage and mayhem had proved so shatteringly linked when the wedding of the Catholic French princess Marguerite to the Protestant Henri of Navarre had precipitated the horror of the St Bartholomew's day massacre. Just as the song of the owl and the cuckoo registers the full range of the cycle of human and natural behaviour, so the play as a whole does not hesitate to confront the necessity for elements of psychological growth which cannot be contained within its own comedic framework – another issue which surfaces again in *All's Well that Ends Well*'s sustained forays into the terrain of closure.

LOVE'S LABOUR'S LOST

From the outset of *Love's Labour's Lost* a note of untimeliness and inappropriateness is sounded. Longaville says of Berowne, 'He weeds the corn, and still lets grow the weeding';[1] this image of the failure of proper husbandry introduces a sustained emphasis on metaphors of infertility and unseasonality associated with the young men's self-denying behaviour. The King says, 'Berowne is like an envious sneaping frost / That bites the first-born infants of the spring' (I.I.100–1), and Berowne does not deny it:

> Well, say I am; why should proud summer boast
> Before the birds have any cause to sing?
> Why should I joy in an abortive birth?
> At Christmas I no more desire a rose
> Than wish a snow in May's new-fangled shows;
> But like of each thing that in season grows.
>
> (I.1.102–7)

This insistence on seasonality will recur with a vengeance at the end of the play. The Princess intimates ultimate success to the king, 'If frosts and fasts, hard lodging and thin weeds, / Nip not the gaudy blossoms of your love' (V.II.791–2), and the changing rhythms of the seasons provide the theme of the owl and the cuckoo song with which the play closes (V.II.884ff). C.L. Barber suggested that 'The songs evoke the daily enjoyments and the daily community out of which special festive occasions were shaped up', and that therefore 'they provide for the conclusion of the comedy what marriage usually provides: an expression of the going-on power of life'.[2] The play itself, however, seems to draw deliberate attention to its omission to provide the comic closure of marriage.

Such an outcome is obviously anticipated from an early stage. Boyet reminds the Princess what the situation demands:

> Yourself, held precious in the world's esteem,
> To parley with the sole inheritor
> Of all perfections that a man may owe,
> Matchless Navarre; the plea of no less weight
> Than Aquitaine, a dowry for a queen.
>
> (II.I.4–8)

Navarre is 'matchless' in both senses, being a paragon who is unmarried; the suggestion that Aquitaine might be a dowry clearly indicates that a marriage would be both personally and politically appropriate. Intimations of the appropriateness of marriage continue to accrue, as we hear that Maria first saw Longaville at a wedding feast (II.I.40–3) and as Rosaline and Boyet swap cuckold jokes. The betrayal of the courtiers' vows does not even lead to friction amongst them, but facilitates still greater male solidarity as Berowne exclaims, 'Sweet lords, sweet lovers, O! let us embrace' (IV.III.211). But as events draw to a close, we discover the existence of an obstacle to marriage which is neither personal nor political, but, it seems, aesthetic. When the King requests, 'Now, at the latest minute of the hour, / Grant us your loves', the Princess responds, 'A time, methinks, too short / To make a world-without-end bargain in' (V.II.777–9). She may well be taken as registering here not merely the shortness of real time but the enforced compression of *dramatic* time, and Berowne makes a similar point about dramatic form in his summing-up:

> Our wooing doth not end like an old play;
> Jack hath not Jill: these ladies' courtesy
> Might well have made our sport a comedy.
>
> (V.II.864–6)

Berowne's distinction works in one sense towards the creation of a kind of realism which would distinguish what we are seeing from hackneyed convention (interestingly, it also denies the play's status as comedy). Equally, though, it is suggestive that he labels marriage as proper specifically to 'an old play'. Shakespeare may well have been trying in *Love's Labour's Lost* to create an innovative dramatic aesthetic which would respect verisimilitude of psychological development as well as generic convention; if so, it is striking to see how rapidly and how completely he abandoned the experiment, and showed himself content to work within the constraints of a teleology of marriage in what seem likely to have been his next few comedies. It is notable, too, to see how completely he identifies such a teleology with conventional comic structure.

MUCH ADO ABOUT NOTHING

Much Ado About Nothing operates in rather different ways. This is a play which focuses strongly on family and social groupings, which are distinctively imaged. Like *The Merchant of Venice*, there is a proliferation of only children – Hero and Beatrice clearly have no siblings, and Claudio and Benedick have none that we know of – whose marriages are the subject of careful planning and supervision by almost all the members of the communities to which they belong. Fertility in Messina may have been limited, it seems, but it is at least carefully cultivated and cherished. But, like *As You Like It*, the play is also interested in brothers: mischief is contrived by Don Pedro's bastard brother, and the comic solution is facilitated by Leonato's legitimate one, though the non-existent 'daughter' whom he produces serves only to highlight the small numbers of the younger generation (accentuated by the wartime background of the play). Moroever, there is an unusual emphasis on other members of families: the opening stage direction includes the ghost character of Innogen, Hero's mother, and Leonato says of Claudio's valiant performance in the wars that 'He hath an uncle here in Messina will be very much glad of it'.[3] It also seems to have been originally envisaged that Antonio should have a son,[4] and we even hear – unusually enough – mention of Beatrice's mother, albeit only that she cried when her child was born. Equally, there are several significant bonds of friendship – there are two separate male groupings linked by strong homosocial bonds, and there is also an unusually large community of young women, all living amicably and intimately together. Thus, although there are no existing marriages in the older generation for us to contextualise the nature and meaning of the lovers' progress towards matrimony, the play pays considerable attention to the structures and operation of kinship and friendship groupings in the facilitating of civilised communal life. Unlike *As You Like It* or *A Midsummer Night's Dream*, the play shows us no alternative mode of existence: no one moves outside the group, and even the Bastard has his own two henchmen, so that we are made sharply aware that, like Euripides' *Bacchae*, this is a play which focuses less on the psyche of the individual than on the collective sociopsychological functioning of the community as its various wholes.

The way that Messina principally regulates its social interactions is through rituals of hospitality and, above all, through the bonding processes of commensality. Images of food run strongly through the play, combining to create a sense of an appetitive, vigorous body politic which functions as the opposite of the starved relationships of *Coriolanus* and as a counterpoint to the cannibalistic imagery of *Othello*. When Beatrice first speaks of Benedick, she demands, 'I pray you, how many hath he killed and eaten in these wars? But how many hath he killed? For indeed I promise to eat all of his killing' (I.I.38–40). Assured that he has distinguished himself on campaign, she ripostes, 'You had musty victual, and he hath holp to eat it: he is a very valiant trencher-man; he hath an excellent stomach' (I.I.45–7); later she exclaims, 'Is it possible disdain should die, while she hath such meet food to feed it as Signor Benedick?' (I.I.110–11). Benedick echoes her when he assures the Prince that if he looks pale it will be '[w]ith anger, with sickness, or with hunger, my lord, not with love' (I.I.230–1), and is again associated with food when he is soon after chosen as the Prince's messenger to assure Leonato that they will be present at his supper (I.I.255–7). The Prince's errand here concerns the proper and regulated consumption of food; by contrast, Conrade advises Don John towards a markedly more disruptive course when he tells him 'It is needful that you frame the season for your own harvest' (I.III.23–4), and Beatrice strikes a similar note when she comments of Don John, 'How tartly that gentleman looks! I never can see him but I am heart-burned an hour after' (II.I.3–4).

As the relationship of Beatrice and Benedick develops, it is increasingly characterised in terms of food. Beatrice tells the disguised Benedick that she has no fear of him:

> he'll but break a comparison or two on me, which, peradventure not marked or not laughed at, strikes him into melancholy; and then there's a partridge wing saved, for the fool will eat no supper that night.
>
> (II.I.136–40)

Benedick says to Claudio of Don Pedro's apparent deception that ''Twas the boy that stole your meat, and you'll beat the post' (II.I.185–6), and he labels Beatrice 'a dish I love not! I cannot endure my Lady Tongue' (II.I.257–8). When Don Pedro induces Claudio, Leonato and Hero to help him snare Benedick, he assures them that 'in despite of his quick wit and his queasy stomach, he shall fall in love with Beatrice' (II.I.361–2). Benedick dismisses Claudio in love with 'his words are a very fantastical banquet, just so many strange dishes' (II.III.20–1), and muses, 'I will not be sworn but love may transform me to an oyster' (II.III.23–4), while Claudio sees him as a fish about to bite on the hook (II.III.109). As Don Pedro goes to send Beatrice to call Benedick into dinner (II.III.210–11), Benedick muses, 'doth not the appetite alter? A man loves the meat in his youth that he cannot endure in his age' (II.III.229–31). Similarly, Ursula too images Beatrice as a fish (III.1.26–9), and Margaret will later observe that Benedick 'swore he would never marry, and yet now in despite of his heart he eats his meat without grudging' (III.IV.82–4).

When the tone of the play abruptly darkens with the cancelled wedding, so does the nature of the food images. Claudio calls Hero 'a rotten orange' (IV.I.31) (he himself has previously been as jealous as an orange (II.I.276–7), Leonato speaks of 'frugal Nature' (IV.I.128) and insists that age has not yet 'eat up my invention' (IV.I.194). Beatrice and Benedick seem initially to strike the old light-hearted note:

Bene. By my sword, Beatrice, thou lovest me.
Beat. Do not swear and eat it.
Bene. I will swear by it that you love me, and I will make him eat it that says I love not you.
Beat. Will you not eat your word?
Bene. With no sauce that can be devised to it. I protest I love thee.

(IV.I.273–9)

But Beatrice abruptly alters the mood with the startling savagery of her exclamation 'O God that I were a man! I would eat his heart in the market-place' (IV.I.305–6). She dismisses Claudio as 'Count Comfect' (IV.I.315), a sweet thing easily consumed, and Claudio himself soon echoes her when he tells the Prince of Benedick's challenge: 'he hath bid me to a calf's head and a capon, the which if I do not carve most curiously, say my knife's naught. Shall I not find a woodcock too?' (V.I.152–5). And the imagery of unappetising food finds its climax with Claudio when, hearing Borachio's confession, he cries, 'I have drunk poison whiles he utter'd it' (V.I.240).

The fact that the relationship between Beatrice and Benedick is so insistently presented in terms of nourishing and appealing food may well seem to suggest that it should be perceived as an entirely wholesome and natural affair, perhaps especially by contrast with the taint associated with the Hero–Claudio intrigue. Nevertheless, modern criticism is often quick to point to the profound artificiality of the way in which Beatrice and Benedick are tricked, manoeuvred and manipulated into subject positions which suit their respective communities, by making them more malleable and conventional. This can essentially be seen as a prime example of interpellation into ideological structures which constrain and preempt individual expressions of emotion and thought: Jean Howard sees the ending as essentially mystificatory, performing 'a sleight of hand' by which 'the aristocratic ideology of arranged property marriages is made to appear seamlessly compatible with emergent middle-class ideologies of love and individual choice as preconditions for marital union', and concludes that by falling for their friends' deception Beatrice and Benedick 'do not so much obey a spontaneous, privately gendered emotion as reveal their successful interpellation into particular positions within a gendered social order'.[5] And on similar lines, Peter Smith argues that 'marriage in *Much Ado* clearly functions to structure the social fabric rather than to give expression to anything as fanciful as love...Marriage is a hard political reality and reputations, male reputations, are at stake.'[6]

Beatrice and Benedick are, at the outset of the play, more than usually adamant that they wish to live single.[7] Benedick's very name connotes bachelorhood, and Beatrice notably revises the distaste which Katherine in *The Taming of the Shrew* feels for spinsterhood when she reappropriates Katherine's image of leading apes in hell and subversively re-encodes it as celebratory symbol of liberation and of the 'blessed' state which her own name encodes (II.I.39–45). We may choose whether to take these stances seriously, or to see them as obviously ironised by the play's comic structure in ways which invite us to see both characters as clearly destined to be altered, and preferably in conjunction with each other.[8] Equally, we could take further Beatrice's use of Katherine's imagery to read this play as a conscious reworking of the form of relationship already presented in *The Taming of the Shrew* – we could note, in this connection, that this play too presents a freely chosen affective relationship in sustained counterpoint to a socially engineered one which proves, in many ways, to be more successful and satisfactory. Certainly, *Much Ado About Nothing* situates the commencement of the Beatrice–Benedick relationship in a past which, whether envisaged theatrically as a prehistory of the play or metatheatrically as the story of the shrew and her suitor, conditions their present and future. Beatrice refers repeatedly to their previous encounters: '[h]e set up his bills here in Messina, and challenged Cupid at the flight; and my uncle's fool, reading the challenge, subscribed for Cupid, and challenged him at the bird-bolt' (I.I.36–8). The likeliest explanation of this would cast Beatrice herself as her uncle's fool, and suggest a previous emotional entanglement with Benedick to which she was more committed than he; and the same thing is also implied by her accusation that 'You always end with a jade's trick, I know you of old' (I.I.133–4). Finally, she unequivocally asserts that Benedick has once before won her heart 'with false dice' (II.I.263). Benedick is noticeably more reticent on the subject, but he does dismiss Hero with the remark that 'there's her cousin, an she were not possessed with a fury, exceeds her as much in beauty as the first of May doth the last of December' (I.I.177–9). It is also suggestive that he asserts, 'I would not marry her, though she were endowed with Adam had left him before he transgressed' (II.I.234–6), when no one but himself has actually suggested the idea.

We may, then, choose to see Beatrice and Benedick as already involved, and the actions of those around them as merely enabling them both to come to a fuller understanding of themselves and to enter a happier state; after all, Beatrice responds to the news of Benedick's alleged affection with 'others say thou dost deserve, and I / Believe it better than reportingly' (III.I.115–16). But even if we are attracted by this recuperative reading, it still leaves unresolved the issue of why Beatrice and Benedick were unable simply to progress towards a relationship of their own volition, and why, in particular, Beatrice, who in other respects verges on the shrew-like, should be so obviously more amenable than the apparently easy-going Benedick.

Part of the answer to this may perhaps lie in what we see of the development of the Hero–Claudio relationship. This, like that of Beatrice and Benedick, has a pre-history: he 'lik'd her ere I went to wars' (I.I.285), 'But lest my liking might too sudden seem, / I would have salv'd it with a longer treatise' (I.I.294–5). 'Treatise' is a telling word here, for it encapsulates precisely the search for authorisation which characterises Claudio's whole attitude towards his courtship of Hero. He is desperately cautious. Some aspects of his concern may be understandable enough – when he asks, 'Hath Leonato any son, my lord?' (I.I.274), he is merely evincing the same kind of financial prudence as Bassanio and Petruchio, but in other areas he seems clearly to be quite abnormally nervous about committing himself. When Don Pedro declares, 'the lady is very well worthy', Claudio replies, ludicrously, 'You speak this to fetch me in, my lord' (I.I.204–6), and the whole intrigue surrounding Don Pedro's apparent bad faith is wantonly unmotivated by any intelligible or overtly articulated consideration. Claudio could perfectly well have proposed to Hero by himself, though Lisa Jardine suggests that what happens here works to reveal the extent to which the society is poised between two models of the marriage relationship:

> Don Pedro correctly intercedes for Claudio with Leonato, since his rank (and Claudio's dependent relationship with him) will make Leonato's consent to the match more likely... His proposal to woo Hero... to gain her *love*, however, confuses his role in the match... Don Pedro has apparently elided old and new forms of alliance formation.[9]

Tellingly, when he suspects that the Prince has betrayed him, it is the woman, rather than his friend, whom he is inclined to blame, declaring, 'beauty is a witch / Against whose charms faith melteth into blood' (II.I.167–8). *Much Ado About Nothing* may not be a problem play, but there are unmistakable similarities between Claudio and Bertram. Though Claudio is certainly less reluctant to substitute marriage for a life of fighting, he may still seem noticeably quick to fall for Don John's trick, and wantonly cruel as Beatrice alleges, and as Benedick ultimately agrees, in the manner of his public repudiation of his bride.

Having turned against Hero, however, Claudio markedly does *not* turn against the whole idea of marriage. He accepts his penance readily, and makes no objection to taking Leonato's supposed niece, even when he is not allowed to see her face in advance. He even defers to her: he calls her 'Sweet' before he knows anything of her but her alleged lineage (V.IV.55), and he promises, 'I am your husband, if you like of me' (V.IV.59). Perhaps Claudio's previously evidenced craving for male approval for his marital choice actually works in his favour here: he may well be happier accepting the bride given him by his elders than with the one he chose by himself. As in *The Taming of the Shrew*, this play presents an individualistic choice and an arranged one, and ultimately endorses the latter – though, in the inventiveness and flexibility of the comic resolution, they are eventually revealed as the same; moreover, the appropriateness of the socially engineered relationship is also affirmed by the successful communal manipulation of Beatrice and Benedick. Even here, though, the play, if not all of its characters, finally holds back from full commitment: we end with dancing, not with the formal wedding, whose celebration is yet again deferred.[10]

It is at Benedick's instigation that it is postponed. Throughout, Benedick has embodied resistance to marriage, which he consistently associates with cuckold jokes. When Leonato identifies his daughter with the old chestnut 'Her mother hath many times told me so', Benedick immediately demands, 'Were you in doubt, sir, that you asked her?' (I.I.97–8), and then ostentatiously deploys the conditional in 'If Signor Leonato be her father...' (I.I.104). He exclaims, 'In faith, hath not the world one man but he will wear his cap without suspicion?' (I.I.183–4), makes game of the bachelorhood implied in his name (I.I.248) and invites the Friar to 'bind me, or undo me – one of them' (V.IV.20). Even at the end, he refuses to dissociate the two as he advises Don Pedro, 'Prince, thou art sad; get thee a wife, get thee a wife! There is no staff more reverend than one tipped with horn' (V.IV.120–2).

Benedick, however, is not the only character to denigrate marriage. When Borachio informs Don John of an imminent wedding, the Bastard – himself the product of a disregard for matrimony – demands, 'Will it serve for any model to build mischief on? What is he for a fool that betroths himself to unquietness?' (I.III.43–5); and Beatrice advises her cousin that after wedding comes repentance (II.I.64–71). Least well established, but perhaps most interesting, is the attitude of Don Pedro. He twice hints that he himself might be interested in Beatrice: 'Will you have me, lady?' (II.I.307) he asks, and later during the deception of Benedick he declares, 'I would she had bestowed this dotage on me, I would have daffed all other respects and made her half myself' (II.III.164–6). The first of these utterances, though, is received by Beatrice as jest, and the second is in the unequivocal context of jest, so that presumably the whole community is well aware of the 'other respects' that have kept the Prince so far celibate.[11] Since his father's siring of a bastard has led to war, he would be well advised to take his marriage seriously.

In fact, almost everyone in the world of Messina does take marriage seriously. Leonato wants to make sure that at the wedding of Hero and Claudio 'all things answer to my mind' (II.I.336–7); Don Pedro defers his departure until the consummation of the marriage (III.II.1–2). Claudio uses the language of the ceremony to request of Don John, 'If there be any impediment, I pray you discover it' (III.II.82–3), and can even be seen as working similarly within its structures when he resolves that 'he would meet her as he was appointed next morning at the temple, and there, before the whole congregation, shame her' (III.III.155–7). Margaret asks, 'Is not marriage honourable in a beggar?' (III.IV.27–8), and Claudio takes a far stricter attitude towards prenuptial sex than his namesake in *Measure for Measure* when he calls it a 'sin', albeit one he thinks can be 'extenuated' (IV.I.50), despite the full and formal public betrothal of himself and Hero. Moreover, the play itself offers the most nearly complete staging of an actual marriage ceremony to be found in the Shakespearean canon,[12] although it also dramatises the disturbing ease with which the wedding can slide into its other as first rite of burial (IV.I.205–6) and then of birth (IV.I.213).[13] Finally, however, the Friar can again summon the congregation to the chapel (V.IV.71) and, with the consent of both Beatrice and Benedick publicly ensured, the ending even retrospectively revises any earlier hints of darker closures as Benedick tells Claudio, 'I did think to have beaten thee, but in that thou art like to be my kinsman, live unbruised' (V.IV.108–10). Beatrice might have longed to eat Claudio's heart in the marketplace, but Benedick, we must now understand, had challenged him with no more serious intent than a bruising, rather than a killing.

Even at the end, however, the Prince is notably not paired off, reflecting the fact that in Messina, marriage, like reproduction, seems to be hard to achieve, though both products may be the more precious for that. As the names of both Beatrice and Benedick remind us, this is a blessed world, gifted with a good fortune, which we simultaneously perceive as gloriously abundant and imperilled and unusual. Situated in a brief interval in a war which still remains to be prosecuted, and which has been occasioned entirely by the social disruption produced by an extramarital liaison, *Much Ado About Nothing* offers us perhaps Shakespeare's least qualified vision of mutuality and enrichment in marriage, but it is also careful to present it as a rare event.[14] Moreover, this play does not, like *A Midsummer Night's Dream*, end with a fertility blessing, or even, like *The Merchant of Venice*, with a bet on the first boy. No children are presaged; no wedding is actually celebrated. Restraint, difficulty and frugality are made prominent to the last.

MEASURE FOR MEASURE

In *Measure for Measure*, by contrast, fertility runs rampant. An unusual number of the women in it are, or have been, pregnant: the very word pregnant (recorded by OED as signifying 'gravid' in 1545) recurs repeatedly.[15] The Duke compliments Escalus, 'the terms / For common justice, y'are as pregnant in / As...any / That we remember';[16] Angelo moralises to Escalus, "Tis very pregnant, / The jewel that we find, we stoop and take't / Because we see it' (II.I.23–5); and Angelo later repents, 'This deed unshapes me quite; makes me unpregnant / And dull to all proceedings' (IV.IV.18–19). When Angelo is first informed that he is to be made deputy, he figures his promotion in terms similar to those employed by Theseus in *A Midsummer Night's Dream* to describe the mechanics of fatherhood:

> Let there be some more test made of my metal,
> Before so noble and so great a figure
> Be stamp'd upon it.
>
> (I.I.48–50)

Similarly, images of pregnancy characterise the growth of Angelo's infatuation with Isabella. He says aside, 'She speaks, and 'tis / Such sense that my sense breeds with it' (II.II.142–3); he finds 'in my heart / The strong and swelling evil of my conception' (II.IV.6–7); and he instructs Isabella, 'Plainly conceive, I love you' (II.IV.140).

The language of reproduction colonises other speakers in the play. Lucio tells Isabella:

> Your brother and his lover have embrac'd;
> As those that feed grow full, as blossoming time
> That from the seedness the bare fallow brings
> To teeming foison, even so her plenteous womb
> Expresseth his full tilth and husbandry.
>
> (I.IV.40–4)

Obviously, images of birth are merely appropriate in a speech announcing a pregnancy; but Lucio presents the fertility of Juliet as part of a general pattern of growth and fruition, and implies an absolute equation between 'husbandry' and child-bearing which is very different from the sparser world of *Much Ado About Nothing*. Other characters similarly view sex as essentially reproductive: Isabella will not sleep with Angelo because 'I had rather my brother die by the law, than my son should be unlawfully born' (III.I.189–90), and Lucio declares, 'this ungenitured agent will unpeople the province with continency' (III.II.167–9). He also tells Isabella, 'I dare not for my head fill my belly: one fruitful meal would set me to't' (IV.III.152–4), where 'fruitful' may well suggest that it is not only Lucio's belly which would be filled in the lush cycle of food and sex which he envisages. This is a world where propagating the species is as automatic as spawning. The Duke images it as a virtually effortless by-product of life itself, warning Claudio:

> Friend hast thou none;
> For thine own bowels which do call thee sire,
> The mere effusion of thy proper loins,
> Do curse the gout, serpigo, and the rheum
> For ending thee no sooner.
>
> (III.I.28–32)

Children come as a 'mere effusion' of the loins, as inevitable an adjunct to a human body as its bowels.

The teeming population explosion envisaged by the play's imagery is confirmed by its striking number of actual pregnancies. As well as Juliet, whose condition triggers much of the plot, we hear of Mistress Elbow, who 'came in great with child; and longing, save your honour's reverence, for stewed prunes' (II.I.88–9), and Lucio's former mistress, Kate Keepdown, who 'was with child by him in the Duke's time. He promised her marriage. His child is a year and a quarter old come Philip and Jacob. I have kept it myself' (III.II.195–6). Here, unusually, we are invited to imagine not only a child but the practicalities of its care, registering an even greater difference between the unfortunate Kate Keepdown and women of an equivalent class in other Shakespearean plays, such as Doll Tearsheet and Mistress Quickly, who are never said to have children (in accord with the long-lived myth that prostitutes bear very few children). We also hear Lucio's speculations on Angelo's own conception – 'Some report, a sea-maid spawned him. Some, that he was begot between two stock-fishes' (III.II.104–5) – and his reflections on the fecundity and abundance which he associates with the Duke's reign: 'Ere he would have hanged a man for the getting of a hundred bastards, he would have paid for the nursing a thousand' (III.II.113–15).

Perhaps even more markedly, the play's world of 'foison' is unaccompanied by any of the usual anxieties about legitimacy, parenthood and, in particular, the role of the father. *Measure for Measure* has neither cuckold jokes nor – except in a highly specialised mode in Isabella's reproach to her brother – queries about paternity, and though never once is a child said to look like its father, blood relationships to fathers are taken largely for granted. Escalus tells Angelo, 'Alas, this gentleman, / Whom I would save, had a most noble father' (II.I.6–7); Pompey introduces Master Froth as 'a man of fourscore pound a year; whose father died at Hallowmas...I hope here be truths' (II.I.122–6); Isabella greets Claudio's resolve with, 'There spake my brother: there my father's grave / Did utter forth a voice' (III.I.85–6). Two of the play's children may be (at least temporarily) subject to the label of bastardy, but in each case the fathers – Claudio and Lucio – acknowledge them, and indeed the term 'bastard' is not used for them.

One reason for this, perhaps, is the extreme disturbance registered throughout *Measure for Measure* to generally acknowledged rites and forms of marriage. A massive body of scholarly discussion has centred on the problematic nature of the three central relationships, none of which is conducted or formalised by precisely the same set of rules as any other, and all of which raise sharply focused questions about what actually constitutes a marriage, both legally and morally speaking. No play more clearly reflects the changes in custom and ceremony which resulted from the clash and interplay of Catholic, Protestant and Puritan attitudes to the meaning of marriage and its spiritual and secular solemnisation. The issue is clearly signalled during our first introduction to the case of Claudio and Juliet, when Claudio tells Lucio:

> Thus stands it with me: upon a true contract
> I got possession of Julietta's bed.
> You know the lady; she is fast my wife
> Save that we do denunciation lack
> Of outward order. This we came not to

> Only for propagation of a dower
> Remaining in the coffer of her friends,
> From whom we thought it meet to hide our love
> Till time had made them for us. But it chances
> The stealth of our most mutual entertainment
> With character too gross is writ on Juliet.
>
> (I.II.134–44)

According to Claudio's own account – which is inherently perfectly probable – neither he nor Juliet have been guilty of anything more grievous than over-optimism in assuming that time *would* soften Juliet's friends. He gives no reason why they thought this, and we can attribute it only to hope, albeit hope of precisely the kind that featured so strongly as a comic virtue in the story of Viola in *Twelfth Night*. But even if we condemn them for this, in all other respects they are, by their lights, blameless. Like the Duchess of Malfi in Webster's play, they have merely taken advantage of the prevailing confusion in marriage rites to suit themselves.

Similar kinds of ambiguity inhere in the story of Mariana and Angelo. The Duke explains Mariana's situation quite clearly to Isabella:

> She should this Angelo have married: was affianced to her oath, and the nuptial appointed. Between which time of the contract and limit of the solemnity, her brother Frederick was wracked at sea, having in that perished vessel the dowry of his sister. But mark how heavily this befell to the poor gentlewoman. There she lost a noble and renowned brother, in his love toward her ever most kind and natural; with him the portion and sinew of her fortune, her marriage dowry; with both, her combinate husband, this well-seeming Angelo.
>
> (III.I.213–23)

Angelo did not of course use the loss of her fortune as his excuse – he cited alleged loose-living on her part – but nevertheless the existence of the betrothal seems to the Duke to be enough to justify the bed-trick:

> He is your husband on a pre-contract:
> To bring you thus together 'tis no sin,

> Sith that the justice of your title to him
> Doth flourish the deceit.
>
> (IV.I.72–5)

In the teeming world of *Measure for Measure*, the Duke's choice of the term 'flourish' is an appropriate one; but he goes one step further than the cheerfully unregulated reproductive practices of most of his subjects by attempting to impose organisation and logic on to the transaction by framing it within a network of 'justice' and 'title'. The difficulty of so doing, however, is only too clearly exposed by the riddling dialogue of his interrogation of Mariana:

> *Mariana.* Pardon, my lord; I will not show my face
> Until my husband bid me.
> *Duke.*   What, are you married?
> *Mariana.* No, my lord.
> *Duke.* Are you a maid?
> *Mariana.* No, my lord.
> *Duke.* A widow, then?
> *Mariana.* Neither, my lord.
> *Duke.* Why, you are nothing then: neither maid, widow, nor wife!
> *Lucio.* My lord, she may be a punk; for many of them are neither maid, widow nor wife.
>
> (V.I.171–81)

Ostensibly, the Duke, like the King in *All's Well that Ends Well*, is nonplussed by Mariana's answers; but in fact it is he who has set up this conversation, and, presumably, inspired her answers – certainly the exchange runs like a rehearsed set-piece. Though Lucio may characterise him as 'the old fantastical Duke of dark corners' (IV.III.156), such a role is – like the rest of what Lucio says about him – entirely alien to his own self-image; indeed he works throughout this scene to eliminate grey areas and to impose the clarity of absolute definition on all situations presented to him.

But just as Lucio's suggestion that Mariana may be a punk disrupts the smooth flow of the stichomythia, so the tensions surrounding definitions of matrimony keep disrupting the smoothness of this scene. Mariana does not wait to be exculpated by the Duke, for she is already sure of her own position:

> As there is sense in truth, and truth in virtue,
> I am affianc'd this man's wife, as strongly
> As words could make up vows. And, my good lord,
> But Tuesday night last gone, in's garden-house
> He knew me as a wife.
>
> (V.I.225-9)

The Duke may, of course, have prompted this speech too; but if he did so, it is seriously detrimental to his project as a whole. Mariana asserts the validity of precisely those informal customs governing marriage which the Renaissance state was working so hard to stamp out; her assurance that the consummation of a betrothal *per verba de futuro* transforms it into a binding marriage tallies with tradition,[17] but radically unsettles notions of state control and state surveillance of its subjects by claiming the importance of a private, subjectively experienced act. Marriages without witnesses had long proved a headache: a particular case in point was the notorious instance of Lady Catherine Grey, younger sister of Lady Jane, who had a claim to the English throne, who contracted a private marriage, bore two sons, but could not afterwards produce any evidence of its legality, since the priest had disappeared and the sole witness had died of consumption. Lady Catherine and her husband had both been confined to the Tower; their children, deemed illegitmate, lost their potential place in the succession. Mariana's case rests on an even more problematic position, since Angelo was unaware that she had taken Isabella's place, and she is thus the only person able to claim certain knowledge that consummation of the earlier betrothal has now taken place.

In the circumstances, it is no surprise that the Duke, who has spent the whole play trying to find out what other people wished to keep concealed, should demand a public celebration of the marriage.[18] He also does the same for Juliet and Claudio, ordering 'She, Claudio, that you wrong'd, look you restore' (V.I.522), even though their contract was presumably *per verba de praesenti* and thus, in traditional practice, perfectly legal by itself. He thus asserts state control, and although his favoured method of so doing is by the apparently benignly paternalist institution of marriage, Lucio, as so often, is on hand to deconstruct assertions, blur distinctions and reveal underlying logic when he protests, 'Marrying a punk, my lord, is pressing to death, / Whipping, and hanging' (V.I.520-

1).[19] For Lucio, marriage provides a culmination only marginally less disastrous than the hanging from which he is so narrowly reprieved; and it has already had similarly ominous overtones in Claudio's promise that 'If I must die, / I will encounter darkness as a bride / And hug it in mine arms' (III.I.82–4), which metaphorically associates marriage with death.

As for the Duke's own marriage, it is perhaps the most problematic of all. Turning, in the last lines of the play, to Isabella, he repeats the proposal he has already hinted at:

> Dear Isabel,
> I have a motion much imports your good;
> Whereto if you'll a willing ear incline,
> What's mine is yours, and what is yours is mine.
> So, bring us to our palace, where we'll show
> What's yet behind, that's meet you all should know.
>
> (V.I.531–6)

Though directors have sometimes chosen to hint at a developing mutual attraction between the Duke and Isabella, it is equally possible to stage the play in ways that make the ending a complete surprise, stripping it of one of the usual staples of comic closure, the fulfilment of anticipation.[20] Does it add to the sense of comic inventiveness and abundance that this marriage should spring out of the generic hat, or should we pay more attention to the fact that Isabella (like Juliet throughout her time on stage in this last scene)[21] is completely silent, and that her consent – so essential in all marriage theory of the period – is not only not given, but barely solicited?[22] And is the ending closed, with Isabella's compliance assumed, or – as often in modern productions – radically open, with the actress either gesturally rejecting the proposal or pointedly neutral on the matter? Moreover, we might well be tempted to ask what it is that marriage can offer to the world of the play.[23] The Duke has already declared himself the possessor of a 'complete bosom' (I.III.3), and procreation, ostensibly one of the prime functions of marriage, has quite clearly already been flourishing in Vienna without benefit of clergy. Isabella, uniquely amongst Shakespeare's heroines, already has a niche securely established in the world, in the convent to which she was apparently whole-heartedly committed; Claudio and Juliet and Angelo and Mariana are pair-bonded in ways that some at least of the audience would be quite ready to recognise as adequately binding, and while Kate Keepdown's reputation will be salved, there is no apparent prospect of material improvement in either her situation or her child's. Marriage may be positively repellent to Lucio, but to the other characters it may well seem little more than an irrelevance; a play that teems with images of fertility may seem more vigorous than the frugal world of *Much Ado About Nothing*, but it has also anticipated and undercut the resonances of its own closure. It is, perhaps, fitting that its final moments should contain the question, but not the answer, of the Duke's proposal, for the play itself has disabled our sense of its own ability to offer closure, conclusion and answer.

4
The Fate of the Nation: Marriage in the History Plays

Marriage in the history plays is less often the focus of critical attention than is the case in the comedies, and commentary has tended primarily to cluster round perhaps the most obviously comic instance of its use, the resolution to *Henry V*. Although crucial in the achievement of closure, however, the relationship between Henry and Catherine is, in fact, curiously marginalised, featuring in only one scene of the play and functioning ultimately more as a coda than a climax. In two others of the history plays, *Richard III* and *King John*, marriage actually features at a much more fundamental level of the text, making significant contributions to thematic and structural elements of the plays. I intend to examine these, but first I want to look at the celebrated union between Henry and Catherine, using a joint examination of the historical figure of Catherine of Valois as she was mediated in Shakespeare's sources, and of the two scenes in which her theatrical counterpart appears, to suggest some of the problematics which structure her use as a character and may, in fact, have contributed to her relative marginalisation.

HENRY V

In his essay 'Invisible Bullets: Renaissance Authority and its Subversion, *Henry IV* and *Henry V*', in the seminal collection *Political Shakespeare*, Stephen Greenblatt comments on how the Earl of Warwick, at 2 *Henry VI* IV.iv.68–78, refers to bawdy talk as a thing that must be learned in order to be known and hated. Warwick means his remarks to refer to the hero of the *Henriad*, Prince Hal / Henry V himself:

> The Prince but studies his companions
> Like a strange tongue, wherein, to gain the language,
> 'Tis needful that the most immodest word
> Be look'd upon and learnt; which once attain'd,
> Your Highness knows, comes to no further use
> But to be known and hated.[1]

Greenblatt, in a typically New Historicist manoeuvre, links Warwick's analysis with Thomas Hariot's attempts to create a glossary of the dialect of the Algonquin Indians.[2] It might also be possible, though, to see another connection with instances of actual language-learning, this time one that takes place within the *Henriad* itself: the scene in which Henry V's prospective bride, the Princess Catherine of France, is being introduced to English by her attendant, Alice.

As is often the case with second language acquisition, Catherine's nascent vocabulary is focused on what is most immediate to her, the parts of her own body, as she learns, in sequence, 'de hand', 'de fingres', 'de nailes', 'de arm', 'd'elbow', 'de nick', 'de chin' (which she pronounces as 'de sin'), 'de foot', and, finally, 'de cown' (her version of 'gown').[3] Part of the point of this scene centres on the comedy of Catherine's mispronunciations, which invest what she says with punning *doubles entendres* of which she herself is unaware: 'nick' can mean 'vulva', 'sin' is obviously suggestive, 'foot' is reminiscent of the French 'foutre', which means 'to fuck', and 'cown' sounds like 'con', the French equivalent of 'cunt'.[4] Here, she echoes the language play of Fluellen's Welsh accent, which leads him to the comic nomenclature of 'Alexander the Pig', as well as the inadvertent humour of Mistress Quickly's description of the death of Falstaff, where there is a similar obscene connotation to the use of the word 'stone', a common term for testicle:

> So a bade me lay more clothes on his feet. I put my hand into the bed and felt them, and they were as cold as any stone. Then I felt to his knees, and so up'ard and up'ard, and all was as cold as any stone.
> (2.3.21–4)

As Jyotsna Singh comments of Mistress Quickly's similar linguistic habits in *Henry IV Part One*, her 'carnivalesque malapropisms mock at the linguistic order buttressing the world of kingly hierarchy'.[5] Clearly, the play in these scenes is demonstrating a comprehensive interest in language, not only as it is manifested within the punning potentialities of everyday English, but also as it relates to the diverse experiences of three people, a Frenchwoman learning it, a Welshman speaking it as a second language, and a tavern hostess using a simple, demotic discourse which, nevertheless, she is unable fully to control, since the double energies of 'stone' invest her speech with a bawdy quality she surely does not intend.

However, there seem also to be other concerns informing this presentation of Catherine. Although she is the generator of comedy here, she, like Mistress Quickly, is not only speaking but also spoken by her own words; we laugh at her rather than with her. Critics are quick to read Ophelia's mad songs as expressions of a previously concealed sexual nature; it is hard to do the same with Catherine, unconscious of her own meanings and a mere parrot of the words offered to her by Alice (who is equally guiltless of deliberate obscenity). Although it would certainly be possible to play this scene as light comedy, there is, perhaps, a more sinister suggestion in the way that these two French women are unknowingly made fools of by the English language. We could read Catherine here as being, albeit in a minor way, a victim of Englishness, just as her countrymen at Harfleur and Agincourt are. She is, after all, asking to learn English for a reason: Henry V's military victories have made it appear likely that she will become his bride. No one in the play has said this yet, but that, surely, is because they do not need to. Catherine's apparently light-hearted language must be seen, then, as traversed by political realities none the less potent for being unarticulated and unacknowledged.

There is also, though, a possibility of another reading, one which would make Catherine appear rather less' a passive victim of events. She and France itself are consistently elided to form a joint prize for Henry at the culmination of his successful campaign: Lisa Jardine suggests that 'The audience's assent to the proposition that England has "won" France legitimately is effected dramatically by the scene in which Henry woos Kate'.[6] By a silent transition, the crown of France, Henry's avowed goal at the outset, becomes metaphorically replaced by its Princess:

> Yet leave our cousin Catherine here with us.
> She is our capital demand, comprised
> Within the fore-rank of our articles.

(5.2.94–6)

Instead of the capital city, Paris, Henry names Catherine as his 'capital demand'. Obviously, this is far more gracious than an overt statement of the brutal political reality which has already assured him everything he chooses to name; Henry here is tactful and shows himself far more adept at a diplomatic glossing over of the political with the personal than had Catherine's brother the Dauphin with his infamous insult of the tennis balls. Nevertheless, not all his rhetorically effective affectation of bluntness can paper over the possibility of a slippage between those two nouns which he has so smoothly tried to conflate, 'Catherine' and 'France'. As conqueror, Henry V may have proved himself invincible, but as the numerous jealous husbands of Renaissance drama attest, when a man embarks on marriage his honour, previously in his own keeping, must be abruptly entrusted to his wife – and was, therefore, consistently seen as desperately vulnerable. If, as *As You Like It* seems to suggest, cuckoldry was an inevitable fact of life, what price marital happiness, diplomatic alliances, the honour of a king or the legitimate succession of a kingdom?

On the surface, the behaviour of the Princess Catherine seems calculated to quell any such doubts. Charmingly unaffected, incapable, precisely because of her limited language skills, of deception, she appears the epitome of modesty and obedience, prepared, like a model daughter, to dispose of her affections entirely at the discretion of her father. Maybe, however, the episode of her language learning should give us pause. What if she too, like her husband, should have learned bawdy language only that it should be 'known and hated'? This would certainly bode well for her fidelity, but what would it imply for her response to her husband – which he does, indeed, seem to have trouble awakening in the closing scene, with her horrified reaction to the prospect of being kissed? Certainly an apparent equation between 'English' and 'bawdry' seems hinted at again when the wooing-scene is interrupted by the return of the negotiators. Henry says, 'Here comes your father' (5.2.270–1), which Kenneth Branagh in his film version played for pure comedy, and Burgundy responds, 'God save your majesty. My royal cousin, teach you our princess English?' (5.2.272–3); and a persistent pun on 'tongue' as both language and instrument of kissing also lurks throughout the scene. Perhaps, under Henry's tutelage, Catherine will progress jointly in proficiency in English and in love; or perhaps, given our memory of Warwick's comments and our knowledge of Fluellen's failure ever fully to master a second language, we can read this play, too, as figuring, however subtly, female reluctance to marry.

The historical Catherine of Valois, as Shakespeare would have known from Holinshed and from his other sources, was troubled by no such reserve. After the death of her husband Henry, her suspected fondness for his cousin Edmund Beaufort led to the passing of a bill to regulate the remarriage of dowager queens, making it effectively subject to the new king's permission (since Henry VI was only a child, this was intended to delay matters until he had at least attained his majority); undeterred, however, Catherine did in fact enter into a secret marriage with a gentleman of her wardrobe, Owen Tudor, who is said to have attracted her attention when he fell drunk into her lap at a ball. Tudor was, as his name suggests, a Welshman; interestingly, the historical Catherine's language learning clearly cannot have progressed very far, for Sir John Wynn of Gwydir claimed:

> Queen Katherine being a French woman born, knew no difference between the English and Welsh nation until her marriage being published, Owen Tudor's kindred and country were objected, to disgrace him, as vile and barbarous.[7]

They had four children, Edmund, Jasper, Owen, who became a monk, and a daughter who died young. Catherine kept the marriage, if marriage it was, a secret until shortly before her death, when it became known to her son from her first marriage, Henry VI. He was kind to his half-brothers, who became his loyal followers; Edmund, the eldest, was given the earldom of Richmond, and in due course married Margaret Beaufort, daughter of the Duke of Somerset, whose descent, like his own, was dubious, since the Beauforts had originally been bastards of John of Gaunt. It was the son of these two, Edmund Tudor and Margaret Beaufort, who was eventually to succeed to the English throne as Henry VII, the first ruler of the House of Tudor, and the grandfather of Elizabeth I.

Catherine of Valois' position in the family tree of the English royal family was, therefore, both dependent on and disgraced by marriage; she was both one of the few royal ancestresses of Elizabeth I (indeed Elizabeth's only direct link to the major royal families of Europe), and a woman whose sexual incontinence had led her to contravene class barriers and to muddy the waters of the succession to the throne. Her own final destiny was curiously emblematic of her uneasy position: after her death at Bermondsey Abbey, her body was taken to Westminster Abbey for interment close to that of her famous husband, but it was later disturbed and lay, gradually mummifying, above ground until well into the seventeenth century, when Pepys kissed it on his birthday. The sadness of her ending is compounded by a contemporary rumour that she died mad, like her father Charles VI and her son Henry VI.[8]

Although the imminent death of Henry V himself is hinted at in the closing lines of Shakespeare's play – Tennenhouse comments that 'the Epilogue continues on past a comedic resolution to remind the Elizabethan audience that the very marriage which secured the peace with France and established the line of succession eventually led to the War of the Roses'[9] – Catherine's future fate is never mentioned. It could, indeed, be seen as one of many significant gaps in the text concerning women, and, in particular, inheritance through the female line. Henry V's mother, Mary Bohun, who gave birth to him at the age of 17 and died in childbed at 24, is also passed over in silence, although there is evidence that she and her husband had had a close and loving marriage, with much joint involvement in their children;[10] so, more understandably, is his stepmother, Joanna of Navarre (memorialised in the splendid tomb she shares with Henry IV in Canterbury Cathedral), whom the king's brother arrested on a charge of witchcraft while he himself was on campaign in France. Indeed, women in general have no place in the young king's life: any elements of the feminine seem to be subsumed within Falstaff's parody of the grotesque maternal body,[11] and Hal's famed sowing of wild oats includes not one single sexual misdemeanour. He does indeed joke to Falstaff that 'Why then, it is like if there come a hot June, and this civil buffeting hold, we shall buy maidenheads as they buy hob-nails, by the hundreds',[12] but he shows no inclination to do so himself. The closest we come to it is Falstaff's allegation in Part Two of Poins' boast that the Prince will marry his sister (II.ii.120–2), and the point of this is that it is a ridiculous suggestion. Immediately after that, proposing to beard Falstaff at the Boar's Head, he enquires first of Bardolph, 'Sup any women with him?' (II.ii.143), and it is not until after he is satisfied that there will be only Doll Tearsheet and Mistress Quickly there that he agrees to go. Apart from the wives of Hotspur and of Mortimer, women have very little place indeed in the male-oriented world of the two *Henry IV* plays, with their peer bonding and their network of father–son relationships.

Women, however, feature almost from the outset in *Henry V*, for it is female inheritance which forms the entire crux of Henry's claim to the throne of France (and, in a parallel which it would have been impossible for the audience to avoid noticing, of the Tudors' claim to the throne of England).[13] An audience ruled by a female sovereign is automatically positioned here to be out of sympathy with the Salic law; nevertheless, they might take note that it was originally established by

> certain French
> Who, holding in disdain the German women,
> For some dishonest manners of their life,
> Established there this law: to wit, no female
> Should be inheritrix in Salic land...
>
> (I.2.47–51)

Even a passage which ostensibly works to legitimise claims through the female line thus intrudes a reminder of the potential instability of that key concept, female 'dishonesty'. And yet the Salic law is simultaneously shown to be ridiculous: what female dishonesty compromises is not the place in the family tree of the women themselves, but that of their husbands, who may find themselves written out of their own lineage if they are tricked into rearing progeny not genetically theirs. If there is doubt about a woman's fidelity, it must affect her sons as much as her daughters. What these lines do is expose the doublethink which displaces such threatening anxieties about paternity onto the demonised figure of the woman, preferably (as in the case of the absent Mary Bohun) by forgetting her altogether while a father–son psychodrama is played out.

It is very easy for a modern perspective (and particularly a feminist one) to demonise and ridicule such concerns about women's role in the reproductive process and their ability to disrupt the transmission of the correct male genes through infidelity. Shakespeare's audience, however, would have been very well aware that one of the female characters of *Henry V* was notorious for perpetrating precisely such disruption. Catherine's mother,

Isabeau of Bavaria, was widely believed to have had an affair with her brother-in-law, Louis, Duke of Orleans, and the king's role in the begetting of at least some of her children was open to substantial doubt. While sleeping with one's brother-in-law does in one sense cause minimal disturbance to transmission of genes, it did not make Isabeau any the less, in contemporary ideology, a whore, and the issue of paternity hung relentlessly over the long fight of Catherine's brother the Dauphin to be recognised as rightful heir. (It is often suggested that the secret confided to him by Joan of Arc, which inspired his ultimate success, was her heaven-guided belief that he was the true son of the king.) This, too, is something on which the play is silent, but the notoriety of Isabeau's sexual misdemeanours, and their pivotal role in the Hundred Years War, was such that Shakespeare might well assume knowledge on the part of his audience of the behaviour of Isabeau as well as of the later history of her daughter Catherine.

For all the worries about female fidelity, however, Henry's marriage to Catherine is the goal towards which the play pushes, resolving the conflicts of the battlefield through the characteristic techniques and teleology of comedy. Relying on the word-play of the language lesson to establish Catherine firmly in the minds of the audience, Shakespeare is able to produce her at the end, like a rabbit out of the generic hat, as a romantic heroine to crown all. The scene in which he does this can be read in various ways – as straightforwardly romantic, as cynical, as a deft weaving of discourses, or as a simple piece of inspired opportunism.[14] On one level, it may well be felt that the entire episode hinges on a sustained mystification of political reality as personal choice; and yet, especially in the theatre, it is almost impossible not to respond to the fact that it is also a very charming scene, and one which offers its audience profound gratifications. Kenneth Branagh's film version of the play is prepared to query war and expose the ruthlessness of which its hero is capable, but when it came to the finale he cast his own wife in a lusciously photographed comic interlude which had two very nice people developing genuine affection for each other; and certainly the scene proved easily susceptible of such an interpretation.

One of the greatest strengths of the scene is, perhaps, that it is prepared to face its weak points. This is not *As You Like It*, where our attention has been on the lovers since Act One, and their marriage has long been established as the only likely outcome;

Catherine is never even heard of before Act III, and even when she is eventually introduced, she appears only once before the finale. The whole thing gives an impression of breakneck speed, in marked contrast to a recent historian's comment that 'the negotiations which preceded the marriage of Henry V and Katherine of Valois...must rank among the most prolonged in the annals of English royal marriages'.[15] Maybe Shakespeare had no time for more scenes with her, or maybe he is in fact highlighting the ways in which her role functions essentially as a plot device. Even in the wooing scene, the underlying realities of the situation are allowed to show through quite clearly, as Henry tells her:

> I speak to thee plain soldier: if thou canst love me for this, take me. If not, to say to thee that I shall die, is true – but for thy love, by the Lord, no. Yet I love thee, too. And while thou livest, dear Kate, take a fellow of plain and uncoined constancy, for he perforce must do thee right, because he hath not the gift to woo in other places.
>
> (5.2.148–53)

For all its vaunted plainness, this actually represents a complex mixture of discourses. On one level, it clearly seems to recall the play to which Pistol had alluded earlier in the cycle, *Tamburlaine the Great*:

> Techelles, women must be flattered;
> But this is she with whom I am in love.[16]

It is a potentially awkward echo – might recollections of Tamburlaine invite comparison between his celebrated brutality to the virgins of Damascus, which is immediately followed by his tenderest apostrophisation of Zenocrate, and Henry's own behaviour at Harfleur?[17] However, it also compactly encapsulates the position of the soldier in the discourse of love which he knows he must use, but which is not his natural language. Tamburlaine opens up a potential gap between language and actuality, only to resolve it in ways which paradoxically both challenge and legitimate the authenticity of his discourse: his flattery may be meaningless, but what he asserts – in, for him, an unusually plain style – is not. Henry attempts a similar bridging.

However, his words also echo those of Rosalind in *As You Like It* (herself at the time alluding to Marlowe, on this occasion to the poet of *Hero and Leander*), who equally does not believe that men have died for love. Henry thus aligns himself with a *female* perspective on the matter, as he perhaps does too when he urges Catherine to 'let thine eye be thy cook' (5.2.147–8), where he speaks the homely language of the kitchen. As with his willingness to adopt franglais, he works here to elide rather than stress the difference between them, holding out the promise of an apparently companionate marriage. At the same time though, his explicit interpellation of her, with the use of the familiar 'Kate', and his implict categorisation of her as a 'place' (5.2.153), also serve as concealed reminders of how very little power she actually has in this scene. The terms of the deal are, in fact, very clearly set out. The marriage is a political necessity; language and behaviour may turn it into something more pleasant, and Henry is prepared to do that if Catherine agrees. Denial, however, would produce her only a worsening of the conditions, not a removal of them. This would be very serious for her, since she has no other arena of action or interest, and, presumably, little more than a minor inconvenience for him, since she could still bear his children and would still constitute a direct genealogical link with the crown of France.

In this sense, there is certainly a gender imbalance inscribed in the scene. Yet Catherine's lot is undoubtedly a far more pleasant one than that of Bardolph, Pistol or Falstaff, and though it would in one way be possible to see all these as victims of Henry, it is equally possible to read them as reaping the rewards of their own inadequacies and choices. In short, there has been much suffering in the play, and Henry's discovery and tactful engineering of a way in which some sense of closure and rejoicing can be achieved may well be as welcome to Catherine as it invariably is to the theatre audience. Like another Kate who makes the best of things (and whose presence seems almost deliberately to be invoked when Henry tells Catherine that 'a good heart, Kate, is the sun and the moon – or rather the sun and not the moon' (5.2.160–1), she kisses.

Catherine's marriage is unique in the history plays in affording the pleasures of comic closure. In the *Henry VI* plays, where the young Shakespeare now seems to have been borrowing heavily from Marlowe, women, such as Joan of Arc and Eleanor of Gloucester, are consistently demonised as whores and witches, with

Margaret of Anjou's infidelity in particular jeopardising the entire succession to the English throne; Coppélia Kahn comments that in the first tetralogy, 'Liaisons with women are invariably disastrous because they subvert or destroy more valued alliances between men.'[18] In *Richard II*, Richard's wife, although made significantly older than the child she historically was and therefore capable of emotional maturity, does little more than provide a counterpoint of lamentation to the king's own sorrows, and is dispatched back to her native France well before the end.[19] In both *Richard III* and *King John*, however, marriage does have a major part to play in structuring the form and mood of the developing narratives.

RICHARD III

One of the most extraordinary features of the character of Richard III is the magnetism he apparently exerts over women. This is perhaps less surprising in modern productions where the role has been taken by an actor such as Laurence Olivier, famous for playing romantic leads like Heathcliff; but it is perhaps noteworthy that the only record we have of Richard Burbage as attracting enthusiastic female response comes from his appearance as Richard III, in the famous anecdote from John Manningham's diary:

> Upon a time when Burbage played Richard III there was a [female] citizen grew so far in liking with him, that before she went from the play she appointed him to come that night unto her by the name of Richard III. Shakespeare, overhearing their conclusion, went before, was entertained and at his game ere Burbage came. The message being brought that Richard III was at the door, Shakespeare caused return to be made that William the Conqueror was before Richard III.[20]

Within the play, Richard is able to overcome or at least temporarily to quell the antagonism of four women who all have good reason to hate him: the Dowager Queen Margaret, Elizabeth Woodville, his own mother, the Duchess of York, and his eventual wife, Anne. From three of these he has taken a son, from one a husband, yet each is, apparently, tamed by him during the course of the play, and none is present in the totally womanless scene at the end, which records his defeat and death and the triumph of Henry of

Richmond. Whatever his failures in other respects, in his dealings with women, at least, he appears totally successful.

One thing that is immediately notable about his tactics when fighting women is that he always aims to separate them. Margaret, Elizabeth, Anne and the Duchess are all united by close family bonds – the Duchess is mother-in-law to Elizabeth and, later, to Anne, the husbands of Margaret and the Duchess were cousins, and Anne was married to Margaret's late son – as well as by the horrific experiences they have all lived through. They seek out each other's company, and frequently appear together in scenes, in groups of two or more; but Richard prefers to encounter them singly. In 1.3, he is, as Margaret points out, quick to play up the causes of antagonism between herself and the others present, so that he himself ceases to be the member of the group who is universally demonised; this is elementary policy. He dismisses Anne's attendants before he woos her, leaving her alone with just himself and the corpse, and he sends Derby to separate her from Elizabeth and the Duchess before the coronation. In his final encounter with women, he deals first with the Duchess before keeping Elizabeth behind to ask for the hand of her daughter. This second wooing scene has often been compared unfavourably with the first, as showing a diminution in Richard's powers of persuasion and confidence, but in fact it merely clarifies something which was already latent, the extent of the separation in Richard's mind between marriage and women. Marriage is an act of political survival, boosting his status and intended to provide him with heirs; women, all his life, have meant nothing but trouble.

Richard's problematic attitude towards marriage is suggested from the very outset of the play. His comment on 'this sun of York' (I.1.2) valorises not just his paternal house but also his brother, who is, punningly, 'the son of York'; women, in contrast, are 'wanton' and 'ambling' (I.2.17), unfit companions for Richard ever since the archetypal female, Nature, cheated him in the womb.[21] Meeting his other brother, he feigns a hail-fellow-well-met manner and is quick to demonise women:

> Why this it is when men are ruled by women;
> 'Tis not the King that sends you to the Tower.
> My Lady Grey his wife, Clarence, 'tis she
> That tempers him to this extremity.
> Was it not she, and that good man of worship,

Anthony Woodville, her brother there,
That made him send Lord Hastings to the Tower,
From whence this present day he is delivered?
We are not safe, Clarence, we are not safe.

(I.1.62–70)

His next target is Mistress Shore, the king's mistress (and a heroine of popular legend), whom he will later blame for the withering of his arm. On one level this may be sheer bad faith – Richard laid half these plots himself, his arm was withered from birth – but on another level it is perhaps suggestive of a profound psychological truth: he emerged from the womb damaged, and for birth, women are responsible.

That there is some kind of psychological gratification being achieved in Richard's dealings with women is suggested by the notable lack of any other attributable motive:

And, if I fail not in my deep intent,
Clarence hath not another day to live;
Which done, God take King Edward to His mercy
And leave the world for me to bustle in!
For then I'll mary Warwick's youngest daughter.
What though I killed her husband and her father?
The readiest way to make the wench amends
Is to become her husband and her father,
The which will I – not all so much for love
As for another secret close intent
By marrying her which I must reach unto.

(I.1.149–59)

Part of the problem here may lie in Shakespeare's close fidelity to his sources: it is this which, for no good reason at all, will make him later bring on Buckingham 'in rotten armour, marvellous ill-favoured' (III.5.s.d.), and have Richard send the Bishop of Ely for strawberries (III.4.32–3). It is, perhaps, this sense that his characters are not wholly his, but already pre-existent in Holinshed, which leads him to present them in this externalised fashion, with their motives and drives not fully imagined. Equally, however, the speech is surely susceptible of at least a mildly psychoanalytic reading in which the 'intent' is secret and close not so much from Shakespeare as from Richard himself, who wants to get rid of his brothers to emerge – as he so suggestively puts it – as a father; as his own father, perhaps, as his attempts to bastardise Edward by stressing his own far greater likeness to the dead York would seem to imply: in Coppélia Kahn's suggestive phrase, 'Shakespeare rarely portrays masculine selfhood without suggesting a filial context for it'.[22]

One of the very few occasions when Richard speaks with consideration and respect of another human being is when he mentions his father. In his account, York becomes positively Christlike:

> The curse my noble father laid on thee
> When thou didst crown his warlike brows with paper
> And with thy scorn drew'st rivers from his eyes,
> And then, to dry them, gave the Duke a clout
> Steeped in the faultless blood of pretty Rutland –
> His curses then, from bitterness of soul
> Denounced against thee, are all fallen upon thee;
> And God, not we, hath plagued thy bloody deed.
>
> (I.3.173–80)

One of the notable omissions from the play is any mention of the son Anne bore to Richard, Edward of Middleham, who died as a child in the penultimate year of his father's reign. Historically, it seems to have been grief for this only child which precipitated the demise of Queen Anne; dramatically, she becomes a victim of her husband, and there is complete silence on the subject of her child, as there is also with Richard's two bastards, John and Katherine. (A popular legend also had him the father of another son, first presented to him on the eve of the battle of Bosworth, who escaped the slaughter and lived peaceably and anonymously as a carpenter well into the Tudor period.) Never a father, rejected by his mother, Shakespeare's Richard seems indeed to sum up the very conditions of his own psychological exile in his most famous utterance, 'Now is the winter of our discontent / Made glorious summer by this sun of York' (I.1.1–2), which forever casts his brother rather than himself as 'this sun of York' and writes him into the shadows.

It is to this crucial idea of fathers that he recurs in his wooing of Anne. It comes early on in the great speech which finally induces her to let fall the sword:

> Those eyes of thine from mine have drawn salt tears,
> Shamed their aspects with store of childish drops.
> Those eyes, which never shed remorseful tear –
> No, when my father York and Edward wept
> To hear the piteous moan that Rutland made
> When black-faced Clifford shook his sword at him;
> Nor when thy warlike father, like a child,
> Told the sad story of my father's death
> And twenty times made pause to sob and weep,
> That all the standers-by had wet their cheeks
> Like trees bedashed with rain – in that sad time
> My manly eyes did scorn an humble tear;
> And what these sorrows could not thence exhale,
> Thy beauty hath, and made them blind with weeping.
>
> (I.2.153–66)

The dazzling psychological substitutions that this speech performs are extraordinary. Who dies in it? First it is Richard's brother, Rutland, slaughtered at the hands of 'black-faced Clifford'; the other brother, Edward, and their father York are bystanders, weeping and impotent. Immediately, however, the scene shifts, and it is York himself who is the victim; but this time, the death is rather differently imagined. There is none of the vividness and circumstantial detail of the black face, the shaken sword and the heard moan: the event is recounted, at another time and another place – possibly because Richard himself was not an eye-witness on this occasion, possibly because the scene is too painful for him to imagine. It is not even coherently recounted, because it is 'twenty times' interrupted, and its teller, Warwick the Kingmaker, is, interestingly enough, imaged as 'like a child'. Indeed he is both father and child in the same line, positioned in his paternal relation to Anne and then immediately dislodged from it by the simile. Richard draws here on the shared past and traditional political and familial affiliations which unite them (one longstanding tradition even had them as childhood sweethearts, with Anne, disguised as a kitchen maid by the grasping Clarence, who wished to prey on her inheritance, discovered and rescued by Richard); as with Henry and Catherine, his strategy is to efface difference, as fathers and children, his father and hers, merge in the telling. Equally, however, the success of his rhetoric depends on an ultimate triumphant reinstatement of that difference when Anne herself is imaged as transcendentally unique, the sole cause capable of prompting him to shed tears. The inscriptions of Anne which take place throughout this speech are indeed powerful enough to make her response hardly surprising, for the combination of flattery and of the revelation of such petrifying vulnerability as Richard's story of his father tells her could certainly move.

But although Richard has set himself to marriage because heterosexual intercourse is now the privileged goal of his society, fuelled by peace and the proclivities of his brother, it can bring him no satisfaction. Its potential for discord is clearly figured in his punning exchange with Lord Rivers about the Queen:

> *Richard*... What may she not? She may, yes, marry, may she –
> *Rivers*. What, marry, may she?
> *Richard*. What, marry, may she? Marry with a king,
> A bachelor and a handsome stripling too!
> Iwis your grandam had a worser match.
>
> (I.3.97–101)

It is Richard's confirmed view that marriage – Edward's marriage with Elizabeth Woodville – has caused all the evils of his world. To this extent, the structure of the play actually approximates to a pattern common in tragedy, of the marriage which inaugurates a series of disasters, like Gertrude's with Claudius or Othello's with Desdemona; but since Richard, who makes no secret of his close affiliations with the morality play vice, has no desire to be a tragic hero, he strives instead towards another pattern, that of marriage as comic closure. He perhaps regards his accession initially as a form of closure; discovering that it is not, almost his first act is to end his marriage, in a manoeuvre ostensibly as unmotivated as his initiation of it is. Faced with the hesitation of Buckingham and the flight of Dorset to Richmond, he says:

> Come hither, Catesby. Rumour it abroad
> That Anne my wife is very grievous sick.
> I will take order for her keeping close.
> Inquirre me out some mean poor gentleman,
> Whom I will marry straight to Clarence' daughter.
> The boy is foolish, and I fear not him.

Look how thou dream'st! I say again, give out
That Anne, my queen, is sick and like to die.

(IV.2.49–58)

Of what does Catesby dream? Maybe the implications of what he has heard give him pause; certainly even Richard appears to have qualms of conscience a few moments later, telling himself, 'Tear-falling pity dwells not in this eye' (IV.2.64). In the celebrated 1984 Stratford-upon-Avon production, Antony Sher swung slowly towards Anne as he spoke of her supposed illness; she gasped and staggered, clearly dying, from the stage. It was a dramatic gesture, but it merely made plain the logic which Catesby, at least, must surely detect: this is an announcement of intent to murder.

Why must Anne die? Certainly it would be massively dangerous for Richard if his niece Elizabeth, heiress of York, were to marry his political rival Henry Tudor, heir of Lancaster, and he makes it plain that one of his primary reasons for being widowed is so that he can foreclose on this possibility by marrying Elizabeth himself. Yet the reference to meanly marrying off the daughter of Clarence seems almost designed to remind us that there is more than one possible way of dealing with the threat of a marriageable heiress. If Clarence's daughter can be so effortlessly disposed of, then why not Elizabeth too? Why does it follow that Richard must marry her himself? He recognises the act as sin, and seems also to acknowledge that were he to carry it through, Elizabeth would be deserving of 'tear-falling pity'. Nevertheless, the attempt to engineer this marriage appears to be his instinctive response to adversity. Perhaps, then, its real appeal lies in the prospect which it perversely holds out of identifying himself ever more closely with his own, dead family, of whom Elizabeth is now the primary representative. At one level at least, what seems to be taking place here is an – in one sense literal – exchange of women of which the real object is, as so often, to strengthen the ties between men. (Interestingly, the same argument could be raised in relation to Henry V: Catherine was the sister of Isabella, wife of Richard II, the man whom Henry V invoked before Agincourt, and whom he was popularly believed to love 'more than his own father').[23] Whereas Anne offered him the opportunity of imaginative reopening access to the combative community of the dead Rutland, York and Warwick, Elizabeth brings in her wake the more recent ghosts of her father Edward, 'this sun of York', and the two boys whom Richard is about to murder.

That Elizabeth can be seen as in some sense substituting for those doomed brothers is suggested by the extraordinary bad taste of Richard's proxy wooing of her mother. When the elder Elizabeth reproaches him 'Yet thou didst kill my children' (IV.4.422), he replies:

> But in your daughter's womb I bury them,
> Where, in that nest of spicery, they will breed
> Selves of themselves, to your recomforture.
>
> (IV.4.423–5)

Hideous though this suggestion is, it appears to have weight with Elizabeth: she immediately replies, 'Shall I go win my daughter to thy will?' (IV.4.426). Although the text clearly suggests that Elizabeth is never in fact persuaded, since it must be almost immediately after this that she consents to her daughter's betrothal to Richmond, this is, nevertheless, the argument which sways her to even an appearance of assent, and it seems to me significant that she, like Anne before her, relents when Richard has abandoned the more conventional discourse of Petrarchan courtly wooing to reveal what, in each case, I take to be a profound psychological truth. By marrying Elizabeth of York, Richard may hope to erase the memory of his foulest crime; he gropes for that most fundamental of strategies for the achievement of comic structure, substitution, the replacement of the old by the new. He seems, indeed, to participate in what Kate McLuskie sees as eventually becoming a general concern of Renaissance tragedy:

> As the concerns of tragic drama shifted from military to sexual honour, women characters became the crucial focus of the action. The exchange of women, which seemed unproblematic in comedy as women passed more or less happily from fathers to husbands, became the problem of the tragic plays.[24]

Richard imagines his marriage with Elizabeth as offering not children of his own, but a means for the dead brothers to breed 'selves of themselves': the woman is primarily a vessel for the transmission of her own blood relatives' familial identity. Since it so happens that these are also *his* blood relatives, marriage with her would therefore be desirable; on this basis, it would be small surprise that he should seek to replace Anne, a mere cousin on the mother's side, with a niece, if what he really wants is closer bonding with the male relatives the women represent. In the face of such fruitless and frightening need, the two women may well wish instinctively to disengage from the conversation – which, with one of Richard's persistence, can only be achieved by at least the appearance of yielding.

The projected marriage with Elizabeth of course never materialises; she is reserved instead to provide a closure of a different sort, by her offstage union with Henry Tudor. (John Barton's *Wars of the Roses* cycle emphasised this point by actually writing in a part for her, as does Ian McKellen's screenplay for the recent Richard Loncraine film, but the text itself keeps her at a discreet distance, perhaps to avoid having to engage with the potentially thorny problem of her own attitude to marriage with her uncle, which the Ricardian apologist Sir George Buc claimed she had actually favoured.) Even had it occurred, however, it is difficult not to feel that it, like Richard's marriage to Anne, would have been doomed from the start, since Richard, its initiator, would have been unable to find in it what he actually wanted. Henry V too had a troubled relationship with his father, but although it takes him two plays to work through, work through it he does; Richard never has, and misrecognising his desire for identification, he is critically handicapped in such an other-directed relationship as marriage.

KING JOHN

Marriage performs a very different structural function in *King John*. The play opens on a world of dislocated marriages: there is no mention of either of King John's two wives, the divorced Isabella of Gloucester and the nubile Isabella of Angoulême; both his mother Eleanor and his sister-in-law Constance are widows; and one of the first things he has to do is arbitrate in a tale of marital infidelity. Moreover, John is himself accused of acting in ways specifically incompatible with the values of marriage:

> But thou from loving England art so far,
> That thou hast underwrought his lawful king,

> Cut off the sequence of posterity,
> Outfaced infant state, and done a rape
> Upon the maiden virtue of the crown.[25]

In reply to this, John's mother Eleanor attempts to disable Arthur's claim to the crown by suggesting that he is a bastard. But this is a dangerous strategy, for Constance is quick to respond, 'My bed was ever to thy son as true / As thine was to thy husband' (II.i.124–5) – alluding, as the note to the Arden edition points out, to the notorious fact that Eleanor was *not* faithful to her first husband. This is a strong weapon for Constance to use, but unfortunately she immediately turns it into a double-edged one:

> My boy a bastard! By my soul, I think
> His father never was so true begot:
> It cannot be and if thou wert his mother.
>
> (II.i.129–31)

Nobody, in short, can be sure of who their father was; and yet the identity of the father is the key to all property and inheritance transactions in this patriarchally-oriented society.

Interestingly, when this very question has been raised earlier in the Faulconbridge inheritance case, attitudes to it have apparently been polarised along gender lines: John, although recognising the face and features of his brother in the supposed heir of Faulconbridge, nevertheless rules that the child of one's wife must be one's heir or social chaos will ensue, but Eleanor sets aside inheritance custom by inviting her grandson to join her retinue, which eventually leads to an informal admission from his mother of his bastardy. In terms of Tudor and Stuart inheritance customs, it is John who is in the right, as a long and very convoluted case over the succession to the earldom of Banbury was to demonstrate; in terms of natural justice, Eleanor's position may well appear instinctively right, but only because in this case the physical resemblance is pronounced enough to admit of no doubt, which is no basis for customary practice. We are back with the dilemma so pithily expressed in the horn song of *As You Like It*: social chaos will ensue unless the unpalatable fact of bastardy can be accepted within the fabric of society.

It is as a resolution to all the most immediate problems of this society that marriage is proposed. The suggestion comes from a relative outsider, a citizen of Angers, the city which the warring factions are cold-bloodedly preparing to raze to the ground:

> That daughter there of Spain, the Lady Blanche,
> Is near to England: look upon the years
> Of Lewis the Dolphin and that lovely maid:
> If lusty love should go in quest of beauty,
> Where should he find it fairer than in Blanche?
> If zealous love should go in search of virtue,
> Where should he find it purer than in Blanche?
> If love ambitious sought a match of birth,
> Whose veins bound richer blood than Lady Blanche?
> Such as she is, in beauty, virtue, birth,
> Is the young Dolphin every way complete:
> If not complete of, say he is not she:
> And she again wants nothing, to name want,
> If want it be not that she is not he:
> He is the half part of a blessed man,
> Left to be finished by such as she;
> And she a fair divided excellence,
> Whose fulness of perfection lies in him.
> O, two such silver currents, when they join,
> Do glorify the banks that bound them in;
> And two such shores, to two such streams made one,
> Two such controlling bounds shall you be, kings,
> To these two princes if you marry them.
> This union shall do more than a battery can
> To our fast-closed gates; for at this match,
> With swifter spleen than powder can enforce,
> The mouth of passage shall we fling wide ope,
> And give you entrance
>
> (II.i.423–50)

The citizen is eloquent; but his speech is nevertheless shadowed by the gaping fissures which this mingling of the discourses of love and power seeks to paper over. Reality is sketched briefly at first – the politics and the ages are right – before a sustained flight of fancy on a woman he can hardly know (notably, Blanche is taken to need a bigger puff than the Dauphin); but it creeps back at the end in a series of insidious underminings of the purported effects of the language. 'If you marry them' gives the verb its less usual force of a directly transitive one; Shakespeare puns on this again in *Much Ado About Nothing*, when Leonato tells the priest, 'To be married to her; Friar, you come to marry her'.[26] It presages danger there, and it may well be seen as doing so here, with its implicit reminder that the act of marriage is envisaged as being for the benefit of others, not for the couple themselves. The 'controlling' bounds may even recall the apparent pun on 'cunt-rolling' which seems to be audible in the sonnets, while 'match' has a definite double meaning, its official sense of 'marriage' haunted by the 'battery' and 'powder' which surround it and which evoke the spark that lights the conflagration. The mouth of passage opened for entrance, with its clear connotations of ruptured virginity, also underscores the twin ideas of violence and of the realities which underlie the rhetoric.

Shakespeare provides his own comment on this doublethink in the shape of the Bastard:

> He speaks plain cannon, fire, and smoke, and bounce;
> He gives the bastinado with his tongue;
> Our ears are cudgell'd; not a word of his
> But buffets better than a fist of France.
> Zounds! I was never so bethump'd with words
> Since I first called my brother's father dad.
>
> (II.i.462–8)

The Bastard not only offers an accurate translation of Hubert's speech as being essentially a discourse of war, he also gets to the nub of the point – the potentially problematic relation between this marriage, proposed as a solution to all evils, and the dysfunctional marriages that characterise the rest of the play. The Bastard's asides similarly deflate the conventional acceptances and words of love that the Dauphin is quick to utter; but even he is less condemnatory than Constance, whose own political ambitions are so badly damaged by the marriage. Explaining that she is herself 'A widow, husbandless, subject to fears' (II.ii.14), she images the marriage entirely in terms of sexual infidelity:

> But fortune, O,
> She is corrupted, chang'd and won from thee;
> Sh'adulterates hourly with thine uncle John,
> And with her golden hand hath pluck'd on France
> To tread down fair respect of sovereignty,
> And made his majesty the bawd to theirs.
>
> (II.ii.54–9)

Constance's talk of bawds and adultery encapsulates the play's twin concerns with broken marriage vows and with legitimate inheritance. It seems no accident that, characterising marriage as debased, she regards her own widowed status as rendering her quasi-sacred, and as her passport to special treatment: 'A widow cries; be husband to me, heavens!' (III.i.34 [108]); and marriage is attacked again when Cardinal Pandulph, who should be its celebrator, becomes rather the agent of its divorce, riding roughshod over the protests of King Philip when he protests that he cannot attack King John because of the recent marriage between Lewis and Blanche (III.i.152–5 [226–9]). The end result of Pandulph's intervention will in fact be the interdict placed on England, which, amongst the other religious rites which it affects, will prevent the solemnisation of marriages in England altogether. The hapless Blanche urges against renewing the fighting 'Upon thy wedding-day' (III.i.226 [300]), beseeching 'what motive may / Be stronger with thee than the name of wife (III.1.239–40 [313–14]).[27] Her husband, however, ignores her altogether for 24 lines, and then says only, 'Lady, with me, with me thy fortune lies' (III.i.263 [337]). Soon, Blanche will be his excuse for laying claim to the English throne, although he knows that the urging of this claim signs Arthur's death-warrant. She herself is banished from the play: we hear no more of her story, and Constance's and Eleanor's are briefly concluded with the reports that they are dead. Blanche's last word is of death, as she exits saying, 'There where my fortune li'es, there my life dies' (III.i.264 [383]), and we have no reason to suppose that the marriage so lauded by Hubert will be, for her, a happy one. Shakespeare's dramatic compression of time to make the cardinal's intervention occur on the wedding-day itself makes the point most forcibly.

In all three of these plays, the very idea of marriage is in serious danger of collapse under the pressures of the dual functions it is asked to perform. It must reconcile public and personal needs; in the case of Richard, it must mediate between accepted social forms and unfulfilled psychological needs which he has not acknowledged even to himself. In both *Richard III* and *King John*, it is transparently obvious that marriage cannot reconcile these diametrical opposites: the union between Blanche and Lewis breaks down on the very day it is celebrated, and neither of the women Richard pursues could satisfy his neediness. In *Henry V* a glorious sleight-of-hand may briefly elide all such difficulties; nevertheless, any modern production may easily upset the balance, suggesting that Henry's true emotional release is found not with his bride but in his soldierly bonding with Fluellen, or inviting a feminist consciousness to query the subject-positions so artfully constructed for Catherine. What is ultimately most apparent is the confusions of purpose which attempt to elevate a male-female bonding ritual to the fundamental building-block of social and national cohesion, and the fragility of the balancing-act by which such a sense of unity must be maintained.

5
Roman Marriage

Even in the most far-flung geographical settings of his comedies, Shakespeare visibly adheres to the norms and mores governing early modern English marriage customs, and he is, to a great extent, equally reliant on the same traditions in his tragedies. Just as a wood outside Athens, in *A Midsummer Night's Dream*, proves home to the insuperably English-sounding Puck, and just as a household in Illyria accommodates characters with the Anglo-Saxon names of Belch and Aguecheek alongside its Feste and its Malvolio, so Shakespeare insistently anglicises the social customs of even the most alien of his communities. Critics have been quick to respond to this; when Ann Jennalie Cook or Diane Elizabeth Dreher comments on the correlation between dramatised betrothals and real ones, she consistently assumes an English norm.[1] In one group of his plays, however, Shakespeare does seem to me consciously to offer an alternative picture of a different kind of marriage, a relationship structured within very different social forms and assumptions. This is in the three Roman plays of his maturity, *Coriolanus*, *Antony and Cleopatra* and *Julius Caesar*, and the early *Titus Andronicus*, which all contain portrayals of marriages which are visibly, in one respect or another, malfunctioning, and which also run along notably different lines from those expected of English marriage.

TITUS ANDRONICUS

Titus Andronicus is a play ostensibly less interested in couples than in children – especially in sons, but daughters too are a focus of concern: Marion Wynne-Davies, commenting on Shakespeare's two major depictions of rape, observes that 'whereas in *Lucrece* female identity is centred exclusively upon marriage, in *Titus* it is seen in a broader familial context; women are mothers and daughters first, wives second.'[2] Titus' own wife is dead, as is the wife of his son Lucius;[3]

the relationship between Tamora and Saturninus is so sketchily treated that we never even see him learn of his cuckolding, and that between Lavinia and Bassianus is forcibly destroyed almost as soon as it begins. By contrast, we hear much of the 24 sons that Titus has lost by the end of the play, as well as of his sole surviving one Lucius; Saturninus stakes his claim to the throne on the basis that 'I am his first-born son that was the last / That ware the imperial diadem of Rome' (I.I.4–5), Tamora pleads 'spare my first-born son' (I.I.20), and Aaron leaps to the defence of 'my first-born son and heir' (IV.II.92).

The very emphasis on the eldest son is, though, validated and underpinned by the institution of marriage. This is clearly indicated by Lucius' labelling of Aaron's son as 'his fruit of bastardy' (V.I.48) and Lavinia's scorn at the Empress' 'goodly gift in horning' (II.III.67). Moreover, Bassianus – and Lavinia's brothers – insist on the validity of his pre-contract with her (I.I.285–6, I.I.405–6); indeed, Lucius suggests he will kill his sister rather than break it (I.I.297–8). The stress, though, is very clearly on the social rather than the personal element of the marital relationship. When Saturninus proposes to marry Lavinia, it is, notably, not *her* consent that he asks: 'Tell me, Andronicus, doth this motion please thee?' (I.I.243); and even though Tamora is at her own disposal, and so must be solicited directly rather than through a father, he assumes her consent and talks for eight lines before he lets her reply to his proposal (I.I.321–9). Moreover, although this relationship is – at least on his part – a genuinely affective one, we are hardly invited to endorse it, while the play's other marriage, between Lavinia and Bassianus, seems presented in deliberately passionless terms: Lavinia, who has already looked on unmoved at her supposed suitor's flattery of another woman before her face (I.I.268–72), denies that she dislikes being called early in the morning on what is effectively her honeymoon (II.III.15–16). Naomi Conn Liebler comments that 'in this Rome, feminine values are eschewed',[4] and certainly in the death of all its female characters and its downplaying of the affective it strongly foreshadows *Coriolanus* (to whose story, indeed, it refers [IV.IV.68]). This is a world in which, once marriage has performed its role by securing the future of the legitimate family, it is, apparently, redundant – and women are therefore disposable.

CORIOLANUS

Coriolanus has often been compared with Macbeth, and the two have been frequently treated together within the critical tradition. There are obvious similarities: both are soldiers, both display minimal compassion or emotion, neither is a character who tends particularly to appeal to the sympathies of audience or readers. However, there are also differences. Macbeth, if he loves and trusts no one else, clearly enjoys a deeply important relationship with his wife; Coriolanus may be superficially affectionate to his wife, but his main emotional energies are undoubtedly invested elsewhere, and he inhabits a world in which the feminine as a whole is profoundly undervalued and, where possible, ignored. Nevertheless, although the hero's marriage may seem to both him and his play to be a matter of only minor importance, I shall argue that Shakespeare reveals this marginalisation of the marriage relationship to be at the heart of the troubles experienced by both Coriolanus and his society.

When Menenius in *Coriolanus* offers his political opponents the analogy of the belly, he produces what is both the most striking and also the most heavily commented-on image of the play. As with Jacques in *As You Like It* and Ulysses in *Troilus and Cressida*, and to a lesser extent John of Gaunt in *Richard II* and Prospero in *The Tempest*, his set-piece speech has taken on a life of its own which has tended to work it free from being considered strictly within the confines of its play. The Seven Ages of Man speech, though, seems to me to provide a particularly useful analogue, for, though often taken as a representation of universal experience, it is in fact, as Carol Thomas Neely points out,[5] openly a representation only of *male* experience. The belly in Menenius' metaphor is similarly, silently but undeniably, male – empty of the child or of the reproductive capacity with which the Renaissance imagination habitually invests the female womb – and the image of the unfertile womb which it encodes unlocks two key strands of concern in the play. First, I suggest, *Coriolanus* dramatises a dangerous elision between the homosocial and the homosexual, caused partly by the same kind of insistent attempts to excise the feminine as are imaged in Menenius' tacit assumption that the belly is universally male. Secondly, I shall argue that, partly through close analogies with *A Midsummer Night's Dream*, *Coriolanus* effects a mystificatory valorisation of aristocratic marriage which links its failure directly to the failure of the crop.

Throughout the recounting and exposition of his fable, Menenius uses the male pronoun to refer to the belly. Moreover, one of the marked features of his narrative is the way in which the belly, normally invisible, is put on display, by analogy with the way the hidden processes of government are ostensibly being laid bare here. By contrast, it is a standard complaint in Renaissance drama that the female belly precisely defies such an anatomising gaze, since the secret of a pregnancy can be successfully concealed for five months at least (in some plays, longer; Webster's Duchess of Malfi appears to be on the point of giving birth by the time Bosola is confident that he has confirmed her pregnancy). We see, then, that the belly of Menenius' fable has no secret; unlike the deceptive womb of the Duchess or of Annabella in *'Tis Pity She's a Whore*,[6] there is no hidden foetus concealed within it. And while this may make it seem an image of transparent failure to conceal, it also makes it a powerful, albeit unstated, symbol of barrenness.

Lynda Boose has recently commented that 'in current scholarship on the politics of the body, the issue of gender has a way of vanishing. What happens is that even scholars like Bakhtin and Elias become "silent on this issue, assuming an 'ungendered' or implicitly single gendered-male body".'[7] This has certainly been strikingly the case in critical writing on Menenius' fable; but in fact this omission merely reflects a standard feature of the considerable corpus of body analogies on which Shakespeare, who knew better than anyone that no man is author of himself, was drawing. Gordon McMullan, in his recent book *The Politics of Unease in the Plays of John Fletcher*, cites a typical example, a sermon by Robert Wilkinson: Wilkinson declares 'for the belly sayth that bread must be had, and the soule subscribeth, that bread must be had too; and though reason may perswade and authoritie command... in case of extreame hunger men will not be perswaded, but they will haue bread'.[8] Here bellies belong to men, as they do also in Edward Forset's *A Comparative Discourse of the Bodies Natural and Politique* of 1606: 'the uttermost of mans understanding, can shape no better forme of ordering the affayres of a State, than by marking and matching of the workes of the finger of God, eyther in the larger volume of the universall, or in the abridgement thereof, the body of man.'[9] In Forset's thought, it is the correspondence between the body of God and the body, specifically, of the man which authorises the gender preference, but other agendas can also be at work: Annabel Patterson, for instance, comments on how 'Allan

Bloom, on the way to showing how "higher education has failed democracy", incorporated the famous body fable into his defence of the body, which involves an attack on women's liberation'.[10]

Were the image of the body to be encountered in a context other than the political, however, Shakespeare's culture would by no means have expected it to be exclusively male. As William Slights points out, 'dismemberment had been a strategy for representing the eroticized female body in poetry since Petrarch's *Rime sparse*... By *dis*membering the beloved in order to remember her, Petrarch set the pattern for subsequent lyric poets' enumeration of idealized but often scattered female body parts – eyes, arms, hair, feet'.[11] Coriolanus when he declines to show his wounds indeed shows himself uneasily aware that his own body is capable of occupying the traditionally female position of eroticised object of the gaze, and it is telling that when he leaves the stage after his abuse of the people Brutus queries, 'Mark'd you his lips and eyes?',[12] focusing precisely on those very parts so often given pride of place in the blazon of the sonnet.[13] Behind the obvious discourse of the male-oriented political fable, then, there lurks the less obvious but equally crucial one of the female-oriented genre of love-poetry. If we miss the echoes of it, we miss part of the point of the play, just as Coriolanus, who does try to ignore the woman's part, seriously misreads his own story and, as a result, finds himself ever more deeply embroiled in situations which are precisely governed by exactly the kinds of discourses and ties which are occluded in Menenius' political language and childless belly.

That *Coriolanus* is, in one sense at least, a love story is clear enough. It does not, of course, centre on the silent Virgilia, the legitimate wife; rather the official story of macho political dealing is shadowed by two which are far less speakable – the Oedipal fixation which binds Coriolanus to Volumnia, and the intense homoerotic attraction which makes Aufidius exclaim:

> but that I see thee here,
> Thou noble thing, more dances my rapt heart
> Than when I first my wedded mistress saw
> Bestride my threshold.
>
> (IV.V.116–19)

Ralph Berry has suggested that in their fight at the end of the play, Coriolanus and Aufidius each lay claim not only to military but to sexual dominance, specifically over each other, when each accuses the other of playing the 'boy', the pathic in the homosexual relationship;[14] weight certainly seems to be lent to this suggestion by Aufidius' delight in the unexpected aggression with which he images his 'wedded mistress' 'Bestrid[ing]' his threshold', in clear contrast to the English folk custom which would have had him carrying her, as well as by Coriolanus' own remark, when asked by a servant if he meddles with their master, that "tis an honester service than to meddle with thy mistress' (IV.V.48–9). Like Aufidius' remark, this apparent endorsement of the values of heterosexuality contains a distinct undercurrent of homosexuality.

It is perhaps Coriolanus' most serious mistake that he consistently underestimates the strength of his bonds with the two people – his enemy and his mother – who are most obviously not available to him as sexual partners,[15] just as he seems happy with the most nominal of relationships with his wife. The play, however, forcefully proves him wrong. The passionate hatred that motivates Aufidius to kill may well seem to be the product of a betrayal as much personal as political,[16] while Volumnia could almost be exemplifying the feminist creed that the personal *is* the political when she forces him to realise that he must put his family ties first. Leonard Tennenhouse interestingly suggests that 'the terms of her argument invert the traditional relationships between public and private. Consequently, what had been public, the war on Rome, is now the private assault on the mother... In effect her strategy places him in her position as mediator.'[17] In Tennenhouse's formulation, Coriolanus has not only been forced to recognise the previously suppressed importance of women; his failure to do so in time has actually feminised him.

Coriolanus' downfall in this respect comes because he has tried to copy the mechanism of Menenius' body fable: suppress and conceal the feminine. Ignoring his wife, he leaves even his apparently adored mother behind when he flees to the all-male world of the Volscian camp. He hopes to deny the processes of birth – 'as if a man were author of himself' (V.III.36) – and furiously resents Aufidius' use of the word 'boy', with its residual reminders of that infantilised state; he shows no consciousness of the sterility inherent of 'standing... as if a man were author of himself', an idea which evokes sexual perfomance, in 'standing', but denies literal fatherhood. Indeed, he takes little interest in his own son or in the relationship between them, perhaps because of the threatening reminders of infantilism which the child embodies. Janet Adelman suggests that 'Coriolanus seems to think of his child less as his son than as the embodiment of his own childhood and of the child that remains within him; even when we are first told about the son, he seems more a comment on Coriolanus' childhood than on his fatherhood'.[18] Additionally, Naomi Conn Liebler has recently pointed out some intriguing parallels between Shakespeare's representation of Coriolanus and the legend of St George and the dragon. She points out that St George 'begins, as in Caxton's 1483 translation of Jacobus de Voragine's *Legenda Aurea*, as an agrarian hero, the rescuer of a princess chosen by lot for sacrifice to a dragon who repeatedly befouled the countryside and destroyed the crops'.[19] Though the St George figure is associated with fertility, however, he was also the cause of its destruction. In the version of the story most widely known during the English Renaissance, George's mother, while pregnant, dreamed that she was carrying a dragon; she eventually had to be delivered by Caesarean section and died, while George was born bearing a bright red birthmark in the shape of a dragon: thus, 'from the outset, hero is identified with monster'.[20] Though Coriolanus pointedly differs from George in not distributing grain to the poor,[21] he does correspond to this remarkable web of links which work troublingly to blur the differences between the dragon, the mother, the son, fertility and death.

When Coriolanus does, unusually, mention his own origins, they are, pointedly, mis-remembered. His mother is seen as 'the honour'd mould / Wherein this trunk was fram'd' (V.III.22–3), where 'this trunk' forces us to see the man's body in place of the baby one, or he imagines himself as a gosling (V.III.35). A Jungian approach would also see the 'lonely dragon' image (IV.I.30) as expressive of Coriolanus' feeling about a threatening identification between himself and his mother: this would show motherhood literally pushed to the very fringes of the natural, and suggest that, rather as St George's mother is said to die 'dismembered', Volumnia is analogously mis-remembered. For Coriolanus, his mother is clearly a figure who is not only intimately associated with the monstrous but who also threatens to make him monstrous. Moreover, the arrival of his mother has not only feminised him; it has also theatricalised him, and made him into a spectacle (a thing, perhaps, to be demonstrated, or shown):

> Like a dull actor now
> I have forgot my part and I am out,
> Even to a full disgrace.
>
> (V.III.40–2)

Conceivably, there is a pun there on what 'part' it is that Coriolanus has forgotten – it is interesting here to consider Laura Levine's argument that the fundamental condition of theatricality is seen to be effeminisation, since this would suggest that it is not exclusively 'dull' acting but *any* form of acting that leads a man to forget his 'part'.[22] Certainly, although *Coriolanus* is not one of Levine's texts, there is an insistent connection proposed here too between theatricality and effeminisation: Janet Adelman argues that 'casting the theatrical as the feminine, Coriolanus himself refuses to participate in it',[23] and the connection lurks tellingly behind Coriolanus' remark that 'When he might act the woman in the scene, / He prov'd best man i'th'field' (II.II.96–7). For Coriolanus, all theatre is indeed 'this unnatural scene' (V.III.184).

The idea of the dull actor thus picks up an important strand of the portrayal of Coriolanus, as a man who both resents the theatre and performs badly in it, and yet is insistently characterised in terms of his relationship to it. Richard Wilson refers to 'his hatred of the stage', and speaks also of Coriolanus' 'inability to act...the play-within-the-play in *Coriolanus* ends with the actor hooted off'.[24] Gordon McMullan implicitly links this idea with the play's more obvious concerns with enclosure when he comments that 'Sicinius uses the language of resistance to enclosure in his denunciation of Coriolanus as a "viper / That would *depopulate* the city and be every man himself"'.[25] But this description also alerts us to another aspect of the portrayal of Coriolanus, for it serves to align him with another Shakespearean figure who acted badly but nevertheless wanted to play all the parts himself – Bottom, in *A Midsummer Night's Dream*.

This may seem a highly improbable coupling. However, in one sense *A Midsummer Night's Dream* and *Coriolanus* are in fact an obvious doubling. Titania's speech on the disastrous climatic effects of the marital estrangement between herself and Oberon has long been recognised as a direct allusion to the real series of bad harvests which, beginning in the 1590s, were eventually to culminate in the very corn shortages and food riots on which

Coriolanus so obviously reflects; between them, the two plays form a sequence which frames the commencement and the climax of the problem. Coriolanus' dismissive 'Rome's mechanics' (V.III.83) echoes closely the designation of *A Midsummer Night's Dream's* mechanicals. Moreover, Bottom shares with Menenius' fable a dependence on I Corinthians 12:14–15,[26] and, as Cole Porter suggested when he advised the kicking of a 'heinous' woman up the 'coriolanus', it is also possible to see a pun linking the two.[27] 'His tale pronounc'd' (V.VI.58) is, in one sense, his tail pronounced. When he conquers Corioli and becomes Coriol-anus, Caius Martius acquires a suffix which, in English, aligns him with the artisan Bottom, and in his own native Latin (as *anus*, an old woman) feminises him. Though the pun may seem far-fetched, there is an analogy in Menenius' play on Aufidius' name in 'I would not have been so 'fidiussed for all the chests in Corioles and the gold that's in them' (II.I.129–31), and there is surely an earlier pun on Martius' name, playing on it as a virtual homophone of Marsyas, when Cominius exclaims 'Who's yonder / That does appear as he were flay'd? O Gods, / He has the stamp of Martius' (1.VI.22–4). Flaying is too insistently connected with the fate of the satyr Marsyas not to bear the same connotation here.

In the very name which is his fame Coriolanus thus finds both his class and his gender position fundamentally threatened. But when ' "Coriolanus" / He would not answer to', then 'He was a kind of nothing' (V.I.11–12, 13); in the reductive either/or logic which characterises his thought, Coriolanus finds himself caught between being an anus – thus feeding directly into Ralph Berry's theories about the pathic connotations of Aufidius' use of the word 'boy' to him – or a nothing, which in Elizabethan slang meant 'vagina'. Laura Levine has recently argued that one reason for the strong anti-theatrical movement in Renaissance England was a fear that acting would *literally* effeminise a man, making him forget his 'part' and forcing him to regress to the feminine state which was thought to be always, threateningly, latent within him. Coriolanus certainly seems to feel himself so threatened, even when he is not acting, in the presence of the female:

> Not of a woman's tenderness to be,
> Requires nor child nor woman's face to see

(V.III.129–30)

Carolyn Williams, arguing that there is in fact no tension, in Marlowe's *Tamburlaine the Great Part Two*, between the aggressive heterosexuality of Tamburlaine's son Calyphas and his alleged effeminacy, has recently suggested that 'in early modern times, the word "effeminate" could be used to describe a man who desired women, or a man who was like women. It was often used in both senses at once, both reflecting and perpetuating a deep-rooted belief that men were weakened, contaminated, and to some degree emasculated by sexual contact with women'.[28] It is this deep-rooted insecurity about the inherent fragility of masculinity, and the danger that it may revert to what Levine terms the 'default state' of femininity, that powers Coriolanus' exclusion of women and informs the essentially homosocial drive of such parts of his psyche as are other-oriented at all. He dreads that he will have to adopt 'Some harlot's spirit' (III.II.112), and might 'by my body's action teach my mind / A most inherent baseness' (III.II.122–3). And that 'baseness' would trebly undo him, robbing him of manhood, of social standing and even, with its associations of harlotry and namelessness, of legitimacy.

For allowing oneself to become an object of the public gaze not only makes a man effeminate, it degrades him. Brutus makes quite clear the reversal of power entailed in the production of Coriolanus as passive object of the plebeian gaze:

> All tongues speak of him, and the bleared sights
> Are spectacled to see him. Your prattling nurse
> Into a rapture lets her baby cry
> While she chats him. The kitchen malkin pins
> Her richest lockram 'bout her reechy neck,
> Clambering the walls to eye him.
>
> (II.I.203–8)

And the implicit erotic dynamics of this looking are also made clear:

> Our veil'd dames
> Commit the war of white and damask in
> Their nicely gawded cheeks to th'wanton spoil
> Of Phoebus' burning kisses.
>
> (II.I.213–16)

The man becomes the object of the woman's gaze. The Coriolanus who assures his wife of his fidelity and describes his lip as having 'virgin'd it' (V.III.48) is unlikely to relish this. Equally distasteful, presumably, would be the way that being paraded in this way proves to be so intimately interconnected with the economy of the marketplace:

> *Cor.* No, sir, 'twas never my desire yet to trouble the poor with begging.
> *Third Cit.* You must think, if we give you anything, we hope to gain by you.
>
> (II.III.70–3)

The distinction which Coriolanus tries to draw between himself and 'the poor' is radically destabilised by Third Citizen's deployment of the discourse of merchandise, which both interpellates him as a person involved in trade with them, and commodifies him as himself something available for barter. Not for nothing does the play associate being watched with being debased in Menenius' threat to the Watch, 'if thou stand'st not i'th'state of hanging, or of some death more long in spectatorship and crueller in suffering...' (V.II.63–5).

But the greatest threat of all is that the falseness inherent in theatricality may in fact be used to reveal the deeper truth. As with Coriolanus' fear that the externals of womanish acting may precipitate the revelation of internal feminisation, so even Coriolanus' supporters see connections between his own labour and that of the workers he despises; Volumnia herself calls him a 'harvest-man' (I.III.36). The pointed parallels between the patrician Coriolanus and members of the more plebeian classes have been extensively noted. Michael Bristol calls him a lenten butcher; Richard Wilson terms him 'a day labourer...[whose] contract casts him in the despised boy's role of "a mistress", the "Bessy" or shemale in the harvest play Aufidius masters', and also argues that 'in the symbolic repertoire of rural culture, Coriolanus is a farm boy "booted" for his blunders'.[29] (It is notable that Aufidius should connect Coriolanus in the same sentence with sexual passion and with his 'threshold'; the Oxford English Dictionary confirms the word's derivation from the processes of threshing.) Bristol's valuable analysis of the play in terms of the grotesque body receives powerful support from Wilson's inspired grounding of the general concept of carnival in the specifics of the popular culture of rural Warwickshire; in the context of my own analysis, I want to lay particular stress on Wilson's suggestion of Coriolanus playing the role of the 'bessy', for, not only an anus but a Latin *anus*, what he discovers is precisely the link between class and gender which leads him, in disregarding one, to lose both.

The occlusion of women, as well as the chaste absence of reference to other elements of the lower body stratum, in Menenius' fable of the belly also points to another aspect of the emotional logic of the text, and to the precise mechanisms whereby the feminine is both repressed and, ultimately, enabled to return. The insistent politicising, in *Coriolanus*, of the processes of feeding leaves no room for overt record that the traditional role of nurturer and food-giver has been predominantly a female one. Through its imagery, however, the play itself insistently reminds us of this, especially in connection with the feeding of infants: Stanley Cavell points to Volumnia's references to nursing,[30] and one of the most incisive analyses of the play, Janet Adelman's '"Anger's my Meat"', has offered a brilliant reading of Coriolanus as the hungry hero, starved of both the food and the affection which Volumnia has systematically denied first to herself and then to him.[31] This emphasis on starvation has led to an insistent move to connect the play very intimately with the literal food shortages caused by the Midlands corn revolts of 1607.[32] Other events, both public and personal, may, however, also have had a bearing on its conception. In 1609 – often thought to be the likeliest date for the play's composition – Shakespeare's own mother died; Rufus Putney tentatively links the two events in an article which argues that it is 'the importance of Coriolanus's struggle to choose between his own or his mother's death...which determines the outcome of the play'.[33] To read the play within the twin contexts of marriage and mothering may lead us to disregard the text's own strategies of banishing motherhood to the fringes of both the natural and the cultural – the lonely dragon, the male belly – and to see it instead as profoundly traversed by discourses of motherhood, of nature, and of their relation to cultural fertility practices both aristocratic and plebeian.

Throughout the play, we are encouraged to expect a public, political climax, but what we get instead is two small-scale, private ones. The sack of Rome in *Coriolanus* is much anticipated, but never occurs; what takes its place instead is a private confrontation between mother and son, in which the mother brings about a series of events encapsulating the very antithesis of her usual role, as she ensures the death of her son and her own survival. This may alert us to a more general pattern of sterility in *Coriolanus*; for although, so unusually in tragedy, both a woman and a child survive (*Macbeth*, a play often critically considered alongside *Coriolanus*, provides the obvious contrast here), the child disappears from the stage, and emphasis is placed instead on the savage irony inherent in the spectacle of the mother who is seen being feted immediately before the destruction of her child, for which he himself has labelled her responsible. The young man is sacrificed, not even in the martial Armageddon he had promised himself, but privately and quietly; the old woman, who has placed no value on any life but her own, continues, and the plebs still starve.

But even before his death, Coriolanus has been denying life; father of only one child, who himself takes delight only in destructiveness, and characterising heterosexuality as a 'nothing', he has displaced it, metaphorically at least, with the sterility of anal intercourse. Here, too, the twinning with *A Midsummer Night's Dream* is suggestive. In that play, it is discord in the marriage of Oberon and Titania which has resulted in crop failure; in *Coriolanus* too, aristocratic marriage fails, and outside the people starve. The politics of *Coriolanus*, then, do not only overtly denigrate the mob; covertly mystifying aristocratic marriage, they propound a residually feudal world-view in which prosperity for all classes is organically linked in an inextricable chain of interdependence. In this sense, Menenius' fable of the belly – the organic metaphor *par excellence* – is radically appropriate. The problem, however, arises because the aristocratic belly is empty – has, indeed, been silently gendered exclusively as male – and the aristocrats themselves have marginalised women from their affections to such an extent that homosociality has blurred with homosexuality, disturbing both personal relationships and, most crucially, fertility both human and general. When the aristocratic belly is empty because the aristocratic marriage has ceased to function, the corn, as Titania says, rots.

JULIUS CAESAR

The same motif of barrenness and the same low-key level of emotional investment in marriage are also found in another Roman play, *Julius Caesar*. *Julius Caesar* pre-dates *Coriolanus* in terms of composition, but the period of Roman history which it dramatises is considerably later, and the ethos and distinctive values of Roman society are that much more strongly established. Although husband and wife relationships play a noticeably small role in the plot, being largely separate from the world of political action which provides the play's central focus, the institution of marriage itself proves on examination to be surprisingly important in the smooth functioning of Roman society. The play does, after all, 'begin at the Feast of the Lupercal, the Roman celebration on 13–15 February which later became St Valentine's day'.[34] The relationships between men which bulk so large in both the emotional and the political world of the play are largely founded on precisely the kinds of family relationships which marriage secures and cements. When Brutus and Cassius so insistently term each other 'brother',[35] they are not merely registering a mutual affection but referring specifically to the fact, recorded by Plutarch, that Cassius was married to Brutus' sister, Junia. Junia herself does not feature in the play and is never even directly mentioned; there is in fact no indication at all that Cassius is married – and yet the marital relationship, emotionally unimportant though it seems to be, radically structures and informs the homosocial bonding with Brutus in which so much of his energy and affection are invested.

When we later meet another brother-in-law of Brutus, Portia's brother young Cato, the fact of the relationship is again not directly mentioned, though it is directly deducible from the text, but once again Cato's entire sense of identity is bound up in the legitimate transmission of name and title which marriage ensures:

> What bastard doth not? Who will go with me?
> I will proclaim my name about the field.
> I am the son of Marcus Cato, ho!
>
> (V.IV.2–4)

Brutus himself has earlier revealed the same assumption, making legitimacy the cornerstone of his personal and civic creeds:

> every drop of blood
> That every Roman bears, and nobly bears,
> Is guilty of a several bastardy,

> If he do break the smallest particle
> Of any promise that hath pass'd from him.
>
> (II.I.136–40)

And adherence to the customs of marriage literally becomes a sign of civil obedience in the interrogation of Cinna the poet:

> *Cinna* ... wisely I say, I am a bachelor.
> 2. *Pleb.* That's as much as to say they are fools that marry. You'll bear me a bang for that, I fear.
>
> (III.III.16–18)

Yet despite the importance placed by Roman society on the institution of marriage, it seems to be very much on a social rather than a personal level that it is expected to function. No man in this play, with the arguable exception of Brutus, seems to have made any kind of emotional investment in his relationship with his wife, and even Brutus is careful to suppress all signs of disturbance when Messala tells him of Portia's death (IV.III.186–90).

The reason for his reticence is perhaps implied in Decius' earlier rebuke to Caesar:

> it were a mock
> Apt to be render'd, for some one to say,
> 'Break up the Senate till another time,
> When Caesar's wife shall meet with better dreams.'
> If Caesar hide himself, shall they not whisper,
> 'Lo, Caesar is afraid'?
>
> (II.II.96–101)

The irrational world of women must not be allowed to obtrude onto the public world of male business, lest it contaminate and effeminise men and make them objects of ridicule. At Decius' prompting, Caesar dismisses Calphurnia's dream – which the play will, ironically, reveal to have been an accurate prediction. This is of a piece with his earlier treatment of her at the ceremonies associated with the Lupercal:

> Forget not, in your speed, Antonius,
> To touch Calphurnia; for our elders say,
> The barren, touched in this holy chase,
> Shake off their sterile curse.
>
> (I.II.6–9)

In this public exhibition of a painful and private matter, Caesar does not even speak to Calphurnia, and is, moreover, careful to lay the blame for their infertility as a couple squarely on her shoulders alone, although the episode as a whole is clearly designed to reinforce the play's image of himself as a man who is personally weak, a kind of Fisher King.[36]

In both these instances of Caesar's interaction with Calphurnia, it is in fact notable how insistently the overall design of the play as a whole encourages us to read the situation very differently from the way Caesar himself sees it: dramatic irony and context allow us to see that blame and guilt cannot simply be displaced onto the woman. The complex structure of the piece supplies, albeit obliquely, a further endorsement of the female viewpoint when anticipation of the outcome of events at the Capitol is heightened as we are forced to share the helpless, immobilised perspective of the waiting Portia in II.IV. Ironically, however, it is precisely this instrumental approach to women, deploying them only when they are convenient, that Portia herself so powerfully critiques in the play's most direct and sustained reflections on marriage:

> Within the bond of marriage, tell me, Brutus,
> Is it excepted I should know no secrets
> That appertain to you? Am I your self
> But, as it were, in sort or limitation,
> To keep with you at meals, comfort your bed,
> And talk to you sometimes? Dwell I but in the suburbs
> Of your good pleasure? If it be no more,
> Portia is Brutus' harlot, not his wife.
>
> (II.I.280–7)

This is a very serious and careful representation of the rights and responsibilities pertaining to marriage, in which Portia, uniquely in the play, seeks to resist the predominantly social role allowed to marriage within her invocation of the concepts of the 'secret' and the 'self'. Equally, however, she too deploys the discourse of the civic in her reference to the 'suburbs', the region of diminished order outside the control of the civic authorities, and ultimately it is on the public and legal recognition of legitimate marriage that she must depend for her claim to personal intimacy. Here, as so often elsewhere in the play, marriage is still strongly fulfilling its allotted role of provider of social cohesion; what it has lost is the elasticity of the affective dimension which, at its best in the comedies, allows it to provide personal fulfilment as well.

ANTONY AND CLEOPATRA

In *Antony and Cleopatra*, some of the key characters of *Julius Caesar* recur. Octavius and Antony are both found again, though the conception of Antony at least is notably different from that of the earlier play; Caesar and Brutus are both heard of, as is Pompey, dead before *Julius Caesar* had begun but a significant presence in the opening scene. Despite the characterological continuity, however, *Antony and Cleopatra* diverges markedly from the other two Roman plays in the depth and scope of its critique of Roman values, and in the extent to which it dramatises an alternative to them; and perhaps its most thoroughgoing interrogation of the Roman world comes in its treatment of the realm of the emotional, particularly in relation to marriage.

In marked contrast to *Julius Caesar*, *Antony and Cleopatra* rings with the twin terms of 'wife' and 'husband'.[37] Egypt represents for Mark Antony the abode of illicit dalliance, the home of his mistress rather than of his wife, but nevertheless the talk in Egypt is heavily centred on marriage. Throughout the first scene Cleopatra harps on the distinction between herself and Antony's legitimate wife, Fulvia, showing quite clearly the extent to which her own position as 'the other woman' preys on her mind. She mentions the name of Fulvia four times in 24 lines: 'Fulvia perchance is angry';[38] 'Where's Fulvia's process? Caesar's I would say.' (I.I.28); 'so thy cheek pays shame / When shrill-tongued Fulvia scolds' (I.I.32); and 'Why did he marry Fulvia, and not love her?' (I.I.41). Interestingly, in another English Renaissance version of the Antony and Cleopatra story, Mary Sidney's translation of the French dramatist Garnier's *The Tragedie of Antonie*, Cleopatra has no such chip on her shoulder, and refers to herself quite unproblematically as Antony's wife: 'Wife, kindhearted, I' (she is also said to be a blonde in this play!).[39] Even in Shakespeare's version, we are reminded that Cleopatra has at least been a wife in the past, when Caesar refers to her as 'the queen of Ptolemy' (I.IV.6) and Pompey as 'Egypt's widow' (II.I.37). Cleopatra herself, however, constantly positions herself as a mistress, and simultaneously suggests that a mistress – even one who is the Queen of Egypt in her own right – must always be less than a wife. In so doing, this royal personage covertly endorses the bourgeois emphasis on the importance of the married state; equally, however, she does so not in the interests of the companionate view of marriage, but of the social one. She and Antony already share the affective dimension of the relationship; what she wants, though, is social and legal recognition of it as a binding and indissoluble contract. It is indeed ironic that what may well seem to be Shakespeare's most conservative endorsement of the old-fashioned advice to get a ring on your finger should come from the lips of his most exotic, transgressive and sexually adventurous female character.

It is not only Cleopatra herself who attaches considerable importance to the idea of marriage, but her women as well. Her scene with Antony is immediately followed by one in which Charmian, Iras and the eunuch Alexas all seek to be told their fortunes – and in each case, interest in the future centres on marriage. Charmian requests:

> Good now, some excellent fortune! Let me be married to three kings in a forenoon, and widow them all: let me have a child at fifty, to whom Herod of Jewry may do homage. Find me to marry with Octavius Caesar, and companion me with my mistress.
> (I.II.25–30)

Iras hopes for an inch of fortune more than Charmian, though 'Not in my husband's nose' (I.II.58); and Charmian thinks of even the eunuch Alexas in terms of marriage, entreating the fortune teller 'Alexas, – come, his fortune, his fortune! O, let him marry a woman that cannot go, sweet Isis, I beseech thee' (I.II.59–62). In such a context, it is little wonder that Cleopatra's mind should run so relentlessly on marriage. In the next scene, she demands of Antony, 'What, says the married woman you may go?' (I.III.20), and then tells him

> Why should I think you can be mine and true
> (Though you in swearing shake the throned gods)
> Who have been false to Fulvia?
>
> (I.III.27–9)

Here she adopts the suggestive strategy of positioning Fulvia not as her opposite but as her double, a tactic which actually allows her to claim for herself, however indirectly, some at least of the consideration due to a wife. This technique of identification becomes even more marked after she has learned of Fulvia's death, and says, 'Now I see, I see, / In Fulvia's death, how mine receiv'd shall be' (I.III.64–5). When Antony then goes on to swear fidelity, she replies:

> So Fulvia told me.
> I prithee turn aside and weep for her;
> Then bid adieu to me, and say the tears
> Belong to Egypt.
>
> (I.III.75–8)

What Cleopatra seems to posit here is virtually a generic position of 'wife', whose actual occupant is unimportant, since the social, once again, is overriding the personal.

In one sense, Antony's view of marriage seems to be remarkably similar. His relation to Fulvia is difficult to establish. He is completely impassive at the news of her death, asking merely, 'Where died she?' (I.II.115), a response in marked contrast to the open surprise of Enobarbus (I.II.157–61). However, we may well remember Brutus' very similar reception of the official announcement of Portia's passing, and there are certainly suggestions that the news may already have been known to Antony – that he may, indeed, even have precipitated Fulvia's demise: 'There's a great spirit gone! Thus did I desire it' (I.II.119), and, even more suggestively, 'she's good, being gone, / The hand could pluck her back that shov'd her on' (I.II.123–4).

Ominously, perhaps, he refers to Fulvia again immediately before he learns of the proposition that he should marry Octavia, saying to Caesar:

> As for my wife,
> I would you had her spirit in such another;

> The third o'th'world is yours, which with a snaffle
> You may pace easy, but not such a wife.
>
> (II.II.62–4)

The play's loose handling of its complex chronology makes it unclear whether Caesar at this moment is conceived of as having no wife at all, or a wife less spirited than Fulvia was. By the end of the play he is certainly married, for Cleopatra refers to Livia, his wife (V.II.168), whose behaviour in that role was sharply criticised by Roman historians like Suetonius. It seems, though, more likely that Antony is not offering such open disrespect as a slighting reference to an existing wife would imply; the point is more probably that Caesar, whose youth is so much harped on, is not married at all yet, and so in one sense has not gained full entry into the world of public men, in which marriage alliances play so crucial a part – a point which is indeed about to be precisely illustrated by Agrippa's suggestion that a marriage between Antony and Octavia is what is needed to cement the relationship between Antony and Caesar.

As with the marriage of Louis and Blanche in *King John*, this is a politically motivated exchange of women with only the thinnest of veneers to suggest any kind of personal involvement: it seems indeed to exemplify the pattern which Peter Smith suggests in the play, that 'the world of Octavius is the world of love inverted: ROMA | AMOR'.[40] The first hint of the idea comes from Caesar, who says 'if I knew / What hoop should hold us staunch from edge to edge / O'th'world, I would pursue it' (II.II.114–16). The 'hoop' that would initially hold a barrel together becomes, in the next line, a rather different kind of hoop, a child's plaything bowling along towards the edges of the world; and Octavia will indeed be a device that first seeks to hold together and then is launched on an endless, unstoppable trajectory of chase and flight, the unattainable object of a boys' game. Agrippa images her both more openly and and also more obviously as a commodity of exchange:

> To hold you in perpetual amity,
> To make you brothers, and to knit your hearts
> With an unslipping knot, take Antony
> Octavia to his wife; whose beauty claims
> No worse a husband than the best of men;

> Whose virtue and whose general graces, speak
> That which none else can utter. By this marriage,
> All little jealousies, which now seem great,
> And all great fears, which now import their dangers,
> Would then be nothing: truths would be tales,
> Where now half-tales be truths: her love to both
> Would each to other and all loves to both,
> Draw after her.
>
> (II.II.125–37)

The feminine 'knitting' which Octavia would perform will make brothers of the two men, but the word 'utter', with the commercial connotations derived from its standard secondary meaning of 'selling', clearly reveals the schematic and social nature of the exchange of women here proposed.[41] The only real 'love' expected in the triad is all to originate from Octavia (although it is elsewhere evident that Caesar is in fact an unusually attentive and affectionate brother). The extent to which this marriage pronounces the death-knell of any real affective potential is suggestively conveyed by the very terms of Caesar's ratification of it: 'A sister I bequeath you' (II.II.150). Not only does this bode ominously for Octavia, but it also serves to mark the distance between the Caesar family and the fertile Egyptian world inhabited by Antony and Cleopatra: later, Cleopatra, who 'cropped' when the earlier Caesar 'plough'd' her (II.II.228), is invited by Caesar's messenger to 'put yourself under his shroud' (III.XIII.71).

Another strain in the language surrounding the Antony/Octavia relationship further indicates how markedly Octavia herself is displaced from it, as Antony takes his leave later on:

> Good night, sir. My Octavia,
> Read not my blemishes in the world's report:
> I have not kept my square, but that to come
> Shall all be done by the rule.
>
> (II.III.4–7)

The word 'square', so often heard in this play, combines with 'rule' to evoke carpentry, a craft which will be vividly imaged again in the play when Cleopatra refers to 'mechanic slaves /

With greasy aprons, rules, and hammers' (V.II.208–9). Nowadays, such words also have clear overtones of one of the most strongly established and institutionalised of all male bonding systems, freemasonry. The early history of freemasonry is obscure, but early versions of it certainly seem to be established by the seventeenth century, and it might well be tempting to imagine Shakespeare as alluding to Antony's use of Octavia to give him entrance to the confraternity. Even if masonic connotations are not admitted, it is still, nevertheless, quite clear that the language Antony uses to Octavia is not that of romance, but of a male profession.

Like Blanche's and Louis' before it, however, the marriage of Antony and Octavia fails in its political objectives; ultimately, it seems, the social relationship of marriage does need a personal underpinning in order to operate successfully. For Cleopatra, though, it is, initially at least, the fact of the marriage alone which counts; she never asks whether Antony loves Octavia, but the word 'married' is repeated six times in the dialogue between her and the messenger (II.V.73–101). Enobarbus, however, sees deeper, as becomes apparent during the dialogue in which he conveys the news to Menas:

> *Eno.* But she is now the wife of Marcus Antonius.
> *Men.* Pray ye, sir?
> *Eno.* 'Tis true.
> *Men.* Then is Caesar and he for ever knit together.
> *Eno.* If I were bound to divine of this unity, I would not prophesy so.
> *Men.* I think the policy of that purpose made more in the marriage than the love of the parties.
> *Eno.* I think so too. But you shall find the band that seems to tie their friendship together will be the very strangler of their amity: Octavia is of a holy, cold, and still conversation.
> *Men.* Who would not have his wife so?
> *Eno.* Not he that himself is not so.
>
> (II.VI.109–22)

To Menas, a wife is a generic possession, considered primarily in her relation with the outside world, and particularly as a potential cuckold-maker, which Octavia's coldness and stillness make her unlikely to be. Enobarbus, though, sees the need for a personal dimension and for compatibility, and moves from the generalities of 'Who' to the particularities of 'he'. Marriage may need to perform a social role, but it cannot do so merely by virtue of its existence. Just as the social cohesion afforded by a king cannot function without the loyalty of his subjects, so marriage requires voluntary adherence by its participants to the structure it provides.

Whatever the failure of the marriage on the personal level, however, Octavia continues to be an important counter in the relationship between Antony and Cleopatra. After their quarrel, Antony rebuffs her with 'let / Patient Octavia plough thy visage up / With her prepared nails' (IV.XII.37–9): he may have neglected his wife, but he assumes that her emotional investment in him will still be so great that she will want revenge on his mistress. Cleopatra, too, continues to valorise the marriage relationship. Even when Antony is dying, she cannot refrain from twitting him with it:

> Your wife Octavia, with her modest eyes,
> And still conclusion, shall acquire no honour
> Demuring upon me.
>
> (IV.XV.27–9)

Even after his death, she still tells Proculeius that she will not 'be chastis'd with the sober eye / Of dull Octavia' (V.II.54–5), and, tellingly, she images the Fortune which has betrayed them as a 'false huswife' (IV.XV.44), another demonisation of a figure encoding legitimate marriage. And yet, ultimately, both Antony and Cleopatra are able to conceive of marriage as transcending worldly laws and offering 'a marriage of true minds' indeed. Antony vows, 'I will be / A bridegroom in my death, and run into't / As to a lover's bed' (IV.XIV.99–101), and Cleopatra in turn cries 'Husband, I come: / Now to that name, my courage prove my title!,' (V.II.286–7). Nevertheless, even a passion as strong as theirs can defeat worldly customs only after life, not during it. This play, which provides the most sustained and compelling depiction of the romance and passion of an extramarital relationship, also offers the most consistent rationale for the enabling support structures provided by marriage; but it tempers this with a powerful reminder that the marriage which works must be one founded on affection, not, as in the earlier Roman plays, the suppression and eradication of it. Though the Roman plays as a whole may provide no clear example of a successful marriage, they do show, in the relationship of Antony and Cleopatra in particular, that the ingredients of one would require a fusion of social and personal purposes in which private affective emotions would be directed and contained in such a way as to facilitate the performance of the public role. They also, of course, show how difficult this may be to achieve.

6
Tragic Marriage

'All comedies end with a marriage,' said the maiden English teacher at my all girls' school, 'and all tragedies begin with them.' In the four great works of Shakespeare's central tragic period, *Hamlet*, *Macbeth*, *Othello* and *King Lear*, marriage functions as a site of stress, disruption and destruction of the individual identity. In three of the four plays, a marriage, or the arrangements for it, directly precipitate a disaster; as Joanna Montgomery Byles comments, 'to some extent, it is the denial of Eros and the destructiveness of family attachments which largely contribute to the fate of Hamlet, Othello, Macbeth and King Lear'.[1] Beginning where the comedies left off, these plays sharply develop the darker hints contained within the comic world.[2]

ROMEO AND JULIET

The tragedy of marriage is perhaps most immediately apparent in *Romeo and Juliet*. Though the lovers' attachment may seem to promise a comic outcome, the opposition of their families, sealed in the double death of Tybalt and Mercutio which follows almost immediately on the wedding ceremony, inextricably intertwines marriage and death within the structure of the play, just as Sampson verbally confounds the loss of virginity with the cutting off of heads.[3] The very word 'married' sounds ominously in the text. Discussing the nubility of Juliet, Paris argues that 'Younger than she are happy mothers made' (I.2.12); Old Capulet immediately responds with 'And too soon marred are those so early made' (I.2.13), where 'marred' and 'made' quibble with 'married' and 'maid' in a way that posits a worrying equivalence between 'married' and 'marred'. When 'married' itself is heard, it is in a similar context, as Lady Capulet exhorts her daughter to observe Paris well, and 'Examine every married lineament' (I.3.84); the next reference has Juliet, seeing Romeo, exclaim, in ironic prophecy, 'If he be married, / My grave is like to be my wedding bed' (I.5.134–5), just as the Friar will later rhyme 'tomb' and 'womb' (II.3.5–6). Though Juliet later associates marriage with honour, in her virtual proposal to Romeo (II.2.143–6), for Romeo it leads precisely to an imagined loss of honour: 'O sweet Juliet, / Thy beauty hath made me effeminate / And in my temper softened valour's steel!' (III.1.113–15).

With savage irony, it is precisely as a counter to the tragedy of Tybalt's death that Old Capulet proposes to cheer his family by hastening Juliet's wedding. Initially, Old Capulet has seemed a very proper father indeed, protecting his child on account of her youth, and exhorting her suitor, 'But woo her, gentle Paris, get her heart. / My will to her consent is but a part' (I.2.16–17). Soon, however, he becomes one of the most peremptory of all Shakespeare's fathers, transgressing social norms as well as disregarding Juliet's reluctance:

'A Thursday, tell her,
She shall be married to this noble earl.
Will you be ready? Do you like this haste?
We'll keep no great ado – a friend or two.

(III.4.20–3)

Naomi Conn Liebler argues that Romeo and Juliet, 'by marrying in secret...prevent their families and their larger community from participating in the marriage rite',[4] but Capulet himself was equally proposing to restrict the element of communal celebration involved. There has been much debate about where the sympathies of Shakespeare's original audience would have lain in the disagreement between Juliet and her father: David Lindley, for instance, suggests that 'there can be little doubt that many a father in the Globe Theatre would have identified with Capulet's feelings. Nor is it clear that the play as a whole endorses the position of Romeo and Juliet themselves.'[5] Diane Elizabeth Dreher suggests that the absence of Capulet from the wedding makes it an unsatisfactory ceremony,[6] and Jonathan Goldberg points out that in this play marriage definitively works *against* homosociality rather than facilitating it:[7] only after the death of the couple themselves are the two fathers able to join in 'a belated public solemnization of the marriage contract'.[8]

What is perhaps most striking, though, is the extent of the paralleling rather than the contrasting in the representation of attitudes to marriage. Thomas Moisan points, for instance, to 'the Nurse's reiterated recollection of the "Ay" Juliet's three-year-old voice gave to but a cruder version of the very question put to her by her mother',[9] and Capulet quite literally speaks with Juliet's voice when he mimics her presumed answer that 'I'll not wed, I cannot love; / I am too young, I pray you pardon me!' (III.5.186–7); he also produces a paralleling of opposites as he recounts how he has worked towards Juliet's marriage 'Day, night; hour, tide, time; work, play; / Alone, in company' (III.5.177–8). There is a similar echoing in Juliet and her mother agreeing to poison Tybalt's assassin (III.5.96–9). Though Juliet is actually feigning here, the passage is a multiply suggestive one: it will again stress similarity rather than difference when Romeo in turn decides to buy poison, and it also evokes the story of Tristan and Iseult, where Iseult and her mother concoct a similar scheme against the killer of the mother's brother. The comparison is an interesting one, working both to elevate the lovers by association, and also to point up the fact that their own relationship is a legitimate one, not dependent on Tristan and Iseult's transgression of the marriage bond. It also works to reinforce an association between poison and women,[10] which may further be hinted at in the suggestive phrasing of the Apothecary, 'Mantua's law / Is death to any he that utters them' (V.1.66–7). When Romeo takes poison and Juliet wields his dagger, we may thus indeed be tempted to feel that their unlicensed love has not only made him effeminate, but her – at least temporarily – mannish. Leading the living to lie in tombs, sons to die before their fathers, and Romeo to figure death as birth (V.1.62–5), their marriage consistently generates inversion (Lynda Boose argues that the whole of the latter half of the play 'progresses as a series of inverted and disordered epithalamia'),[11] but it just as insistently leads to the revelation of parallels – both trends being contained in its final effect of healing the feud, as Capulet says 'O brother Montague, give me thy hand' (V.3.296).

One reason for the essentially homologising effect of the marriage lies in Romeo and Juliet's own basic similarity. Unlike, say, Othello and Desdemona, or even Hamlet and Ophelia, they are close in rank, years and status, and are members of the same community, which would indeed benefit from their marriage, if their parents would only sanction it. Despite their youth, they behave in a way that is, arguably, more mature than their own parents' conduct (a comparison which is actually suggested by the play's profusion of parallels). Romeo may kill Tybalt, but only because he was trying to prevent violence and make peace, and neither of the lovers thinks of consummating the relationship before they have had it blessed by the church (which, in the person of Friar Laurence, thoroughly supports their actions). With old heads on young shoulders, they in fact work only towards aims that are in tune with their society (in contrast, perhaps, to Mercutio, whom some readings see as punished by premature death for a homoerotic orientation unconducive to social rituals of bonding and reproduction). Moreover, the love of Romeo and Juliet will ultimately benefit their community by procuring the ending of the feud. This early tragedy has often been criticised for the apparently contingent nature of the tragic outcome – essentially, disaster strikes first because Romeo's arm accidentally got in Mercutio's way, and secondly because the letter goes astray – which does not spring from any *hamartia* on the part of the hero or any feeling that society as a whole has lost its way. This certainly seems to be true of the central relationship, for this was a marriage that need not have failed, a marriage that could have been equally at home in the comic world. In Shakespeare's more mature work, there will be a radical shift in conception, for there the seeds of tragedy will lie in the marital relationship itself.

HAMLET

In *Hamlet*, we enter the world of Denmark in the immediate aftermath of the marriage of Claudius and Gertrude – a ceremony which, in Hamlet's eyes at least, was ominously conflated with a funeral, and which has certainly sounded the death-knell of his own peace of mind – Janet Adelman points to 'the logic of the play's alternative name for poison: "union"',[12] while Terence Hawkes observes that the verb 'to marry' is 'the one the play seems to turn on'.[13] There can be no doubt at all that to the Renaissance mind, the marriage of Claudius and Gertrude was indeed both improper and, as Gertrude herself says, 'o'er hasty': Roland Mushat Frye points out that 'in Tudor sermons and theological tracts, marriages such as that of Gertrude and Claudius are invariably classified as adultery, even if whitewashed by a marriage ceremony', and that 'the marriage followed the funeral almost at once, because it was impossible to bury a king or queen in Renaissance England in less than a month after the death, or at least it was never done more promptly'.[14] Even so, however, the extent of the disorder which it precipitates is striking.

Unlike the marriages of male characters in comedies, Claudius' alliance with Gertrude notably fails to facilitate his bonding with other men, proving particularly destructive in his relationship with Hamlet, whose goodwill is of particular importance to him since the Prince is not only his nephew but the heir presumptive to his throne. Claudius even seems to be himself uneasy about the marriage. Although no one has ever doubted that he loves Gertrude, the occasions on which he speaks of his relationship with her can all be seen as encoding ominous undertones. His initial description of her as 'Th'imperial jointress to this warlike state'[15] has given rise to much speculation about the precise political significance of their relationship, and whether, if Gertrude had some kind of purchase on government, Claudius perhaps stood to gain by the marriage as well as being motivated by affection. Claudius later cites his continued possession of his wife as a reason for his inability to repent, and speaks of Gertrude to Laertes in terms characterised by a radical ambivalence:

> My virtue or my plague, be it either which -
> She is so conjunctive to my life and soul
> That, as the star moves not but in his sphere,
> I could not but by her.
>
> (IV.vii.13–16)

The person most adversely affected by the marriage, however, is Hamlet. Throughout the play, he experiences difficulty in reconciling his twin images of his mother as mother and as wife; he also reverses the traditional patterns of comedy by his increasing alienation from Ophelia, his own potential wife – Lisa Jardine underlines this teleology of separation when she points to Ophelia's return of Hamlet's gifts as 'a sign of a betrothal broken off'.[16] For him, the problematics of identification with the father cannot be mediated by women, and Ophelia, whose name so ironically signifies 'help' in Greek, can function as nothing more than a hindrance on his psychological quest, perpetually doubling both his language and his life-events but radically divorced from sharing them with him.

If Hamlet himself fails to connect with Ophelia, moreover, it often seems as if the play itself does not do so either. *Hamlet*, notoriously, is nothing without its prince, and it has often been remarked that not only does the prince himself habitually dislocate responsibility for his troubles onto women, but that the play relentlessly invites us to share his own perspective on the female characters, to such an extent that traditional critical response to both Ophelia and Gertrude has been radically conditioned by Hamlet's own response to them.[17] Ophelia's soliloquy at the end of the nunnery scene briefly reverses this process by offering us her summing-up of his present condition, but it is rare to take the question of *Gertrude's* view of Hamlet very much further than A.C. Bradley's careless characterisation of her as like a sheep in the sun, wanting to be happy herself and vaguely desirous of seeing her fellow-sheep happy too. Nevertheless, since Gertrude is one of the very few examples in the Shakespearean canon of a woman who has survived one long marriage and has recently embarked on another, it might well be worth looking for a moment at 'what says the married woman'.

Of Gertrude's attitude to her previous husband we know little or nothing, except, perhaps, what we could deduce from the portrayal of her represented by the Player Queen in *The Murder of Gonzago*. Of her attitude to her son we know a great deal, and it is very suggestive. The first exchange between them that we hear involves her publicly reproaching him for his dress and his behaviour; the last includes her comment that 'He's fat and scant of breath' (V.II.290). For all the apparent affection between them, and for all the warmth which led Ernest Jones to advance his famous suggestion that Hamlet was suffering from an unresolved Oedipus complex, there are other suggestions that a keynote of the relationship between them is denigration and rejection, considerably pre-dating the more obviously disruptive advent of Claudius. When the Player Queen concludes a speech with the line 'None wed the second but who kill'd the first' (III.II.175), Hamlet mutters aside, 'That's wormwood' (III.II.176). Wormwood, as Juliet's nurse reminds us, was the substance traditionally applied to the nipple to impart a bitter taste and deter the infant from further suckling; as such, it functions as the sign of the first and most shattering rejection by the mother of the child. That such an association is indeed present here is suggested by the Player Queen's almost immediately preceding assurance that *'Such love must needs be treason in my breast'*

(III.II.173); treason in the breast is what Hamlet seems to be remembering, a betrayal by his mother not only of his father but also of his infant self, but which he can now revenge by submitting her to this public exposure of her husband's guilt and her own. Suggestively, he also echoes here his father's description of the operations of the poison: 'with a sudden vigour it doth posset / And curd, like eager droppings into milk, / The thin and wholesome blood' (I.V.68–70). Both men envisage their fate as fundamentally informed by images of milk spoiled and milk denied, in a minor-image cluster reinforcing the play's larger narrative moves towards the disruption rather than the perpetuation and flourishing of family groups.

Imaging himself, perhaps with some justification, as rejected by his mother, Hamlet never seems likely to move towards forming a family of his own. If there is a sketched suggestion of malfunctioning lactation, there is a strongly sustained one of a general failure of fertility and of blight and waste. Claudius' view of nature is that its 'common theme / Is death of fathers' (I.ii.103–4); Horatio uses the language of fertility to suggest guilt when he wonders whether the Ghost has 'uphoarded in thy life / Extorted treasure in the womb of earth' (I.i.139–40). For Laertes, 'birth' is used to figure the constraints of Hamlet's rank (I.iii.18), and for Hamlet all breeding produces sinners, and so is best avoided (III.i.121–4); Naomi Conn Liebler points out that Hamlet's lament for the forgotten hobby-horse also encodes a failure of fertility, since the traditional hobby-horse 'was specifically a man dressed in a horse mask and a hoop-like skirt under which he caught and then released village maids in an aggressively mimed fertility dance'.[18] Hamlet wants 'no mo marriage' (III.i.149), and associates all marriage with curses, cuckoldry, error and the blighted growth of 'a mildew'd ear' (III.i.136–41, III.ii.245–6 and III.iv.64). In this, he resembles his counterparts in the comedies, but the difference is that he cannot mould his perspective into a basis for joking and for male camaraderie, since he shares it only with women – all his invectives on the subject are directed either to Gertrude or Ophelia. To Claudius, he can offer only a riddle – 'My mother. Father and mother is man and wife, man and wife is one flesh; so my mother' (IV.iv.54–5) – which, because it takes dangerous obliterations of difference as its theme, cannot work to effect any such joining itself.

Other characters also figure marriage as being, at the best, problematic, both to achieve and in its operations. Both Laertes and

Polonius doubt that Ophelia would be able to become Hamlet's bride; later, Ophelia herself sings of how women may be deceived by fale promises of matrimony (IV.v.62–6), and she also hints at the dangers of hypergamy, or marriage with a person below one's own station, when she says in her madness 'It is the false steward that stole his master's daughter' (IV.v.170–1). Bridget Gellert Lyons comments that 'deathly coldness or seclusion ("Be thou as chaste as ice..." "Get thee to a nunnery") on the other, are presented to a young girl as the only sexual alternatives'.[19] The floral imagery that clusters round the scenes of Ophelia's madness and death clearly evokes a parodic and subverted wedding rite, with the accompanying suggestion of sterility and waste. Moreover, images of illegitimacy and of unlicensed sexuality abound: Laertes exclaims, 'That drop of blood that's calm proclaims me bastard, / Cries cuckold to my father' (IV.v.117–18), and Hamlet tells Laertes, 'I am afeard you make a wanton of me' (V.ii.303). The Player Queen, representing Gertrude, protests, '*In second husband let me be accurst; / None wed the second but who kill'd the first*' (III.ii.174–5), and Gertrude herself gives a brief clue to her own marital history when she cries, 'O, this is counter, you false Danish dogs' (IV.v.110). Clearly implying that she herself is *not* Danish, she reminds us of the political rather than the personal nature of the imperatives which would have structured her alliance with Old Hamlet. Swiftly though this is suggested, it is an important idea, since it refers to the importance of marriage as a crucial element of social and national substructure. Once marriages have been broken, illegitimately contracted, or become impossible, the failure and the repercussions are not merely private and personal: something is indeed rotten in the state of Denmark as a whole.

It is these ideas of rottenness, of decay and of failure to flourish which permeate the imagery of the play. The green world is present in *Hamlet* only in ghastly parody, in the 'unweeded garden' (I.II.135) of the hero's imagination, in the barren plot imaged as serving Fortinbras' followers as a grave and in the literal graveyard itself, and in the pastoral landscape of Ophelia's death; the 'country' to Hamlet is always hideously conflated with the pun on 'cuntry'.[20] None of these affords growth and renewal; even resurrection is invoked only to be deflated in the disinterment of Yorick's skull. A society which, in Hamlet's terms, celebrates a marriage with cold meat (left over from a funeral), and where the central relationship involves a woman presumably well past child-bearing age, kills its children, but begets no new ones. Instead, it anatomises its central marriage from a perspective never previously available in the plays – that of the child, radically excluded – and it shifts attention from social and ideological function to psychological cost. It shows us a Claudius who perceives his own uxoriousness as dangerous weakness (and who will later keep silent and let his wife die, rather than betray his own guilt by warning her against the poisoned cup); a Gertrude who, at any rate according to her son and her first husband, has been coarsened and diminished by her second marriage, and a child whose bitter disappointment in his mother and fraught imaginings of his father leave him paralysed, misogynist and sterile. Even when the state passes to the new rule of Fortinbras, the crisis in the state of marriage is not resolved, for Fortinbras, like Hal before him and Malcolm and Edgar after him, is a saviour conspicuously free from any contact with women. Marriage, though it carries within it the seeds of its own renewal, does not prove easy to restore in the tragic world when it has been once disrupted.

KING LEAR

If *Hamlet* treats marriage predominantly from the point of view of the child, *King Lear* deals with the perspectives and experiences of the father – in this case a father for whom the marriage of his youngest and favourite child seems to be proving a source of great stress.[21] Although the opening scene of the play is ostensibly concerned primarily with the major political issues of abdication and succession, both these are mediated through questions of marriage – are, indeed, staged to some extent as a wedding ceremony,[22] onto which Lear attempts to map his own meanings. Even before the subject of Cordelia's betrothal has been mentioned, we hear of marriage vows made – and broken, as Gloucester introduces his bastard son to Kent:

> Kent. I cannot conceive you.
> Glou. Sir, this young fellow's mother could; whereupon she grew round-womb'd, and had, indeed, Sir, a son for her cradle ere she had a husband for her bed. Do you smell a fault?
> Kent. I cannot wish the fault undone, the issue of it being so proper.

Glou. But I have a son, Sir, by order of law, some year elder than this, who yet is no dearer in my account: though this knave came something saucily to the world before he was sent for, yet was his mother fair; there was good sport at his making, and the whoreson must be acknowledged.[23]

The reference to Edgar's age makes it quite clear that Gloucester's relationship was an adulterous one, and this will later be seen by Edgar as the direct and operative clause for all Gloucester's suffering:

> The Gods are just, and of our pleasant vices
> Make instruments to plague us;
> The dark and vicious place where thee he got
> Cost him his eyes.
>
> (V.III.169–72)

Less noticeable than the fact of the transgression, but equally troubling, is Gloucester's reference to his sons' respective places in his 'account', a word which in turn causes 'dearer' to resonate not only with the language of love but with the language of cost. In a low-key way, he uses exactly the same discourse of quantity rather than quality which will later characterise Lear's approach to his children, so that encoded in this passage is not only a cheapening of the marriage relationship but an approach to the parent-child one patterned as a transaction rather than as an emotional response.

Both these elements are even more strongly marked in Lear's dealings with his daughters. From the outset, the scene is riddled with tensions between the rehearsed and the spontaneous, the genuine and the expedient. Lear inaugurates the proceedings with the ominous line 'Meantime, we shall express our darker purpose' (I.i.35). The idea connoted by 'express' seems to make it quite clear that what is to be unfolded is something already decided, but 'darker' suggests not only something previously concealed but something inherently sinister, a meaning, indeed, which may have been unsuspected even by Lear himself until he discovers that it has found expression; certainly there seems to be a deep-seated unease about the prospect of Cordelia's marriage which will later lead him, quite irrationally, to condemn France as 'hot-blooded' and to refuse absolutely to 'knee his throne' (II.iv.210, 212).[24] On the surface, the 'purpose' seems a straightforward and sensible one:

> We have this hour a constant will to publish
> Our daughters' several dowers, that future strife
> May be prevented now.
>
> (I.i.41–3)

Nevertheless, there is again a darker note sounded in Lear's unquestioned assumption that 'future strife' *would* follow if dowry business were left unsettled. In his mind, marriage already figures as a focus for stress and disruption.

It becomes even more of a threat to him when his youngest daughter unequivocally tells him that her imminent marriage is going to diminish the amount of affection she feels for him:

> Good my Lord,
> You have begot me, bred me, lov'd me: I
> Return those duties back as are right fit,
> Obey you, love you, and most honour you.
> Why have my sisters husbands, if they say
> They love you all? Haply, when I shall wed,
> That lord whose hand must take my plight shall carry
> Half my love with him, half my care and duty:
> Sure I shall never marry like my sisters,
> To love my father all.
>
> (I.i.94–103)

Though Cordelia's caution here is intended as a corrective to the extravagance and exaggerations of Goneril and Regan, it also partakes of the same discourse of reckoning as characterised Gloucester's approach to affection (and which is so scorned by Antony in his first exchange with Cleopatra): Cordelia conceives of love not as boundless, but as demarcated and rationed. She may implicitly reject her sisters' language of cost and price, but she also, to some extent, shares it, and she is indeed to find herself virtually echoed in Goneril's final advice to her:

> Let your study
> Be to content your lord, who hath receiv'd you
> At Fortune's alms; you have obedience scanted,
> And well are worth the want that you have wanted.
>
> (I.i.275–8)

On the terms to which both Goneril and Cordelia have subscribed, it is indeed Goneril who sounds the more dutiful here, and seems to have the more generous and compliant conception of the marriage relationship.

Any such view of the sisters is of course soon challenged, as the behaviour of Goneril and Regan sharply deteriorates. It is notable that their disobedience to the (literally) patriarchal structures of behaviour enjoined by their father is repeatedly figured as an attack not primarily on the relationship between father and child, but on that between husband and wife. In the first scene, there is no hint that there is anything amiss between either couple, but trouble soon begins to surface: Goneril declares, 'I must change arms at home, and give the distaff / Into my husband's hands' (IV.ii.17–18), and even Regan, though her relationship with Cornwall seems far more secure, shows occasional signs of impatience with him – the Arden editor suggests that on their arrival at Gloucester's castle, 'Regan takes the words out of her husband's mouth, and thereby shows that he is subordinate' (II.i.118 note). More strikingly, the daughters' disobedience is actually interpreted as a retrospective assault on the sanctity of their *parents'* marriage: Lear terms Goneril a 'Degenerate bastard' (I.iv.251), and tells Regan that if her behaviour were to resemble her sister's, 'I would divorce me from thy mother's tomb, / Sepulchring an adult'ress' (II.iv.128–9) (the Arden note comments that the source-play of *Leir* starts with the funeral of the queen). Bastardy is again invoked as the ultimate social evil when Albany uses it to forbid Regan's marriage to Edmund: when Edmund declares that Albany has no jurisdiction over them, Albany retorts 'Half-blooded fellow, yes' (V.iii.81). In a play that questions many things, the absolute distinction between marriage and adultery remains sacrosanct, and marriage is invoked as a fundamental guarantor of the continuation of civilised society; nevertheless, marking as it does the progression to maturity of a new generation, it is a rite of passage fraught with a peculiar melancholy for those whose lives are waning. It is, as much as anything, the marriage of his youngest child which disempowers Lear.

MACBETH

In *Othello* and *Macbeth*, the focus switches from the generations not personally involved in marriage to those which are, and *Macbeth* in particular presents perhaps the Shakespearean canon's most sustained and probing portrait of an individual marriage – and one which, for all the brevity of the play, is particularly attentive to changes in the relationship over time. The institution of marriage radically fashions not only the individual life of Macbeth, but also the whole mindset of the society in which he lives. Violent and unsettled as it may be, it nevertheless adheres strictly to the rituals which surround kinship and the home. Notably, the Captain initially figures Macdonwald's rebellion precisely in terms of unlicensed sexuality: 'fortune on his damned quarrel smiling / Showed like a rebel's whore',[25] whereas Macbeth, fighting for the rightful king, is 'That Bellona's bridegroom' (I.2.56). Even if loyalty has been forfeited and rebellion broached, legitimate marriage, it seems, remains available as an absolute demarcator. Even heaven is figured as structured by it in Banquo's homely image, 'There's husbandry in heaven, / Their candles are all out' (II.1.4–5).

Marriage – and the legitimacy of offspring which, at least in theory, it ensures – also lies at the heart of the play in a different way. It is a critical commonplace that Shakespeare's choice of subject in *Macbeth* surely represents a response to the accession of James VI of Scotland to the throne of England, and the resultant heightened awareness of all things Scottish. James's claim to the throne derived entirely from the principles of primogeniture and hereditary succession of legitimate offspring; and these are precisely the considerations which are set aside when Macbeth is crowned king in preference to either of the sons of Duncan. However, under the Scottish custom of tanistry, whereby the throne passed not to the son of the previous ruler but to a suitable adult male relative, Macbeth's succession is perfectly legal; it could indeed be said to be Duncan who outrages convention by unilaterally designating Malcolm as Prince of Cumberland, and thus as his probable successor, apparently without prior consultation with his magnates. If blood-relationship alone is sufficient, marriage becomes relatively unimportant, but if, as in the case of James VI and I, it is legitimate descent which is prioritised, then marriage becomes the cornerstone of the royal succession. It is notable that during the course of *Macbeth* Scottish society seems to undergo a clear shift from the first model to the second. There is no initial challenge to Macbeth's claim to the throne, but by the end of the play it seems to be tacitly assumed that the right of Malcolm, as the eldest son of Duncan, is unquestionable. Moreover, Malcolm himself prominently foregrounds the ritual force of marriage in his discussion of his suitability for the kingship. The first sin that he claims is voluptuousness (IV.3.60ff), and he warns Macduff that 'Your wives, your daughters, / Your matrons, and your maids, could not fill up / The cistern of my lust' (IV.3.61–3). Macduff's growing horror draws precisely on the idea of legitimate succession and continuity of good citizenship which marriage should ensure, but which Malcolm, it seems, is monstrously transgressing:

> Thy royal father
> Was a most sainted king; the queen that bore thee,
> Oftener upon her knees than on her feet,
> Died every day she lived.
>
> (IV.3.108–11)

In the end, of course, such a marriage of a virtuous king and a virtuous queen is indeed vindicated as having produced desirable offspring; but immediately after Malcolm's self-revelation we hear of the savage destruction of Macduff's own marriage, and all its progeny. As the grief sinks in, it is Malcolm's turn to give counsel, as he exhorts Macduff, 'Dispute it like a man' (IV.3.219) – an echo, perhaps, of the latent fear that all association with women, even within the legalised context of marriage, carries the threat of effeminisation.

Though Malcolm's unsatisfactoriness as an offspring of his parents' apparently perfect marriage proves eventually to be only illusory, it does nevertheless accord with a strongly marked pattern, in the play as a whole, of sterility and of blighted progeny. Initially, the world of the play does indeed seem to promise fertility and growth, as Duncan says to Macbeth, 'Welcome hither. / I have begun to plant thee, and will labour / To make thee full of growing' (I.4.28–30). But soon such images of the cycle of the natural world are perverted as Lady Macbeth advises her husband, 'look like the innocent flower, / But be the serpent under't' (I.5.63–4). For her, reminders of the green world occur only in abuse:

> Was the hope drunk
> Wherein you dressed yourself? Hath it slept since?
> And wakes it now to look so green and pale
> At what it did so freely?
>
> (I.7.35–8)

Her use of 'green' connotes nausea, not viridescence. Macbeth too will come to revel in the obliteration of the potential for growth, his determination intact 'though the treasure of nature's germens tumble all together / Even till destruction sicken' (IV.1.57–9). In his kingdom, Macduff's 'chickens' will fall victim to a 'kite', and babies will be cooked in the witches' stew.

In contrast, Macbeth's enemies come increasingly to be identified as figures of regeneration and the renewal of fertility. Lennox announces that they come 'To dew the sovereign flower and drown the weeds' (V.2.29–30). While Macbeth laments that 'my way of life / Is fallen into the sere, the yellow leaf' (V.3.22–3), and threatens to make a hideous parody of the normal processes of fruit-bearing by hanging the messenger on a tree 'Till famine cling thee' (V.5.40), Malcolm's army advances with its boughs like the green world come to life to take its revenge on the figure who has threatened it.[26] In a final confirmation of his increasing identification with the anti-natural, Macbeth responds to the approach of Birnam wood with an invocation of the apocalypse:

> I 'gin to be aweary of the sun,
> And wish the estate o'the world were now undone. –
> Ring the alarum bell! – Blow wind, come wrack...
>
> (V.5.49–51)

Most noticeably, of course, Macbeth is identified from the outset as an emblem of his sterility by his own childlessness. The apparent contradiction between this and his wife's memories of giving suck has aroused the spilling of much critical ink (the simplest explanation is in fact Shakespeare's awareness that Gruoch, the historical

Lady Macbeth, had a son, Lulach the Fool, from an earlier marriage); but its dramatic and thematic functions are clear enough. It allows not only for a stress on the eventual passing of the Scottish throne to the Stuart line, but also for the presentation of Macbeth (and pointedly him, rather than the couple as a whole) as an incarnation of barrenness[27] – a point often made in production.[28]

Despite their childlessness, however, there can be no doubt that the Macbeths' relationship is – initially at least – a happy one. Barbara Everett calls them 'probably Shakespeare's most thoroughly married couple',[29] and as a couple, they function in striking contrast to the Macduffs' marriage, in which the husband inexplicably abandons wife and children in his flight to England, and the wife responds with bitter recrimination and open criticism of him in front of the children. Even when she is most grossly provoked, by Macbeth's extraordinary behaviour in the banquet scene, Lady Macbeth never does this, desperately trying instead to find excuses for him; indeed A.C. Bradley famously remarked that 'strange and almost ludicrous as the statement may sound, she is, up to her light, a perfect wife'.[30] In the theatre, it is customary to present their relationship as an explosively erotic one – indeed, in Philip Franks' production at the Crucible Theatre, Sheffield, in November 1995, Lady Macbeth's backless purple gown was so striking that the actress appeared in it, in character, in the Celebrity Wardrobe column of the Sheffield *Star*, explaining that it was her 'seduction outfit'. It is, however, perhaps precisely this sexual charge which proves the undoing of the relationship as well as its distinctive strength, for Lady Macbeth's view of marriage, while in some ways companionate, is also relentlessly premised on sharply drawn sexual distinctions. For her, men are men – exhortations to be a 'man', and accusations of failure of manhood, punctuate her exhortations to her husband – and women are Other,[31] creatures whose best hope of full achievement lies in being unsexed. Known only by the name of her husband, affectionately remembering her father, Lady Macbeth is fully interpellated into patriarchal ideology. Never seen outside her own house, she even dies within it, and the most horrific of her actions are nevertheless clearly inserted within a framework, however transgressive and paradoxical, which clearly asserts her femininity: even the laying out of the grooms' daggers parodies her 'proper' duty of table-setting, and her invocation of darkness is couched in the language of breastfeeding.[32] Thus by driving her husband to definitive, 'manly' action she has inevitably set in motion the processes which will confine them to radically demarcated separate spheres. Anny Crunelle-Vanrigh notes the extent to which 'womanhood becomes significantly prominent in Shakespeare's character development of [Lady Macbeth]: she is seen walking in her sleep in her night gown and her talk is all of the perfumes of Arabia';[33] conversely, Coppélia Kahn points to the extent of Macbeth's eventual separation from the world of women when she suggests that when Macduff 'cows' his opponent's better part of man 'it is Macduff's bond with the feminine which triumphs over Macbeth's manly valour'.[34] What the Macbeths' relationship shows us, then, is perhaps that when the genders are kept so firmly apart, and when what lies at the heart of marriage is a sexual relationship so clearly predicated on sexual difference, it can work to break down the companionship and union altogether.

OTHELLO

The marital relationship in *Othello*, on the other hand, is, notoriously, by no means so clearly identified as sexual. Nicholas Brooke comments that '*Macbeth* is unique among Shakespeare's tragedies in centring on an intimate marriage (Othello's was never that)',[35] and there has even been extensive critical debate about whether the marriage of Othello and Desdemona ever actually achieves consummation,[36] while Stephen Greenblatt has commented perceptively on 'the syntactic ambiguity' in Iago's lines 'to abuse Othello's ear / That he is too familiar with his wife', where it could as well be Othello himself as much as Cassio who is figured as over-intimate with Desdemona.[37] Michael Hattaway, too, notes that even when he is killing Desdemona, Othello can still refer to himself as being yet to 'pluck her rose', which, he argues, clearly connotes her virginity.[38]

It is certainly quite clear that Othello does not unequivocally embrace the married state. He tells Iago:

> I fetch my life and being
> From men of royal siege, and my demerits
> May speak unbonneted to as proud a fortune
> As this that I have reach'd; for know, Iago,
> But that I love the gentle Desdemona,
> I would not my unhoused free condition

Put into circumscription and confine
For the sea's worth.[39]

In Othello's account, marriage has offered him nothing:[40] already Desdemona's social superior because of his royal ancestry, he has merely succeeded in forfeiting his freedom, an action which he figures by reference to the sea, which, throughout the play, will recur as an image of unpredictability, insatiability and instability. The only redeeming feature, it seems, is his 'love' for the 'gentle Desdemona', and love, in Shakespeare, rarely proves enough to sustain a marriage. Moreover, even Othello's description of his feelings may sound an ominous note; even if 'gentle' does not suggest a noticeable rank difference from his own 'royal' condition, in this marriage of dissimilarities, it certainly suggests a conditionality in Othello's love, which will endure only as long as he finds her 'gentle' (and Desdemona, even more than Shakespeare's other heroines, is a woman whom men are continually finding suspect).[41] This is clearly not the language of an eager bridegroom, and even the act of warning his wife of his departure is characterised in terms suggestive of effort and cost: 'I will but spend a word here in the house' (I.ii.48).

Interestingly, Desdemona, too, is described by her father as initially averse to marriage:

> a maid so tender, fair, and happy,
> So opposite to marriage, that she shunn'd
> The wealthy curled darlings of our nation
>
> (I.ii.66–9)

There is a forceful implicit logic to Brabantio's paratactic structure here, for the syntax draws no distinction between the various elements of his list, presenting 'opposite to marriage' as precisely the same kind of quality as 'tender', 'fair' and 'happy'; the effect is that it, too, becomes an item in his praise of her, implicitly aligning Brabantio himself with his daughter's alleged repugnance to marriage. Iago, also, registers such a dislike, dismissing Cassio as 'A fellow almost damn'd in a fair wife' (I.i.21), a passage that has aroused much critical debate since the suggestion that Cassio is either married or about to be so never occurs again. Suggestively, the 'almost' of Iago's indictment of Cassio is echoed by his assumption that Othello's own marriage may be merely provisional, shown when he questions his general:

> but I pray, sir,
> Are you fast married? For be sure of this,
> That the magnifico is much belov'd,
> And hath in his effect a voice potential
> As double as the duke's; he will divorce you,
> Or put upon what restraint, and grievance,
> That law (with all his might to enforce it on)
> Will give him cable.
>
> (I.ii.10–17)

The triple alliteration of 'double', 'duke' and 'divorce' may perhaps serve to underline the potential ambiguity of 'double', which, in Renaissance English, connotes 'duplicitous' as often as 'duplication'. Moreover, here again syntax and imagery work to disturbing effect. For Iago, 'divorce' is envisioned as an alternative to 'restraint' and 'grievance' which would operate *within* marriage; and marriage itself is best 'fast', although that very 'fastness' associates it with precisely the same kind of tethering idea as is present in the 'enforce'd 'cable' of the law which Brabantio might invoke as punishment. Iago's terms are ominous indeed, suggestive of nothing but trouble whatever the outcome may be.

Similar danger signals continue to gather round the couple's unfolding story, to the extent, indeed, that Michael Bristol has brilliantly compared the whole play to the performance of a charivari, a popular ritual performed to deprecate a marriage not to the satisfaction of the community.[42] What we hear of their courtship resonates heavily with the language of manipulation: Othello recalls that he 'Took once a pliant hour, and found good *means* to *draw* from her...' (I.iii.151–2), that he 'did *beguile* her of her tears' (I.iii.156), and, finally, that 'Upon this *hint* I spake' (I.iii.165; my italics in all cases). Brabantio is appalled by what he hears:

> If she confess that she was half the wooer,
> Destruction light on me, if my bad blame
> Light on the man!
>
> (I.iii.176–8)

The focus of his anger is telling. The hints and counter-hints which characterised the couple's courtship may seem to us to be informed with a mutuality which is profoundly appealing; but Brabantio's point is precisely that there should be no such mutuality in male-female relationships, and while modern sensibilities may disagree, we should be aware that, from one point of view, he is right: in a misogynistic society, what Desdemona has done is dangerous. Her behaviour may have arisen from pleasing motives, but it will lay her open to exactly the kind of misconstruction which will, in fact, dog her whole career. Additionally, she will soon find out that the 'division' which she experiences between father and husband is in fact a spurious distinction, since both will operate within the same actantial role of patriarch: as Brabantio warns Othello, demonstrating a degree of same-sex identification which ironically transcends their individual conflict, 'Look to her, Moor, have a quick eye to see: / She has deceiv'd her father, may do thee' (I.iii.292–3).

Desdemona responds to her father's accusations in terms strongly reminiscent of Cordelia: 'My noble father, / I do perceive here a divided duty' (I.iii.175–6). To some extent, her argument fails just as Cordelia's had done, since the angry father is not appeased, but it also functions in a different way, for whereas Cordelia did retain a considerable emotional investment in her father, Desdemona's commitment will, in practice, be entirely to her husband, and will indeed go further than simple 'duty' might prescribe:

> So that, dear lords, if I be left behind,
> A moth of peace, and he go to the war,
> The rites for which I love him are bereft me
>
> (I.iii.255–7)

Not only does she press to accompany him; she, as Othello had done earlier, assigns a reason for her love – the performance of love's 'rites'.[43] Where Othello seeks gentleness, Desdemona desires performance; unfortunately, there seems to be a radical mismatch between the couple's expectations of each other and what each offers. Ironically, they might in fact do better to reverse the polarities and value the 'gentleness' of Othello and Desdemona's dedication to 'rites', in which case they might hope for the kind of eclectic but fulfilling mutual exchanges which characterised the relationship of Antony and Cleopatra – except that they too would find, like Antony and Cleopatra, that theirs is a society which does not easily countenance such failure to adhere to traditional gender roles.

That there is indeed a marked difference in their attitude to love's 'rites' is clearly indicated by Othello's response to Desdemona's speech:

> Your voices, Lords: beseech you, let her will
> Have a free way; I therefore beg it not
> To please the palate of my appetite,
> Nor to comply with heat, the young affects
> In my defunct, and proper satisfation,
> But to be free and bounteous of her mind;
> And heaven defend your good souls that you think
> I will your serious and great business scant,
> For she is with me.
>
> (I.iii.260–8)

There is certainly at least a tolerance of Desdemona's evident sexuality here, and it is easy to hear a standard Renaissance pun on both male and female sexual organs in Othello's plea 'let her *will* / Have a free way'. Nevertheless, Othello goes out of his way to discount the influence of his *own* 'appetite' and 'heat', which seem (the passage is a notoriously difficult one to construe) to be 'defunct' now that he is no longer young. Moreover, when the Duke orders that their departure should take place immediately, Desdemona queries it – 'Tonight, my Lord?' (I.iii.277), but Othello positively embraces the haste which will, in effect, defer his embracements of Desdemona: 'With all my heart' (I.iii.277).

Even when the couple are safely reunited in Cyprus, Othello is still noticeably willing to postpone the moment of consummation:

> If it were now to die,
> 'Twere now to be most happy, for I fear
> My soul hath her content so absolute,
> That not another comfort, like to this
> Succeeds in unknown fate.
>
> (II.i.189–93)

Though the standard pun on 'die' certainly enforces a suggestion here that it is the moment of orgasm that he is so impatient for, Othello's persistent efforts to divorce mind and soul from body equally inform 'die' with an idea that it is *real* death, in a classical instance of the Freudian death-wish, that he craves. Desdemona's attitude, though, is once again visibly differentiated from his when she responds, 'The heavens forbid / But that our love and comforts should increase, / Even as our days do grow' (II.i.193–5). Here, she takes on the eschatological overtones of Othello's concern with death, fates and souls, but recasts them into the image of the 'heavens' which, as well as being the abode of God, are also responsible for the regulation of the cycles of time and weather, so that the image-pattern shifts towards the temporal promise implied by 'increase' and 'grow'.

Desdemona's figures of fertility are, however, doomed even before they are spoken, for in direct opposition to her own vision of beneficent heavens, the audience have already heard of the only kind of fruition that will take place in the play in Iago's triumphant declaration 'I ha't, it is engender'd; Hell and night / Must bring this monstrous birth to the world's light' (I.iii.401–2). Iago's 'engendering' and 'birth' will be the play's only examples of parturition, and they, like Frankenstein's monster, will be born of a radical misogyny that seeks persistently to exclude and demonise women. Condemning the whole sex as 'Players in your housewifery; and housewives in your beds' (II.i.112), Iago sees sexual misconduct, gender role reversal and sexual failure everywhere he looks: 'For that I do suspect the lustful Moor / Hath leap'd into my seat' (I.ii.290–1); 'Our general's wife is now the general' (II.iii.305–6); 'her appetite shall play the god / With his weak function' (II.iii.37–8). Even his account of Bianca is subtly skewed, when he calls her 'A housewife that by selling her desires / Buys herself bread and clothes' (IV.i.94–5); what Bianca actually obtains from the economic transaction may be bread and clothes, but for Iago, what she wants is, perversely, not what she buys but what she *sells*, and he reads her as motivated not by need but by desire. This is consistent with his usual pattern of imagining an aggressive sexuality for all around him – indeed the vigour with which he describes Cassio's supposed dream-advances to himself (III.iii.424–32) has led many critics to suspect that what is at work is indeed, as Emilia terms it, his 'fantasy' (III.iii.303), and that what really motivates him is a repressed homosexual desire for either Othello or Cassio. If such were indeed the case, then his failure to achieve such a liaison would be another instance of the fact that, as the perversion and sterility of his own imagery of birth implies, Iago can only create from what is there already. He can feed desires, but he cannot implant them; he may reap the harvest of Desdemona and Othello's mismatched relationship, but the seeds were sown already.

Throughout the scenes dramatising Iago's manipulation of events, there is in fact a carefully controlled balance between the damage done by his provocation and the damage which the couple bring upon themselves. Iago may prompt Cassio's appeal to Desdemona, but he could hardly have hoped for such a disastrously self-destructive response as Desdemona spontaneously makes to the suggestion:

> my lord shall never rest,
> I'll watch him tame, and talk him out of patience;
> His bed shall seem a school, his board a shrift,
> I'll intermingle everything he does
> With Cassio's suit.
>
> (III.iii.22-6)

However briefly, Desdemona here is unmistakably proposing to exhibit the stereotypical behaviour of the shrew, and laying herself open, in Renaissance ideologies, to appropriate punishment: unlike Emilia, who obeys her husband even when (as in the case of the handkerchief) his commands are morally dubious, Desdemona is, at least in some sense, wilful.[44] She will combine immoderate talking, a standard attribute of both shrew and loose woman, with inappropriate sexual behaviour, for she will talk her husband 'tame' – i.e. reduce him to impotence. The appearance of such a word in such a context must surely remind us that it might well be Desdemona herself who would be seen, like Kate, as in need of 'taming' here. Once again, a gesture of unguarded generosity on Desdemona's part exposes her to serious charges of deviancy and tempts patriarchal wrath.

Desdemona's campaign continues along these unpromising lines when she mounts her attack on Othello. Not satisfied with some signs of softening on his part, she warns him:

> nay, when I have a suit
> Wherein I mean to touch your love indeed,
> It shall be full of poise and difficulty,
> And fearful to be granted.
>
> (III.iii.81–4)

What is notable here is Desdemona's insistent use of indicative and future tenses, rather than conditionals: she confidently anticipates a time when she *will* make such a demand of Othello, and she puts it to him as a test of his love. It is perhaps unsurprising that Othello's own use of the future tense in a rather similar situation suggests that he is already mentally prepared to fail that test:

> Excellent wretch, perdition catch my soul,
> But I do love thee, and when I love thee not,
> Chaos is come again.
>
> (III.iii.92–4)

The Arden editor's note says that it would be wrong to read any suggestion of futurity into 'when', but the language clearly invites it, as it does again when Othello tells Iago 'I'll see before I doubt, when I doubt, prove' (III.iii.194). Certainly he listens to Iago, but his own psychic processes are at work as well. When Iago reminds him, 'She did deceive her father, marrying you' (III.iii.210), he immediately assents, 'And so she did' (III.iii.212), and he is soon exclaiming, 'Even then this forked plague is fated to us, / When we do quicken' (III.iii.280–1). Othello here mentally links conception and cuckoldry, just as when he later tells Desdemona:

> This argues fruitfulness, and liberal heart;
> Hot, hot, and moist, this hand of yours requires
> A sequester from liberty; fasting and praying
>
> (III.iv.34–6)

He has, moreover, given his wife a handkerchief which, in one version of its origins, was deliberately designed to secure the marital chastity of his own parents, which he clearly imagines as threatened (though in that relationship it was the husband who was thought likely to stray). For Othello, it seems, the love of fathers and mothers is likely to deteriorate, and yet sex is always likely to turn husbands and wives into fathers and mothers. Perhaps this is why this play which includes three childless women figures its births as monstrous and hellish, so that even Emilia hopes that Othello's distraction is caused merely by state-matters, 'And no conception, nor no jealous toy / Concerning you' (III.iv.154–5).

Emilia in general functions in sustained counterpoint to her husband, defending female sexuality in contrast to his attacks on it, and asserting stoutly, 'But I do think it is their husbands' faults / If wives do fall' (I.viii.86–7), a clear and sane articulation of a perspective that does not always seek to make women a focus of blame. Her words will take on a bitter ring, however, in the play's final demonstration of how even Desdemona's best intentions are always vulnerable to indictment: after his wife has sought to exculpate him of her murder, Othello cries savagely, 'She's like a liar gone to burning hell, / 'Twas I that killed her' (V.ii.130–1). While Emilia dies echoing another 'lie' of Desdemona's that was nevertheless profoundly expressive of truth, the Willow Song, Othello reverts to a scale of values that marriage with Desdemona had perhaps barely disrupted. He exclaims:

> Behold, I have a weapon,
> A better never did itself sustain
> Upon a soldier's thigh
>
> (V.ii.260–2)

'Weapon', the idea of 'itself sustain' and 'thigh' might all suggest, in another context, the penis; but for Othello, the sword has perhaps always been better. His brief marital career disastrously concluded, he reclaims his preferred identification as a soldier. Even when he joins Desdemona on the bed, the presence of Emilia robs the scene of intimacy.

Obviously, events have been precipitated by Iago's lies and manipulations. Nevertheless, the seeds of trouble have been clearly there from the beginning, and they may well be thought to lie primarily in the conflicting sets of expectations which characterise Othello's and Desdemona's approach to their relationship. It is notable that, when Othello comes to believe in Desdemona's infidelity, he finds that he has a positive superfluity of causes to which to attribute her apparent change of heart: he imagines that his colour, his age, his cultural difference and his military background all separate him from her, and indeed in terms of the cultural norms espoused by Shakespeare's own society and in many of his other plays, he has a point. Othello *does* seem to be old to marry – older than any of the Shakespearean characters who make a successful marriage, with the highly dubious exception of Claudius in *Hamlet*, and perhaps Paulina and Camillo in *The Winter's Tale*. He has, notably, not renounced his military career, which Bertram in *All's Well* needed to do before he could commit himself to his wife; he does indeed find that his differing cultural expectations cause him problems in understanding the probable causes of his wife's behaviour, though he himself does not really understand this until it is too late. And having married as it were in a cultural vacuum, without the support of either her family or his, they find that they have no one to turn to when difficulties begin – there is only Emilia, whose advice is well meant but ill-informed, and Iago, who is out to destroy them.

Shakespeare need not have been a racist to suggest that a marriage between an older black soldier and a young white Venetian woman was unlikely to survive in such circumstances and in such a setting – he need only have been a realist.[45] He presents Othello as, in many respects, a dignified, noble figure, and Desdemona as loving and lively; he lets us see what attracted each to the other. But marriage in Shakespeare is above all a social relationship as well as a personal one, and where the social infrastructure is lacking the personal interaction is simply not enough to sustain the bond. If Othello at the outset seems to think that marriage has surprisingly little to offer to him personally, what is abundantly clear throughout the play is that his relationship with Desdemona has nothing at all to offer to the society around it – indeed its first effect was to kill her father, a potent emblem of its failure to feed the community and the needs of the patriarchy.

The patriarchy, however, is amply revenged, for in one sense the failure of the relationship could be said to be little to do with purely personal traits, but to be radically conditioned by the very success with which both Othello and Desdemona had previously inhabited their socially allotted roles. So complete is their interpellation within these that they, as characters, seem completely unaware of the extent to which they conform to such sets of expectations; but on the metatheatrical level the audience is repeatedly reminded of the extent to which both Othello and Desdemona have, as it were, their parts already scripted for them. When Othello speaks of the supposedly authentic, personal experiences of his journeys, the audience will actually hear echoes of the fictional accounts of Sir John Mandeville; when Desdemona talks of 'taming', she as a character is oblivious to any intertextual echoes of the earlier play, but we as audience are acutely alive to them. Indeed every act of close reading depends on the belief that the hearer can perceive resonances and themes in the speech of which the fictional speaker himself must be supposed to be unaware. In the cases of Othello and Desdemona, what I think I have heard is unconscious adherence to a psychological pattern which is not purely personal, but social, for it seems to me that each has internalised, in different ways, a set of ideas about female behaviour which read it as always already likely to be deviant.

In Othello's case, this has manifested itself as a fear of commitment – with, arguably, a concomitant fear of consummation and perhaps of conception – and, despite his protestations of not being easily jealous, an underlying readiness to believe in the slanders that a man, and a comrade, tells him about his wife. In Desdemona, the effects seem to me to be both more subtle and more pernicious. Quite unintentionally, Desdemona throughout the play consistently behaves in ways that allow of a hostile construction: openly called 'whore', she is also vulnerable to charges of deceit, of being a bad daughter, of being sexually voracious, and of being a shrew; even after her death, when the audience, who are fully convinced of her innocence of adultery, have seen her nobly attempt to shield her husband from blame, we must still hear that husband call her a liar – *and indeed we have to agree with the accusation,* in a technical sense at least. What Desdemona does, then, is repeatedly find herself inhabiting, as if to the manner born, all the most reductively misogynistic stereotypes that her culture has to offer.[46] Whenever she attempts to speak, she is, unwittingly, 'spoken by' a socially authorised counter-discourse which labels her and demonises her. If it is true to say that the marriage between Othello and Desdemona is doomed partly by a culture clash, then her culture is, ultimately, at least as deeply implicated as his in the destruction of love and hope. Indeed what one sees in all these four tragedies, where discourses of misogyny and of extreme gender differentiation can be so rapidly and so effectively mobilised, is the self-destructiveness of a cultural reflex that, by demonising feminity, disables men too, dooming both individuals and the mutuality of marriage, along with the green world of fertility and renewal which it represents. Nevertheless, marriage does not function in this tragic world as an ideal to be unequivocally defended: as the greed of the Macbeths, the incest of Claudius and Gertrude, and the elements of disparity between Othello and Desdemona so clearly show, marriage, if it is to be worth anything at all, must always function as a social unit, rather than as a purely personal relationship.

7
The Wedding of the Daughter: Marriage in the Last Plays

Shakespeare's last four plays have always defied easy generic pigeonholing, for elements of both comedy and tragedy are deeply rooted in them: *The Winter's Tale* ends in reconciliation and marriage, but it is irrevocably shadowed by the death of its teller Mamilius; Prospero renounces his art and thinks of his grave; Cymbeline finds his sons but loses his queen; and Pericles regains his family only after years of grief and isolation. In blending these two genres, Shakespeare may seem to owe something to the increasingly flourishing art of Beaumont and Fletcher, as exemplified in plays like *The Maid's Tragedy, A King and No King* and *Philaster*; but there are also clear differences. Beaumont and Fletcher's tragi-comedies characteristically combine a cracking pace, much use of disguise, mistaken identity and cross-dressing, and a wildly unpredictable plot, structured by dramatic and unexpected reversals of fortune and, often, of attitude. An audience may be consistently surprised and amused, and may often admire the ingenuity and the political daring of many of the plot developments, but it is very rarely moved. Indeed, there is a sense in which Fletcher's own definition of his preferred tragi-comic form as offering 'the danger, not the death' precludes any significant emotional response: if we know that danger will always be averted, we are, in effect, in much the same fantasy mode as that inhabited by Batman or Indiana Jones.

In Shakespeare's late romances, however, the danger is not always averted. Though the main characters invariably survive, most of them are profoundly changed by their experiences, and many have suffered losses that will not be healed. All of these plays end with one or more marriages, and, in that, they clearly declare their kinship with the earlier world of the comedies; but the comic pattern is seriously modified by the inclusion of waste, death and, above all, the passage of time. In two of the plays, *The Winter's Tale* and *Pericles*, the traditional closure of marriage is significantly affected by the fact that, in each case, the hero is actually re-solemnising a marital relationship that has been totally in abeyance for the past 16 years; we are also aware of the presence of the widowed Paulina on stage, reinforcing the knowledge that marriages can be broken. In all these plays, comedy and tragedy are profoundly interwoven, forcing a quality of emotional response which is, for most readers and audiences, far richer and far more deeply-rooted than that evoked by the rather more mechanical plotting of Beaumont and Fletcher.

THE WINTER'S TALE

This sense of an organic bond between the comic and the tragic worlds is perhaps most fully articulated in *The Winter's Tale*. Paradoxically, the play's structure seems, at first sight, actually to suggest precisely the opposite, a radical divorce between the two: with Father Time providing an obvious hinge, the play seems almost to divide itself into two discrete parts. As in the early comedy *As You Like It*, it appears that the court can be clearly labelled as a place of jealousy and brotherly rivalry (much emphasis is placed on the quasi-fraternal relationship between Polixenes and Leontes), while the movement to Bohemia, perceived solely as a pastoral location, precipitates reconciliation. Such a schema of binary opposition is, though – as so often in Shakespeare – too simple. Though Bohemia may afford a vision of the *literally* pastoral, Sicily (as befits the setting of Theocritus) proves to be insistently steeped in the *literary* pastoral. Polixenes' first lines take us straight into the world of the eclogue and *The Shepheards Calendar*:

> Nine changes of the watery star hath been
> The shepherd's note since we have left our throne
> Without a burden.[1]

The flowing sentence, with its simple grammatical structure and regular iambic beat, establishes a gentle, lyrical note well suited to the evocation of the pastoral world. Even the reference to the cares of power and rule is unusually muted: Polixenes is, after all, a king who can comfortably manage a nine months' absence, and the word 'burden' refers not to anything that he must *carry* but to what he himself *is*, to his throne – and could, moreover, even hint at a suggestion of the 'burden' of a song, in tune with the earlier reference to 'The shepherd's note'.

At the same time, though, this passage does hint, proleptically, at a heavier 'burden'. Polixenes has been in Sicily nine months – a dangerously appropriate amount of time to feed Leontes' suspicions that Polixenes is responsible for Hermione's pregnancy, though in fact when Hermione does give birth Emilia says 'She is, something before her time, deliver'd' (II.II.25), which seems clearly to rule out any suggestion of Polixenes' involvement. Polixenes' speech may appear innocent, but to a Leontes searching for evidence of sexual misdemeanour, it may prove susceptible of a different interpretation, just as the pastoral will again be interrupted by the sexual in Polixenes' description of the two kings' boyhoods:

> We were as twinn'd lambs that did frisk i'th'sun,
> And bleat the one at th'other: what we changed
> Was innocence for innocence: we knew not
> The doctrine of ill-doing, nor dream'd
> That any did. Had we pursued that life,
> And our weak spirits ne'er been higher rear'd
> With stronger blood, we should have answered heaven
> Boldly 'not guilty', the imposition clear'd
> Hereditary ours.
>
> (I.II.67–75)

The habitual Renaissance connotations of 'spirits' and 'blood' make it quite clear that it is, specifically, sexual knowledge which occasions their fall from innocence, as Hermione assumes in her bantering reply.

Similarly, it is an awareness of sexuality which will colour Leontes' assessment of the current situation, leading to the eradication of birth, fertility and children from his court and making it instead into a wintry one. For him, the innocence figured by lambs will soon give place to the bestiality of their 'dams', and such a perceptual slippage has indeed been implicit from the outset of the play, when Camillo says:

Sicilia cannot show himself over-kind to Bohemia. They were trained together in their childhoods, and there rooted between them then such an affection which cannot choose but branch now.
(I.1.21–4)

'Trained', richly, can imply both formal education and the gradual – and mutual – using of one plant to support another; but what does 'branch' mean? Does it continue the natural, fertile potential of that second meaning of 'trained' by suggesting the flourishing of a tree, or does it rather connote divergence, a 'branching out' – or even the branching antlers of the horned beast, which find acceptance in the horn-song of Arden, but which prove so immeasurably threatening to Leontes?

It is notable that we are not told where it was that this joint 'training' of the two kings took place, and whether it was the Sicilian Leontes who received a Bohemian education, or the Bohemian Polixenes who received a Sicilian one. In one way, however, this simply does not matter, for the two are so deeply imbricated in each other's cultures. We meet actual shepherds only in Bohemia, but we hear of them in Sicily; similarly, though real bears and real sheep are confined to Bohemia, Leontes' frenzied animal imagery finds a ready echo in the language of his court. Antigonus protests that if Hermione is guilty, 'I'll keep my stables where / I lodge my wife; I'll go in couples with her' (II.I.134–5). Even when Antigonus is esentially commending the actions of Paulina, his figuring of her is still in terms of the animal: 'When she will take the rein, I let her run; / But she'll not stumble' (II.III.51–2). In a stroke of deft brilliance, Shakespeare seems to have taken the Sicily that was so favoured a location of classical pastoral, and invented for it an afterlife in which its golden age is over, but in which it continues to display a pastoral habit of mind. Just as Leontes and Polixenes have moved on from the innocence of lambs through knowledge of women, so now the mindset of post-pastoral Sicily continues to see an animal, natural world – but sees it with fallen eyes.

It is, as Antigonus' speeches suggest, primarily women who are seen in these animal terms. Antigonus himself will eventually come to believe in Hermione's guilt – and it is peculiarly appropriate that his punishment for this is to be devoured by a bear. Antigonus, too, alerts the audience to a crucial facet in the representation of Leontes' jealousy. In many respects, this story of a man who becomes erroneously but uncontrollably jealous of his wife clearly recalls *Othello* (Hermione even has an attendant named Emilia); but there is the vital difference that Leontes needs no Iago. We are pointedly reminded of this when Antigonus tells him, 'You are abus'd, and by some putter-on / That will be damn'd for't' (II.I.141–2). Here he virtually echoes Emilia in the earlier play, who ironically guesses at the existence of such a man but cannot identify him as her own husband; but Antigonus is wrong. There is no such 'putter-on', nor does there need to be, for this is a world where, as Polixenes has already shown, women are associated with sin, with animality, and with the death of innocence. Thus, even though the lords cannot believe in Hermione's guilt, they do not openly defy the king; it is only Paulina who will do that, and though Leontes attempts to demonise her with the tag 'A mankind witch!' (II.III.67) – exactly the kind of accusation which, in Shakespeare's earliest plays, did such harm to women like Joan of Arc – the other men are noticeably much more restrained in their attitude to her, and the overall development of the plot endorses her, as Leontes himself comes to do, as courageous and inventive. The apostle Paul may have recommended the subjection of women to their husbands, but Paulina diagrees, and is allowed by the play to function as a channel of grace which is indeed pauline in its resonances.[2] She is even 'rewarded' at the end by marriage, and though this could be interpreted as the classic patriarchal silencing technique, there are signs that it should perhaps be viewed in a rather different light. Leontes tells her, 'I'll not seek far – / For him, I partly know his mind – to find thee / An honourable husband' (V.III.141–4). In one way this is merely ludicrous: are we to suppose that Camillo has been nurturing some kind of passion for Paulina since before his departure from Sicily 16 years ago, and that Leontes knows so? Nevertheless, it does at least pay lip-service to the desirability of affection in marriage, and it also offers Paulina the double compliment of calling her 'thee' – a mark of intimacy and favour – and of promising her a husband who will be 'honourable'. Both of these manoeuvres clearly work to increase her status, rather than to diminish it – and we have, additionally, already seen that Paulina is easily equal to any attempts by a husband to dominate her. Finally, the simple decision to view Paulina as marriageable at all suggests in itself that women's use and desirability does not cease when their capacity for breeding does, and simultaneously reinforces the suggestion that Leontes will still value Hermione despite her wrinkles. As Carol Thomas Neely comments, 'Marriage here is not a punishment or a convention but a hard-earned fulfillment.'[3]

The play's overall tolerance and support for the potentially deviant Paulina seems reinforced in one of its mellowest passages, the Shepherd's reminiscences of his own wife:

> Fie, daughter! when my old wife liv'd, upon
> This day she was both pantler, butler, cook,
> Both dame and servant; welcom'd all, serv'd all;
> Would sing her song and dance her turn; now here
> At upper end o'th'table, now i'th'middle;
> On his shoulder, and his; her face o'fire
> With labour, and the thing she took to quench it
> She would to each one sip. You are retired,
> As if you were a feasted one, and not
> The hostess of the meeting.
>
> (IV.IV.55-64)

In many ways, Perdita's reticence might seem appropriate for a modest young woman, but the shepherd nevertheless thinks fondly of his energetic, extrovert wife, with her taste for physical contact and her uninhibited drinking. Once again, the play represents women as valued, even when they behave in unconventional ways.

It is not clear whether Perdita ever met the shepherd's wife, or whether the wife was already dead when her husband found the child; nevertheless, it comes as no surprise that Perdita should behave very differently, for in her nature has conclusively triumphed over nurture. Knowing this, the audience are especially well placed to savour the multiple layers of irony in her debate with Polixenes about breeding practices:

> You see, sweet maid, we marry
> A gentler scion to the wildest stock,
> And make conceive a bark of baser kind
> By bud of nobler race. This is an art
> Which does mend nature – change it rather – but
> The art itself is nature.
>
> (IV.IV.92-7)

Polixenes himself will soon be undercutting his own argument in his outrage at his son's choice of bride – 'Thou a sceptre's heir, / That thus affects a sheep-hook!' (IV.IV.420–1) – but its force has in any case already been undone by the dramatic logic of the play, for it is in fact Perdita's inherent royalty and noble nature which have so attracted Florizel. We are thus never asked to confront the question of whether an inter-class alliance really would be desirable, for, once again, Shakespeare's dramaturgy works to avoid such a problem. It is notable, however, that although the young lovers are prepared to overlook the apparent differential, neither of their fathers is, for the shepherd too assumes equivalence of station:

> Take hands, a bargain!
> And, friends unknown, you shall bear witness to't.
> I give my daughter to him, and will make
> Her portion equal his.
>
> (IV.IV.384–7)

In the case of Polixenes, it is not in fact clear how much of his anger is occasioned simply by Perdita's station, and how much is provoked by his own exclusion from the proceedings. In the classic pattern of folktale, he repeatedly encourages Florizel to seek his father's blessing:

> reason my son
> Should choose himself a wife, but as good reason
> The father (all whose joy is nothing else
> But fair posterity) should hold some counsel
> In such a business.
>
> (IV.IV.407–11)

Since he is prepared to allow for affection, we might perhaps assume that he would have been less adamantly opposed to the marriage had he been properly informed of it. Certainly his rage against the father, brother and the bride herself is never translated into action; though his threats are terrible, he, like Leontes when he is rational, is no tyrant, and there is no indication that they will actually be carried out. Nevertheless, our prior knowledge of Perdita's royalty means that the question of hypergamy can be, effectively, finessed.

The revelation of Perdita's identity will in fact solve all the play's problems. Paulina may advise Leontes, 'Care not for issue; / The crown will find an heir' (V.I.46–7), but, as we later learn from Hermione, this is spoken in the belief that Perdita is indeed still alive, and Leontes' own belief in the importance of a lineal heir is clearly indicated in his greeting of Florizel:

> Your mother was most true to wedlock, prince;
> For she did print your royal father off,
> Conceiving you.
>
> (V.I.123–5)

It is only with the recovery of his own legitimate heir that Leontes can regain his wife, his peace of mind, his friend and the safe succession of his kingdom. Before he can do so, however, he has to pass a test – and a test which his fictional predecessor Pandosto, the Leontes-figure in Shakespeare's source, had failed. Told by Florizel that Polixenes would grant him anything, Leontes replies, 'I'd beg your precious mistress' (V.I.222). Here, Shakespeare clearly gestures to the fact that in Robert Greene's prose romance, Pandosto had indeed fallen incestuously in love with his own daughter, and, before he became aware of her identity, consummated the relationship. Leontes, however, is kept safe by Paulina, to whom he has already vowed, 'No more such wives; therefore, no wife' (V.I.56). The grace represented by Paulina forestalls the sin of incest, and the play is able to conclude with the triple celebration of the expected weddings of Perdita and Florizel and Paulina and Camillo, and the reconciliation of Hermione and Leontes. But Mamillius is still dead, and we have already seen that a marriage may not stay happy forever.

CYMBELINE

In *Cymbeline*, the sons do not stay dead, and though the wicked stepmother and her son are sacrificed in their stead, the loss is scarcely felt in the abundance of recoveries and reconciliations which conclude the play. Although the marriage of Imogen and

Posthumus is ultimately restored, however, there are some notable anomalies in the way it is represented in the play. The very description of it seems consistently to cause problems: the First Gentleman refers to Posthumus as 'he that hath her / (I mean that married her, alack good man)',[4] the Queen refers to 'The hand-fast' (I.VI.78), and Cloten, terming the marriage a 'contract', denies its validity:

> for
> The contract you pretend with that base wretch,
> One bred of alms, and foster'd with cold dishes,
> With scraps o'th'court, it is no contract, none;
> And though it be allowed in meaner parties
> (Yet who than he more mean?) to knit their souls
> (On whom there is no more dependency
> But brats and beggary) in self-figur'd knot;
> Yet you are curb'd from that enlargement, by
> The consequence o'th'crown
>
> (2.III.113–22)

Diane Elizabeth Dreher dismisses Cloten's comments, saying 'there was certainly not one law for aristocrats and another for the common people',[5] but he does reflect an attitude prevalent in the play that Imogen's marriage to Posthumus has indeed verged on disparagement, and may perhaps be dissolved – a Lord speaking refers to 'that horrid act / Of the divorce, he'ld make' (2.II.63–4). Unlike Perdita, Posthumus never turns out to be more nobly born than was initially assumed, and can at best take rank from his wife. The First Gentleman comments, 'his virtue / By her election may be truly read / What kind of man he is' (I.I.52–4), and Jachimo refers to 'This matter of marrying his king's daughter, wherein he must be weighed rather by her value than his own' (I.IV.14–16). Even Imogen wishes for her lost brothers, for 'then had my prize / Been less, and so more equal ballasting / To thee, Posthumus' (III.VII.49–51). Moreover, even within the marriage there is a slightly jarring emphasis on female reluctance when Posthumus apparently values Imogen all the more because 'Me of my lawful pleasure she restrain'd, / And pray'd me oft forbearance' (II.IV.161–2).

The twin emphases on inequality and unwillingness to consummate may well recall *Othello* again, and other elements of the plot do so even more clearly (the departing Posthumus even waves a handkerchief). Initially, however, this is an *Othello* in reverse, as Jachimo tries to inflame the jealousy of Imogen, and she indeed responds precisely as Othello had done, by begging him to be clearer (I.VII.87–8). The inversion is complete when Jachimo exhorts her 'Be reveng'd, / Or she that bore you was no queen, and you / Recoil from your great stock' (I.VII.126–8). No amount of sexual infidelity can disrupt the mother-daughter link, as Paulina tells Leontes; the suggestion figures a gender reversal also encoded in Jachimo's relenting characterisation of Posthumus as 'a holy witch' (I.VII.166). It is particularly disheartening that one effect of this exchange is to make Posthumus' own denunciation 'We are all bastards' (II.IV.154) seem merely normative in its adoption of the standard practice of dislocating blame onto women; later, Arviragus will display a similar reflex when he says of Fidele, 'I'll make't my comfort / He is a man, I'll love him as my brother' (III.VII.43–4).

It is, however, an indication of the extent to which this is a forgiving play that Posthumus should relent towards Imogen well *before* he is certified of her actual fidelity. He cautions the audience:

> You married ones,
> If each of you should take this course, how many
> Must murder wives much better than themselves
> For wrying but a little?
>
> (V.I.2–5)

In a play unusually careful to memorialise mothers, Posthumus is even afforded a vision of his own lost family; when his mother protests, 'With marriage wherefore was he mock'd' (V.IV.58), Jupiter promises kindness because 'Our Jovial star reign'd at his birth, and in / Our temple was he married' (V.IV.105–6). There is indeed a quality of joviality about the ending, in which the unusual bitterness of Cymbeline's wrath against his daughter, which had blighted her marriage as 'the tyrannous breathing of the north, / Shakes all our buds from growing' (I.V.36–7), gives way to an instinctive, 'natural' love. Although there is no wedding – Imogen, the only woman left alive, being already married – there are, perhaps to compensate for this absence, an unusual number of references to marriages past, present and figural. The First Gaoler says of Posthumus, 'Unless a man would marry a gallows, and beget young gibbets, I never saw one so prone' (V.IV.204–5), though here, perhaps ominously, it is in fact death for which Posthumus is eager. The next reference is scarcely more cheering, when the Doctor informs Cymbeline that the Queen 'Married your royalty, was wife to your place: / Abhorr'd your person' (V.V.39–40), while Jachimo refers oddly to 'that hook of wiving' (V.V.167). There is, though, a far richer promise in Posthumus' welcome to Imogen – 'Hang there like fruit, my soul, / Till the tree die' (V.V.263–4) – and we also hear that in the case of Euriphile at least, marriage was imagined as a reward (V.V.342). As alliance is sealed with Rome, families are, as far as possible, reunited and figured as promising further increase, even though the unusual degree of recollection of women is perhaps offset by the presence on stage of only one actual woman, who is indeed in boy's clothing and who is not even a bride. Here, indeed, marriage may well seem to have ceased to be the primary constitutive relationship in a family, with a greater emphasis on continuity across and between the generations.

PERICLES

In the strange and terrible beauty of *Pericles*, the incest threatened in *The Winter's Tale* is not avoided.[6] As in *Oedipus Tyrannus*, we are, from the outset, made hideously aware of the possibility of this ultimate familial dysfunction, as the opening Chorus introduces the story of Antiochus and his daughter. Suggestively, the opening mention of them is remarkably formal:

> This king unto him took a peer,
> Who died and left a female heir[7]

In part, the diction here is deliberately archaicising to reflect the use of Gower as narrator. It is still, though, notable that every member of the family is described not in terms of familial relationship, but of rank: the king, his peer and their female heir, rather than man, wife and daughter. This consistent emphasis should alert us to the fact that a seventeenth-century family is indeed as much a social grouping as a personal one, and that the higher the status of the head of the household, the more important its successful functioning in this capacity. The mention of the daughter as a 'female heir', moreover, not only taps into what Lisa Jardine has identified as a widespread social anxiety about precisely this phenomenon,[8] but also immediately raises the question of finding a husband for such an heir. The inheritrix of a kingdom, unless she was that magnificent exception Elizabeth I, needed automatically to be available for the forming of marital and political bonds, and the king is wrong in transgressing this dynastic imperative by retaining his daughter's sexual services solely within his own family. His is a social as well as a moral crime, and the use of formal titles reminds us of that.

The political dimension of the situation is made even more apparent when the Chorus comes to describe the consequences of the incestuous relationship:

> The beauty of this sinful dame
> Made many princes thither frame,
> To seek her as a bed-fellow,
> In marriage-pleasures play-fellow;
> Which to prevent he made a law,
> To keep her still, and men in awe;
> That whoso ask'd her for his wife,
> His riddle told not, lost his life.
> So for her many a wight did die,
> As yon grim looks do testify.
>
> (Act I Chorus, 31–40)

These 'princes' seek to combine the personal fruitfully with the political by looking for an appropriate partner for 'marriage-pleasures', but the law of the father has prevented them – and I use the Lacanian terminology advisedly here, for the combination of riddle and incest motifs are so richly suggestive not only of the original Oedipus story but also of the uses that our own culture has made of it. This indictment of misused patriarchy sits interestingly alongside the deictic indicator of 'yon grim looks': is Gower evoking the brutal realities of the journey from London to Southwark, where the Globe was situated, punctuated as it was by the traitors' heads displayed on London Bridge? And what about that phrase 'keep...men in awe', which so closely echoes the accusation brought by Richard Baines against Shakespeare's great predecessor Christopher Marlowe, that Marlowe subscribed to the atheist doctrine that 'the first beginning of religion was only to keep men in awe'?[9] Taken together, Gower's apparently safe, old-world language could in fact be read as providing a threefold indictment of state power, state execution, and state religion.

If so, though, any threat of subversion is soon dispelled by the entrance of a wiser, juster king, and by the fact that the solution to the riddle is an insistence on normative family relationships. To live, Pericles needs precisely to be able to differentiate between the social and familial roles of 'father, son, and husband mild;/ ...mother, wife, and yet his child' (I.I.69–70). As he does so, and indeed in all his wooing arrangements, the language insistently reminds us of his royalty. He says of Antiochus' daughter, 'Graces her subjects, and her thoughts the king / Of every virtue gives renown to men!' (I.I.14–15); later, when he is courting Thaisa incognito, she declares that she hopes to 'crown you king of this day's happiness' (II.III.11), and Simonides in turn says to her, 'Come, queen o'th'feast' (II.III.17). Simonides muses aside 'By Jove, I wonder, that is king of thoughts, / These cates resist me, he not thought upon' (II.III.28–9), showing, moreover, a sense of strong personal satisfaction and indeed quasi-homoerotic attraction that serve to cement our sense that this appropriate alliance will, as in all Shakespeare's best marriages, allow for the fulfilment of homosocial imperatives as well as heterosexual ones. Thaisa, in turn, remarks to herself:

> By Juno, that is queen of marriage,
> All viands that I eat do seem unsavoury,
> Wishing him my meat. – Sure, he's a gallant gentleman.
>
> (II.III.30–2)

Offering personal, political, familial and social satisfaction to all, the marriage of Pericles and Thaisa is indeed a site of plenitude, as is appropriate for a king who has already emblematised fertility in his bringing of corn to relieve the suffering of Cleon's starving subjects, preventing them from eating their children and spouses (I.IV.42–6), and whose appproachability has been similarly imaged by Helicanus: 'the plants look up to heaven, / From whence they have their nourishment' (I.II.56–7).

The almost magical abundance that graces Pericles' marriage to Thaisa is strongly emphasised by the play's fairy-tale feel at this point. Although Pericles is himself a king, he is travelling in disguise, and the episode of his wooing is richly resonant of such motifs as the George and the Dragon story and the humble suitor who wins the king's daughter through valour:

> *Per.* He is a happy king, since he gains from his subjects the name of good by his government. How far is his court distant from this shore?
> *1. Fish.* Marry, sir, half a day's journey. And I'll tell you, he hath a fair daughter, and to-morrow is her birthday; and there are princes and knights come from all parts of the world to joust and tourney for her love.
> *Per.* Were my fortunes equal to my desires, I could wish to make one there.
>
> (II.I.102–11)

Pericles' reluctance to reveal his true identity also precipitates another element that is common to all four last plays, of a father either disapproving or pretending to disapprove of his child's choice in marriage (the prevalence of the 'pretence' pattern may in fact farther suggest that Polixenes' opposition is less vehement than it immediately appears). Simonides' decision to appear to oppose the match seems virtually unmotivated:

> now to my daughter's letter:
> She tells me here, she'll wed the stranger knight,
> Or never more to view nor day nor light.
> 'Tis well, mistress; your choice agrees with mine;
> I like that well: nay, how absolute she's in't,
> Not minding whether I dislike or no!
> Well, I do commend her choice,
> And will no longer have it be delay'd.
> Soft, here he comes: I must dissemble it.
>
> (II.V.15–23)

Why must he 'dissemble it'? Perhaps it is because he does not know that Pericles is royal, or perhaps because he is unsure of the young man's feelings – but we can only speculate, for Shakespeare has provided no reason, and the prevalence of the 'parental opposition' motif in the last plays may well suggest that it is operating at a level of the pattern deeper than reason, and fulfilling an important role in the journey to grace which characterises all these plots.

Unlike Polixenes, Simonides is not inflamed even when he finds his own opinion effectively disregarded. He continues, though, to appear inflexible:

> Yea, mistress, are you so peremptory?
> *Aside.* I am glad on't with all my heart. –
> I'll tame you, I'll bring you in subjection.
> Will you, not having my consent,
> Bestow your love and your affections
> Upon a stranger? *Aside.* who, for aught I know,
> May be (nor can I think the contrary)
> As great in blood as I myself. –
> Therefore hear you, mistress: either frame
> Your will to mine; and you, sir, hear you:
> Either be rul'd by me, or I'll make you –
> Man and wife.
> Nay, come, your hands and lips must seal it too;
> And being join'd, I'll thus your hopes destroy,
> And for further grief, – God give you joy!
> What, are you both pleas'd?
>
> (II.V.72–87)

Simonides articulates the standard Renaissance view on parental consent – but suddenly it no longer seems to matter. The reason, though, is clear: essentially, Pericles' innate royalty has shone through, so that Simonides, in some texts, cannot 'think the contrary'. Rather than simply valorising the will of the child, this passage works equally strongly to promote a mystique of royalty which allows it to transcend normal considerations; and, after all, Simonides' generosity also works to make him complete master of the situation. If this speech seems to chip away at parental power, it powerfully enhances that of the ultimate patriarch, the king.

Simonides rounds off this betrothal scene with the jovial, 'I will see you wed; / And then, with what haste you can, get you to bed' (II.V.91–2). Having thus set in train the breeding of the next generation, he himself becomes redundant; he is not seen again, and Thaisa too, having produced her child, soon disappears, as we follow the fortunes of the family rather than of the individual. Even when Marina is still an infant, it is, above all, as a site of future fertility, with strong ritual significance, that her father sees her:

> Till she be married, madam,
> By bright Diana, whom we honour, all
> Unscissor'd shall this hair of mine remain

(III.III.27-9)

But almost as soon as it begins, this momentum of reproduction and replacement is arrested by a sudden concentration on the individual. Marina is taken to a place where she would, indeed, most certainly be able to breed, if breeding were the only consideration: the Bawd of the brothel has brought up eleven bastards, though only, as Boult replies, 'to eleven, and then brought them down again' (IV.II.15). This cycle of woman's progress from birth to giving birth may initially seem to be precisely what the play itself has effected with its sudden replacement of Thaisa by Marina, but a new consideration is abruptly introduced when the Pander tells the Bawd, 'Wife, take her in' (IV.II.50). Even in a brothel, the married state is registered as honourable in itself. Moroever, while the Bawd's objection to Marina – 'She's able to freeze the god Priapus, and undo a whole generation' (IV.VI.3-4) – may initially seem to have something of the same force of teeming life as characterises the brothels of Vienna in *Measure for Measure*, the actions of Dionyza, who has, as she thinks, killed to further her child's prospects, also remind us that motherhood alone will not guarantee the continuation of civilised society.

Nevertheless, birth and breeding continue to be of major importance. Boult clearly images her as a site of potential fertility: 'An if she were a thornier piece of ground than she is, she shall be plough'd' (IV.VI.144-5). For Lysimachus, it is Marina's own breeding which will prove crucial. Lysimachus provides something of a challenge for the dramatist, for the plot demands that he must first encounter Marina in a brothel, and he certainly seems to identify himself with their habitual 'resorters' (IV.VI.22); however, there are clear attempts to dissociate him from the taint of prostitution as he protests, albeit rather feebly, 'Had I brought hither a corrupted mind, / Thy speech had alter'd it' (IV.VI.103–4), and 'For me, be you thoughten / That I came with no ill intent' (IV.VI.108–9). These speeches at least establish that Lysimachus feels shame at being found in a brothel, even if they are not felt to be particularly convincing exculpations; but whatever his nervousness about his own position, he is nevertheless not prepared to disregard hers:

> She's such a one that, were I well assur'd
> Came of a gentle kind and noble stock,
> I'd wish no better choice, and think me rarely wed

(V.I.67–9)

In fact, of course, Marina does come of such stock, and that will shortly be proved. Notably, the revelation of her identity is itself conceived of as a birth: Pericles on first seeing her says, 'I am great with woe / And shall deliver weeping' (V.I.105–6), and, discovering who she is, calls her 'Thou that beget'st him that did thee beget' (V.I.195). Similarly, the rediscovery of Thaisa is also resonant of a wedding, as she tells Pericles:

> Now I know you better.
> When we with tears parted Pentapolis,
> The king my father gave you such a ring.

(V.III.37–9)

The ring functions as both proof of identity, reminder and renewal of the wedding, and as a final reminder of the strong bond and continuity conferred by the approval of Simonides. The period of the original wedding is again referred to as Pericles resolves now to shave off his beard: 'And what this fourteen years no razor touch'd / To grace thy marriage-day I'll beautify' (V.III.75–6). With this act, Pericles effectively resumes his original identity; as in *The Winter's Tale*, the wedding of the daughter has facilitated the spiritual rebirth of the father and the restoration of the parents' own marriage, and in this case, too, the element of continuity with the grandfather Simonides is also stressed.

THE TEMPEST

In *The Tempest*, the motif of the father pretending to oppose the marriage recurs again, but this time it does so against a background of marriages and families which are irretrievably fragmented. Prospero's wife will not come back to life,[10] and his reconciliation with his brother is at best half-hearted; Caliban, a bastard, lost his only relative in his mother, and is frustrated in his desire to reproduce himself with Miranda;[11] the King of Naples' daughter lives too far away ever to be seen again, and he remains unaware that his brother is false to him; even Prospero does not gain a new lease of life from Miranda's wedding, focusing instead on his own future death. The note is struck right from the beginning, with the mariners' cries of ' "Mercy on us!" – "We split, we split!" – "Farewell, my wife and children!" – "Farewell, brother!" – "We split, we split, we split!" ' (I.1.55–8); and Sebastian echoes this when he accuses his brother, albeit erroneously, 'Milan and Naples have / More widows in them of this business' making / Than we bring men to comfort them' (II.1.134–6). They were, moreover, coming from the country of 'widow Dido' (II.1.78).

Alongside these recurrent images of broken families comes an insistent fetishisation of female chastity. This has been largely in abeyance in the other two plays, at least for the daughters' generation: no one questions Perdita's virtue, and Lysimachus is quite convinced of Marina's even though he meets her in a brothel. In *The Tempest*, however, Miranda's chastity has already been assaulted even though there is only one other man on the island, and her conversation with her father shows her always nervously aware of the possibility of sexual sin. When he informs her that 'twelve year since, / Thy father was the Duke of Milan and / A prince of power' (I.2.53–5), she immediately responds, 'Sir, are not you my father?' (I.2.55), to which Prospero trots out the standard joke, 'Thy mother was a piece of virtue, and / She said thou wast my daughter' (I.2.56–7). It can clearly only be because she has picked up on her father's attitudes that Miranda makes so literal a response to her father's surprise that his own brother could betray him:

> I should sin
> To think but nobly of my grandmother.
> Good wombs have borne bad sons.
>
> (I.2.118–20)

Miranda has faith in female virtue, and for a girl brought up on a desert island, she registers a surprisingly strong sense of family solidarity. Nevertheless, her belief that a good woman can produce bad children works counter to this general sense of orthodoxy, for it poses a radical challenge to the eugenically motivated telos of the production of kingly offspring towards which all these last plays work.

For all that her very name Miranda, with its translation from the Latin of 'to be admired', sets her up as a passive object of the gaze, Miranda not infrequently challenges implicit orthodoxies. It is she who labels the Europeans as creatures of 'a new world', reversing the assumed superiority of the 'old world', and she calmly disregards traditional gender codes when she assures Ferdinand that she too could carry logs:

> It would become me
> As well as it does you; and I should do it
> With much more ease; for my good will is to it,
> And yours it is against.
>
> (III.1.28–31)

She even proposes to him:

> Hence, bashful cunning!
> And prompt me, plain and holy innocence.
> I am your wife, if you will marry me.
> If not, I'll die your maid. To be your fellow
> You may deny me, but I'll be your servant
> Whether you will or no.
>
> (III.1.81–6)

And if inverting gender norms by making such a suggestion is not enough, Miranda goes one step further by offering to disregard social hierarchies too: she, a princess, is willing to work as a servant.

In order to make this offer, Miranda puns on 'maid', wresting it from its customary denotation of 'virgin' to suggest, interestingly enough, the subservience of a maidservant. However suggestive such an association may be in itself – and however appropriate to the sexual politics of the culture which she must now enter – this is certainly not the meaning given to 'maid' by Ferdinand and Prospero: for both of them, what is overridingly important is physical virginity. Ferdinand tells her, 'My prime request, / Which I do last pronounce, is – O you wonder! – / If you be maid or no?' (I.2.426–8), and shortly after he promises 'O, if a virgin, / And your affection not gone forth, I'll make you / The Queen of Naples' (I.2.448–50). Prospero, overhearing, is pleased enough at the proposal, but is effectively worried that what is easily procured will be undervalued: 'this swift business / I must uneasy make, lest too light winning / Make the prize light' (I.2.451–3). Presumably, this refers primarily to how Ferdinand might account Miranda, but the syntax is also susceptible of a different interpretation: since Miranda herself is the 'prize' who has been won, she *herself* might become light.

It is, however, the sexual appetite he attributes to Ferdinand which principally causes Prospero concern, and which leads him to threaten a curse reminiscent of King Lear's:

> If thou dost break her virgin-knot before
> All sanctimonious ceremonies may
> With full and holy rite be ministered,
> No sweet aspersion shall the heavens let fall
> To make this contract grow; but barren hate,
> Sour-eyed disdain and discord shall bestrew
> The union of your bed with weeds so loathly
> That you shall hate it both. Therefore take heed,
> As Hymen's lamps shall light you.
>
> (IV.1.15–23)

Moments later, he repeats his warnings:

> Look thou be true. Do not give dalliance
> Too much the rein. The strongest oaths are straw
> To th'fire i'th'blood. Be more abstemious,
> Or else, good night your vow.
>
> (IV.1.51–4)

He even builds it into the theme of the masque. Iris, explaining the absence of Venus and Cupid, who as god and goddess of love might be thought particularly appropriate for the occasion, comments:

Marriage in the Last Plays 181

> Here thought they to have done
> Some wanton charm upon this man and maid,
> Whose vows are, that no bed-right shall be paid
> Till Hymen's torch be lighted: but in vain.
>
> (IV.1.94–7)

Again, syntax threatens to undercut sense: it is Venus' and Cupid's thought that was in vain, but Ferdinand's and Miranda's 'vows' are much closer in the sentence, and might equally be read as the subject for the complement 'in vain'. In fact, though, it is clear that it is a chaste betrothal which is being celebrated here, presided over by the goddess not of love but of marriage, Juno Pronuba; specifically identified as 'the wife of Jupiter' (IV.1.77), she invokes the sedate gifts of 'Honour, riches, marriage blessing, / Long continuance, and increasing' (IV.1.106–7). Indeed Ceres, goddess of fertility, will not even attend a wedding blessed by Venus: love, it seems, is figured as having no part in an alliance predicated on the values of marriage and fertility.[12] Nor will Ferdinand and Miranda's wait be a short one: Prospero explicitly wishes to defer it until arrival at Naples (V.1.308). Ferdinand at least, though, registers no discontent, and comments (in most editions) 'So rare a wondered father and a wise / Makes this place Paradise' (IV.1.123–4), stressing once more the homosocial bonding that marriage facilitates – even though some copies of the Folio, suggestively enough, are said actually to read not 'wise' but 'wife'![13]

Marrying, then, and the subsequent begetting of lawful issue, are the values towards which this play works,[14] and which indeed seem to have been a large part of Prospero's original motivation in causing the tempest. Though Gonzalo proposes to eradicate marriage from his dystopia, Antonio is adamant that this can lead only to a population composed entirely of 'whores and knaves' (II.1.170–1); and Prospero is careful to point out Caliban's bastardy (V.1.273), whatever the precise implications of his own reluctant 'acknowledgement' of him. Indeed, in a play where access to power is so strictly controlled by application of the rules of primogeniture, an emphasis on legitimate descent must be paramount – even though brothers may be so different, and, as Miranda so hauntingly reminds us, good wombs have borne bad sons.

THE TWO NOBLE KINSMEN

The Two Noble Kinsmen, which Shakespeare co-wrote with Fletcher, is entirely structured around marriage. In a sense, the whole play is sandwiched between two weddings, since it takes up 'where *A Midsummer Night's Dream* left off, with celebration of Theseus's wedding', and 'ends with a funeral overlaid with wedding festival'.[15] The note is sounded, though, even before that, in the opening Prologue:

> New plays and maidenheads are near akin,
> Much followed both, for both much money gi'en,
> If they stand sound and well. And a good play –
> Whose modest scenes blush on his marriage day,
> And shake to lose his honour – is like her
> That after holy tie and first night's stir
> Yet still is modesty, and still retains
> More of the maid to sight than husband's pains.
> We pray our play may be so; for I am sure
> It has a noble breeder, and a pure[16]

This offers a sustained series of images of the transition from virginity to marriage, and the possibility of sexual disease (stand sound and well) or prostitution (money given for maidenheads) which may interrupt the processes of 'noble breeding'. It provides a fitting preamble to a play which begins with the stage direction '*Enter Hymen with a torch burning... then Hippolyta the bride*' (I.1.s.d.), and where the Boy's opening song includes the lines 'All dear Nature's children sweet, / Lie 'fore bride and bridegroom's feet' (ll.13–14). The stage is described as a 'bridehouse' (I.1.22), but the wedding is suddenly interrupted by the arrival of the three widowed queens who, as in *Hamlet*, seek to intersperse the marriage rites with those of funerals. But marriage is not to be so easily displaced: Theseus says to the first queen,

> King Capaneus was your lord; the day
> That he should marry you, at such a season
> As now it is with me, I met your groom

(I.1.59–61)

Even when he finally agrees to campaign against Creon, the outward form of the wedding itself is not abandoned, as he orders Pirithous 'omit not anything / In the pretended celebration' (I.1.209–10). For Theseus, after all, marriage is 'This grand act of our life, this daring deed / Of fate in wedlock' (I.1.164–5), and 'a service... / Greater than any war; it more imports me / Than all the actions that I have foregone / Or futurely can cope' (I.1.171–4).

One of the reasons why marriage is taken so seriously is that it is in this play that the case for marriage as a disrupter rather than as a promoter of homosocial relationships is most systematically mounted. It is heard first from Emilia, who, recalling the closeness of her childhood friendship with Flavina, remembers:

> the flower that I would pluck
> And put between my breasts – O, then but beginning
> To swell about the blossom – she would long
> Till she had such another, and commit it
> To the like innocent cradle, where phoenix-like
> They died in perfume
>
> (I.3.66–71)

The emphases here on breasts, on picked blossoms and on 'dies', with its habitual connotation of orgasm, prepare us to be unsurprised at Emilia's eventual conclusion that 'the true love 'tween maid and maid may be / More than in sex dividual' (I.3.81–2);[17] but Hippolyta, for all her Amazonian upbringing, brushes away the suggestion:

> Now alack, weak sister,
> I must no more believe thee in this point,
> Though in't I know thou dost believe thyself,
> Than I will trust a sickly appetite
> That loathes even as it longs.
>
> (I.3.85–90)

Even Emilia herself, moreover, will soon assume the rightness of heterosexual coupling when she says of Narcissus, 'That was a fair boy, certainly, but a fool / To love himself; were there not maids enough' (II.1.174–5).

When it comes to Palamon and Arcite, the language carefully registers a much more clear distinction between the homosocial and the possibility of the homosexual. Arcite says,

> here age must find us,
> And – which is heaviest, Palamon – unmarried.
> The sweet embraces of a loving wife,
> Loaden with kisses, armed with thousand cupids,
> Shall never clasp our necks; no issue know us
>
> (II.1.82–6)

Nevertheless, Arcite also suggests – albeit in his attempt to palliate the discomforts of a prison – that 'Were we at liberty, / A wife might part us lawfully, or business' (II.1.142–3); and they soon find that, even in prison, the love of a woman can indeed come between their friendship, ultimately to prove the death of one of them. Perhaps suggestively, though, the one who will survive this experience best is the one who is the more prepared to espouse the values and ethos of marriage. While Arcite appeals to Mars, Palamon prays to Venus, and cites in his own favour his past faith in women (V.1.115–18); moreover, he and his friends intend their last acts on earth to be their contributions towards the marriage portion of the Gaoler's Daughter (V.4.30ff), whose devotion to Palamon has further singled him out as a figure associated with love. This growing emphasis on Palamon is complemented by the flattening effect of Pirithous' account of Arcite's death (V.4.48ff), with its stress almost more on the horse than on the man, and eventually allows the play to avoid a sense of tragedy and concentrate instead on fertility, with its observance of the rites of May (II.4.49–52) and the Schoolmaster's injunction to the ladies to eat the stag's testicles (III.5.155). Even the Gaoler's Daughter makes a recovery, by some means which are never quite clear, and moves on to the socially suitable marriage which has been so properly arranged between her father and suitor (II.1.7–14). In her case, it is, interestingly enough, her suitor's tolerance of her erotomania and her wild and wandering behaviour which saves her, just as it is Palamon's faith in women's virtue which operates in his favour. It is, moreover, notable that while the Hippolyta of *A Midsummer Night's Dream* may have been thought reluctant for marriage, her counterpart in this play expresses far more enthusiasm about her relationship with Theseus. Where difference and even deviance can be tolerated, it seems, marriage can still work for the good of both individual and community, though a fixation on one potential marriage partner – particularly, perhaps, as a way of mediating a quasi-homoerotic rivalry – can still lead to disaster.

HENRY VIII

Shakespeare's other collaboration with Fletcher, *Henry VIII*, although equally classifiable as a history play, certainly shares with the late plays the strong emphasis on regeneration through the daughter, for it culminates with Cranmer's paean of praise over the infant Elizabeth I. It also treats of the highly problematic marital arrangements of Henry VIII himself, covering the period of his divorce from Katherine of Aragon and his marriage to Anne Boleyn, which were indeed events that were to change the shape of English marriage practices forever in their break from the Church of Rome and the resulting end both of celibacy for clerics and, ultimately, of the concept of indissoluble marriage. It is, therefore, appropriate enough that the word which echoes through this play should be not 'marriage', but 'divorce', heard first when the Duke of Buckingham speaks of his impending execution as 'the long divorce of steel',[18] and heard insistently thereafter. The very Prologue concludes with the ominous line 'A man may weep upon his wedding day' (Prologue, 32), albeit this is offered as an instance of something improbable, and the dread of hypergamy is figured in Norfolk's description of the Field of the Cloth of Gold as showing pomp 'now married / To one above itself' (I.1.16–17) – later, Anne will speak of Pomp as something which Fortune will 'divorce / ...from the bearer' (II.3.14–15).

In the treatment of the actual divorce, the authors seem to be at pains to be, as far as possible, even-handed. Katherine stresses her own good wifely behaviour (though her very emphasis in this matter may perhaps in itself militate against the impression of her meekness), and no one ever contradicts her. Henry is initially courteous to her – 'you have half our power' (I.2.11) – and repeatedly explains that he has no complaint against her personally:

> O, my lord,
> Would it not grieve an able man to leave
> So sweet a bedfellow? But conscience, conscience!
>
> (II.2.29–41)

We have, though, already heard Suffolk's remark that 'his conscience / Has crept too near another lady' (II.2.16–17), and there is even a hint of very unexpected self-parody in Henry's reproach to Wolsey:

> You have scarce time
> To steal from spiritual leisure a brief span
> To keep your earthly audit. Sure, in that
> I deem you an ill husband, and am glad
> To have you therein my companion.
>
> (III.2.39–43)

Certainly the Second and Third Gentlemen assume that it is carnal desire rather than conscience which primarily motivates Henry's relationship with Anne, and the language which they use to describe her coronation is not altogether recuperative:

> Our King has all the Indies in his arms,
> And more, and richer, when he strains that lady.
> I cannot blame his conscience.
>
> (IV.1.46–8)

> No man living
> Could say 'This is my wife' there, all were woven
> So strangely in one piece.
>
> (IV.1.79–81)

Anne is figured as something rich, but strange, and is, appropriately enough, associated with a blurring of distinction in wifehood. (Interestingly, women are similarly imaged as faintly alien when Surrey refers to Wolsey kissing 'the brown wench' [III.2.294].)

Anne is, however, thoroughly recuperated in her capacity as mother of Elizabeth. As her confinement draws near, the imagery of estrangement gives way to the language of nature:

> The fruit she goes with
> I pray for heartily, that it may find
> Good time, and live; but, for the stock, Sir Thomas,
> I wish it grubbed up now.
>
> (V.1.20–3)

Here, though, a clear distinction is drawn between Anne herself and the fruit of her womb. Suggestively, the speaker here is Gardiner, whose name will be again played on when he refers to Cranmer as 'a rank weed' (V.1.54); but Gardiner, ironically, is a bad gardener. Indeed, there seems to be a small but marked degree of progression through the images of nature, for the next we hear comes from the Old Lady, who describes Elizabeth as 'as like you / As cherry is to cherry' (V.1.168–9). This speech may initially seem both a refreshing change from the predominant use of print imagery to denote father–child resemblance,[19] and also to suggest the cherry-tree carol associated with the birth of Jesus; but its effect is rather undercut when we immediately afterwards hear the Old Lady lamenting it because she was not paid more. It is not until the great final speech of Cranmer that imagery of fruit, corn and fertility can be heard untainted (V.5.31ff), and that, ironically, is applied to a virgin who will never personally be fruitful. Certainly with hindsight, such a suggestion of withering and blight can only seem appropriate, for the play records not only a divorce, but the marriage which was to put England on the road to divorce.

Conclusion

Only twice in his career does Shakespeare seriously contemplate a world without marriage. In *Troilus and Cressida*, the marital relationship has, in effect, ceased to have a present meaning. As in the Chaucerian original, Troilus never once contemplates preventing Cressida's exchange by marrying her, and indeed the entire question of any marriage between them is simply never raised. The play is, in this respect, the polar opposite of *Romeo and Juliet*, as Troilus introduces his suit with the simple assumption that 'I cannot come to Cressid but by Pandar'.[1] Though Cressida is well aware of the possibility of extra-marital pregnancy (I.II.272–5, III.2.104–5), she does not seem unduly disturbed by it, and the lack even of any betrothal between them is sharply pointed up by the alternative quasi-legal formulation of Pandarus' mock-blessing, 'Here's "In witness whereof the parties interchangeably"' (III.II.58 – a point that is not likely to have been wasted on the play's original audience of lawyers).

Conceivably, the question of marriage fails to arise because of a social distance between the two, but the play never says this, and Cressida is indeed considered of sufficient rank to be exchanged for the invaluable Antenor. A more plausible suggestion for the complete disregard of marriage comes from the distinctly unfavourable tone of Troilus' few references both to it and, indeed, to lasting emotional commitment:

> I take today a wife, and my election
> Is led on in the conduct of my will:
> My will enkindled by mine eyes and ears,
> Two traded pilots 'twixt the dangerous shores
> Of will and judgement – how may I avoid,
> Although my will distaste what it elected,
> The wife I choose?
>
> (II.II.62–8)

Troilus' 'will' carries the usual Renaissance connotation of 'male organ', and he is afraid that it will 'distaste what it elected'. The verb that he uses with the word 'wife' is 'avoid'. Similarly, he later tells Cressida that he hopes that 'my integrity and truth to you / Might be affronted with the match and weight / Of such a winnow'd purity in love' (III.II.163–5); here, too, 'affronted' seems a revealing choice of term in a man who considers his own 'truth' in love to be 'my vice, my fault' (IV.IV.100) and who seems positively to expect betrayal (IV.IV.72ff). Cressida, too, is similarly nervous of commitment: 'That she was never yet who ever knew / Love got so sweet as when desire did sue' (I.II.295–6).

In one sense, betrayal is indeed necessary to Troilus' identity: he, Cressida and Pandarus all self-consciously draw attention to their future reputations, and the keystone of Troilus' is indeed bound up with the falseness of Cressida – Barbara Everett calls him 'a betrayee'.[2] This is a play where identity is problematic – Pandarus exclaims, 'Himself? Alas poor Troilus, I would he were' (I.II.72), and Troilus will later famously declare that 'This is, and is not, Cressid' (V.II.145). Perhaps, therefore, the role of lover betrayed offers at least the security of identity, and one, moreover, that is less notorious than that of husband betrayed, as the perpetual mention of Menelaus' status as cuckold indicates (e.g. III.III.64). Moreover, as well as the obvious marital disaster of Helen and Menelaus, we are constantly reminded of other unsuccessful or unachieved marriages: whenever we see or hear of Hector and his wife Andromache, he is chiding her (I.II.6, V.III.4, V.III.77–8), the god Vulcan (whose status as cuckold was in any case notorious)[3] and his wife are referred to as 'near as the extremest ends of parallels' (I.III.167–8), and those who remembered the *Iliad* would be well aware that the mooted marriage between Achilles and Polyxena will never take place. This is, indeed, ill-omened from the beginning: Patroclus is openly said to be 'Achilles' male varlet' (V.I.15), and though Patroclus is said to be eager to hear of whores (V.II.190–1) and is well aware of Achilles' marriage plans (V.I.36–41), other elements of the text certainly work to support the suggestion. There is obvious homoeroticism in the encounter of Hector and Achilles – 'I will the second time, / As I would buy thee, view thee limb by limb' (IV.V.236–7); Ulysses openly jokes, 'better would it fit Achilles much / To throw down Hector than Polyxena' (III.III.206–7);[4] and Achilles displays a mysterious inability to remember the terms of a challenge focusing on female beauty

(II.I.128). We may well conclude that this is indeed Shakespeare's most open dramatic picture of a homosexual relationship, and that Achilles, like Troilus, has found for himself a mode of existence which can continue equally happily without the institution of marriage.

But although there may be few current marriages in the play, the shadow of previous ones is still long. Helen may live in Troy, but Hector when talking to Menelaus refers to her as 'your quondam wife' (IV.V.178), and Troilus figures his brother as 'The forked one' (I.II.166), while Pandarus puns obsessively on Helen's status as queen/quean (III.I.47ff). Hector demands, 'What nearer debt in all humanity / Than wife is to the husband?' (II.II.176–7), and Thersites repeatedly pours scorn on 'those that war for a placket' (II.III.20–1). Moreover, marriage is still the guarantor and demarcator of relationships: Aeneas remembers his parents when he says, 'by Anchises' life, / Welcome indeed! By Venus' hand I swear' (IV.I.22–3 – later, at IV.IV.143, he will refer to 'a bridegroom's fresh alacrity'), and he reminds the Greeks that 'This Ajax is half made of Hector's blood' (IV.V.83). Equally, though Priam famously had 50 sons, the difference of Margarelon, his bastard, is still recognised, and indeed insisted on (V.V.7, V.VII.15). Fear of bastardy seems, indeed, to be a prime reason for marriage: Diomedes says scornfully to Paris, 'You, like a lecher, out of whorish loins / Are pleas'd to breed out your inheritors' (IV.I.64–5), and Thersites offers us a picture of a nightmare world indeed when he tells Margarelon, 'I am a bastard, too: I love bastards. I am bastard begot, bastard instructed, bastard in mind, bastard in valour, in everything illegitimate' (V.VII.16–18). As Mary Beth Rose observes, 'insofar as the future in *Troilus and Cressida* is suggested, it is associated with marriage: but that future is belittled, rejected, and like Andromache, shunted aside'.[5]

In *Timon of Athens*, accusations of bastardy and whoredom similarly recur,[6] and Timon also fulminates against second marriage (IV.III.38–42). Alone in the Shakespearean canon, this play features no wives; the only two women we meet are Alcibiades' whores, so that, as Margaret Loftus Ranald comments, 'in his bleakest play, *Timon of Athens*, Shakespeare... demonstrates the horror of a world completely devoid of marital love'.[7] Even the young woman whose marriage to Lucilius Timon (notably usurping the role of the bride's father) arranges does not appear. Nevertheless, the ideology of marriage is still recognisably intact. When Timon calls gold

Conclusion

'thou sweet king-killer, and dear divorce / 'Twixt natural son and sire, thou bright defiler of Hymen's purest bed' (IV.III.384–6), he registers the desirability of normative relations, and indeed that is encoded even in Apemantus's persistent assertions of their failure to operate. Marriage may be gone in this world, but it is not forgotten; and it is perhaps in these two visions of a world without it that we come closest to understanding how deeply it was rooted in Shakespeare's understanding of his culture. Marriage in his plays may not guarantee personal happiness or even individual fertility, but it is, nevertheless, the simplest way of ensuring the continuation of civilised society, and for that purpose if no other, it is so highly valued as to be indispensable. Where the ultimate insult is 'bastard', marriage must always be the transcendental authenticator.

Notes

INTRODUCTION: SHAKESPEARE AND CONTEMPORARY MARRIAGE

1. Alison Findlay, *Illegitimate Power: Bastards in Renaissance Drama* (Manchester: Manchester University Press, 1994), p. 23.
2. See Martin Ingram, 'Spousals Litigation in the English Ecclesiastical Courts, c.1350–1640', in R.B. Outhwaite, ed., *Marriage and Society* (London: Europa, 1981), pp. 35–57.
3. On the indispensability of consent, see Alan Macfarlane, *Marriage and Love in England* (Oxford: Basil Blackwell, 1986), pp. 128–30. On the actual form of the marriage ceremony, see N.H. Keeble, ed., *The Cultural Identity of Seventeenth-Century Woman* (London: Routledge, 1994), pp. 121–5, and 'The Making of Marriage' in Ralph A. Houlbrooke, *The English Family 1450–1700* (Harlow: Longman, 1984).
4. Frances E. Dolan, *Dangerous Familiars: Representations of Domestic Crime in England 1550–1700* (Ithaca, NY: Cornell University Press, 1994), p. 17.
5. For an alternative view which stresses continuity rather than change, however, see Kathleen M. Davies, 'Continuity and Change in Literary Advice on Marriage', in Outhwaite, *Marriage and Society*, pp. 58–80, and Ann Jennalie Cook, *Making a Match: Courtship in Shakespeare and his Society* (Princeton, NJ: Princeton University Press, 1991), p. 13. My own argument depends less on whether Puritan doctrines were new than on their existence, which is not contested. The issues of love and control in marriage are lucidly addressed in David Lindley, *The Trials of Frances Howard* (London: Routledge, 1993), pp. 32–3 and pp. 38–9; there is a succinct account of differing views about change in Keeble, *The Cultural Identity of Seventeenth-Century Woman*, pp. 115–17. See also Phyllis Rackin, 'Androgyny, Mimesis, and the Marriage of the Boy Heroine on the English Renaissance Stage', *Publications of the Modern Language Association of America* 102 (1987), pp. 29–41, p. 32, and Mary Beth Rose, *The Expense of Spirit: Love and Sexuality in English Renaissance Drama* (Ithaca, NY: Cornell University Press, 1988), especially p. 14, for a discussion of whether the balance falls on change or continuity.
6. Sir Philip Sidney, *The Countess of Pembroke's Arcadia*, ed. Maurice Evans (Harmondsworth: Penguin, 1977), pp. 814–15.
7. Elspeth Graham, Hilary Hinds, Elaine Hobby and Helen Wilcox, eds, *Her Own Life* (London: Routledge, 1989), p. 16; see also Dolan, *Dangerous Familiars*, p. 24.

8. Interestingly, in view of the persistent speculations that Shakespeare himself may have been a Catholic, Arthur Kirsch comments, '[t]hough not a sacrament in the Anglican liturgy, marriage always in Shakespeare has sacramental value' (*Shakespeare and the Experience of Love* [Cambridge: Cambridge University Press, 1981], p. 98).
9. Graham et al., *Her Own Life*, p. 8.
10. Diane Elizabeth Dreher, *Domination and Defiance: Fathers and Daughters in Shakespeare* (Lexington: University Press of Kentucky, 1986), p. 33. For discussion of *The Taming of the Shrew* in precisely these terms, see Graham Holderness, *Shakespeare in Performance: The Taming of the Shrew* (Manchester: Manchester University Press, 1989), pp. 21–2 and 111.
11. Juliet Dusinberre, *Shakespeare and the Nature of Women* (Basingstoke: Macmillan, 1975); see especially, pp. 2–4, but this is the burden of Dusinberre's argument throughout the book.
12. Dympna Callaghan, 'The Ideology of Romantic Love: The Case of *Romeo and Juliet*', in Dympna Callaghan, Lorraine Helms and Jyotsna Singh, *The Weyward Sisters: Shakespeare and Feminist Politics* (Oxford: Basil Blackwell, 1994), pp. 59–101, p. 79.
13. Catherine Belsey, *The Subject of Tragedy* (London: Methuen, 1985; reprinted Routledge, 1991), p. 135. See also Dolan, *Dangerous Familiars*, pp. 4–5.
14. Kathleen McLuskie, *Renaissance Dramatists* (Atlantic Highlands, NJ: Humanities Press International, 1989), p. 49.
15. Lisa Jardine, *Still Harping on Daughters: Women and Drama in the Age of Shakespeare* (Brighton: Harvester, 1983), p. 43. For additional comment on the negative side of Puritan ideologies, see Akiko Kusunoki, '"Their Testament at their Apron-strings": The Representation of Puritan Women in Early Seventeenth-Century England', in *Gloriana's Face*, ed. S.P. Cerasano and Marion Wynne-Davies (London: Routledge, 1992), pp. 185–204, p. 186–7.
16. Graham Holderness, '"A Woman's War": A Feminist Reading of *Richard II*', in *Shakespeare Left and Right*, ed. Ivo Kamps (London: Routledge, 1991), pp. 167–83, p. 182.
17. Heather Dubrow, *A Happier Eden: The Politics of Marriage in the Stuart Epithalamium* (Ithaca, NY: Cornell University Press, 1990), p. 2.
18. Catherine Belsey, 'Desire's Excess and the English Renaissance Theatre: *Edward II, Troilus and Cressida, Othello*', in *Erotic Politics*, ed. Susan Zimmerman (London: Routledge, 1992), pp. 84–102, p. 95.
19. David M. Bergeron, *Shakespeare's Romances and the Royal Family* (Lawrence: University of Kansas Press, 1985), p. 77.
20. See, for instance, Richard Wilson, *Will Power: Essays on Shakespearean Authority* (Hemel Hempstead: Harvester Wheatsheaf, 1993), p. 19.
21. On this subject see also Cook, *Making a Match*. pp. 8–9, and the instances afforded by the Howard family as described in Lindley, *Frances Howard*, p. 13.
22. See Wilson, *Will Power*, p. 184.
23. Jonathan Goldberg, 'Romeo and Juliet's Open Rs', in *Queering the Renaissance*, ed. Jonathan Goldberg (Durham, NC: Duke University Press, 1994), pp. 218–35, p. 222.

24. Stephen Booth, ed., *Shakespeare's Sonnets* (New Haven, CT: Yale University Press, 1977), Sonnet 10.
25. See Gwyn Williams, 'Shakespeare's Phoenix', *The National Library of Wales Journal*, 22 (1982), pp. 277–81.
26. See, for instance, the cases cited in Cook, *Making a Match*, p. 45. For alternative perspectives on the question of Shakespeare's possible allegiances to either aristocratic or popular positions, see Richard Wilson, 'Is Shakespeare a Feudal Propagandist?', in John Elsom, ed., *Is Shakespeare Still Our Contemporary?* (London: Routledge, 1989), esp. p. 149, and Annabel Patterson, *Shakespeare and the Popular Voice* (Oxford: Basil Blackwell, 1989), esp. p. 6. An interesting analysis of *Twelfth Night* as encoding some of the values of aristocratic marriage is offered by Cristina Malcolmson, '"What You Will": Social Mobility and Gender in *Twelfth Night*', in *The Matter of Difference*, ed. Valerie Wayne (Hemel Hempstead: Harvester Wheatsheaf, 1991), pp. 29–57.
27. See Carol Thomas Neely, *Broken Nuptials in Shakespeare's Plays*, 2nd edition (Urbana, IL: Illini Books, 1993), p. 10.
28. Lindley, *Frances Howard*, p. 80.
29. Marianne Novy, *Love's Argument: Gender Relations in Shakespeare* (Chapel Hill, NC and London: University of North Carolina Press, 1984), p. 5.
30. Lawrence Stone, *The Crisis of the Aristocracy 1558–1641* (Oxford: Oxford University Press, 1965), p. 661.
31. Macfarlane, *Marriage and Love*, pp. 133–4, 132, 161.
32. See J.W. Draper, 'The Queen Makes a Match and Shakespeare a Comedy', *Yearbook of English Studies*, 2 (1972), pp. 61–7, p. 62, and Steven May, 'A Midsummer Night's Dream and the Carey-Berkeley Wedding', *Renaissance Papers* (1983), pp. 43–52, p. 50.
33. David N. Durant, *Bess of Hardwick* [1977] (Newark: The Cromwell Press, 1988), p. 57.
34. Durant, *Bess of Hardwick*, p. 127.
35. See Roger Sales, *Christopher Marlowe* (Basingstoke: Macmillan, 1991), p. 52.
36. *Edward III*, ed. George Parfitt (Nottingham: Nottingham Drama Texts, 1985), II.i.596–600.
37. For an alternative view, which suggests that 'Romantic love in Shakespearean drama is the human image of the charity that St Paul describes...like St. Paul, Shakespeare...associate[s] such love with the process of becoming a man', see Kirsch, *Shakespeare and the Experience of Love*, p. 180.
38. See Eve Kosofsky Sedgwick, *Between Men: English Literature and Male Homosocial Desire* (New York: Columbia University Press, 1985), p. 3. For arguments that homosocial bonds work to the advantage of men but the disadvantage of women, see for instance Louis Adrian Montrose, '"The Place of a Brother" in *As You Like It*: Social Process and Comic Form', *Shakespeare Quarterly* 32 (1981), pp. 28–54, pp. 28–9, Harry Berger, Jr, 'Against the Sink-a-Pace: Sexual and Family Politics in *Much Ado About Nothing*', *Shakespeare Quarterly* 33 (1982), pp. 302–

13, p. 312, and Peter J. Smith, *Social Shakespeare* (Basingstoke: Macmillan, 1995), pp. 33–4.
39. Linda Woodbridge, *Women and the English Renaissance: Literature and the Nature of Womankind, 1540–1620* (Brighton: Harvester, 1984), p. 237.
40. See for instance Lindley, *Frances Howard*, pp. 14 and 26–7.
41. Carol Rutter, *Clamorous Voices: Shakespeare's Women Today* (London: The Women's Press, 1988), pp. xxvi and xxvii.

1 MARRIAGE AS COMIC CLOSURE

1. See Ejner J. Jensen, *Shakespeare and the Ends of Comedy* (Bloomington: Indiana University Press, 1991), p. 2, on the importance attached by the critical tradition to the ends of comedies.
2. This is noted by Nigel Wood ('Endpiece', in *Theory in Practice: Hamlet*, edi. Peter J. Smith and Nigel Wood [Buckingham: Open University Press, 1996], pp. 24–54, p. 137), in response to Brian Vickers' assertion to the contrary.
3. For the Elizabethan expectation that the birth of a child would inevitably result from sex, see Lisa Jardine, *Still Harping on Daughters: Women and Drama in the Age of Shakespeare* (Brighton: Harvester, 1983), p. 130.
4. William Shakespeare, *As You Like It*, ed. Agnes Latham [1957] (London: Routledge, 1987), I.III.11. All future quotations from the play will be taken from this edition and reference will be given in the text.
5. Katharine Eisaman Maus, in 'Transfer of Title in *Love's Labour's Lost*: Language, Individualism, Gender', in *Shakespeare Left and Right*, ed. Ivo Kamps (London: Routledge, 1991), pp. 205–23, sees Navarre's academy as an attempt to repress 'the involvement of women in the process of title transfer' (p. 215).
6. The extent to which *As You Like It* is generally perceived as a play riddled with marriages is interestingly indicated by the Oxford and Cambridge 'O' level board question on the play cited by Alan Sinfield, 'Write an editorial for the *Arden Gazette* on the recent outbreak of marriage in the district' ('Give an account of Shakespeare and Education, showing why you think they are effective and what you have appreciated about them. Support your comments with precise references', in *Political Shakespeare*, ed. Jonathan Dollimore and Alan Sinfield [Manchester: Manchester University Press, 1985], pp. 134–57, p. 150).
7. William Shakespeare, *As You Like It*, ed. H.J. Oliver (Harmondsworth: Penguin, 1968), V.4.104s.d.
8. That there is a genuine ambiguity here is something that has become very clear to me when teaching this text, and an assumption either way can produce very different readings, as in Malcolm Evans' discussion of the play in *Signifying Nothing: Truth's True Contents in Shakespeare's Texts*, 2nd edition (Hemel Hempstead: Harvester

Wheatsheaf, 1989), where it is taken for granted that it is indisputably the god Hymen who appears. (Evans does not discuss the performance aspect.)

9. Diane Elizabeth Dreher, *Domination and Defiance: Fathers and Daughters in Shakespeare* (Lexington: University of Kentucky Press, 1986), p. 123.
10. Dreher, *Domination and Defiance*, p. 122.
11. See Richard Wilson, *Will Power: Essays on Shakespearean Authority* (Hemel Hempstead: Harvester Wheatsheaf, 1993), p. 75.
12. See Adelman, *Suffocating Mothers*, pp. 13–14.
13. Barbara J. Bono points out, however, that the forest of Arden echoes the maiden name of Shakespeare's mother Mary Arden, and that the play encodes a recognition of human origin in a maternal body which precludes knowledge of the father ('Mixed Gender, Mixed Genre in Shakespeare's *As You Like It*', in *Renaissance Genres: Essays on Theory, History, and Interpretation*, ed. Barbara Kiefer Lewalski [Cambridge, MA: Harvard University Press, 1986], pp. 189–212, pp. 194 and 211). On absent mothers in Shakespearean drama generally, see most particularly Mary Beth Rose, 'Where are the Mothers in Shakespeare? Options for Gender Representation in the English Renaissance', *Shakespeare Quarterly* 42:3 (Fall 1991), pp. 291–314.
14. See Wilson, *Will Power*, p. 76, on the patriarchal values encoded in 'thy father's father'.
15. See Louis Adrian Montrose, '"The Place of a Brother" in *As You Like It*: Social Process and Comic Form', *Shakespeare Quarterly* 32 (1981), pp. 28–54, p. 50. Montrose also offers a brilliant analysis of the workings of male bonding mechanisms in the play in general and in the horn song scene in particular, which he terms a 'charivari' (p. 49). He sees the play as a whole as working to diminish the power of women. For additional comment on the snake and lioness, see Valerie Traub, 'Desire and the Differences it Makes', in *The Matter of Difference*, ed. Valerie Wayne (Hemel Hempstead: Harvester Wheatsheaf, 1991), pp. 81–114, p. 105.
16. William Shakespeare, *A Midsummer Night's Dream*, ed. Harold F. Brooks (London: Methuen, 1979), I.1.1–11. All further quotations from the play will be taken from this edition and reference will be given in the text.
17. For the argument that Shakespeare might be alluding here to the presence of actual dowagers in the audience, see Steven May, 'A *Midsummer Night's Dream* and the Carey–Berkeley Wedding', *Renaissance Papers* (1983), pp. 43–52, pp. 46–7.
18. For an ingenious reading of *A Midsummer Night's Dream* as structured around the fear and avoidance of older women, see Terence Hawkes, 'Or', in *Meaning by Shakespeare* (London: Routledge, 1992). On the absence of mothers in Shakespeare's plays, see Carol Thomas Neely, *Broken Nuptials in Shakespeare's Plays*, p. 171.
19. See Paula Louise Scalingi, 'The Scepter or the Distaff: The Question of Female Sovereignty, 1516–1607', *The Historian*, 41:1 (1975), pp. 59–75, p. 64. Semiramis is referred to twice in *Titus Andronicus* (II.I.22

and II.III.118), and so is Pyramus (II.III.231), which increases the probability of an allusion to her in *Dream*.

20. On lesbian desire in the play, see Valerie Traub, 'The (In)significance of "Lesbian" Desire in Early Modern England', in *Erotic Politics*, ed. Susan Zimmerman, pp. 150–69, p. 157. For an argument that all Shakespearean comedy is fundamentally informed by homoeroticism, see Jardine, *Still Harping on Daughters*, pp. 20–9.

21. For discussions of the difficulties of ascertaining whether, in this and similar situations, the sympathies of the audience would be engaged on behalf of the unruly lovers or of the patriarchal order which they challenge, see Michael Hattaway, 'Drama and Society', in *The Cambridge Companion to English Renaissance Drama*, ed. A.R. Braunmuller and Michael Hattaway (Cambridge: Cambridge University Press, 1990), p. 110, and Richard Levin, *New Readings vs Old Plays* (Chicago: University of Chicago Press, 1979), pp. 151–3.

22. For an account of some pertinent aspects of the cult, see Roy Strong, *The Cult of Elizabeth* (London: Thames and Hudson, 1977); Susan Bassnett, *Elizabeth I: A Feminist Perspective* (Oxford: Berg, 1988); and my own *Elizabeth I and Her Court* (London: Vision Press, 1990). On its potential implications for the play, see particularly Louis Adrian Montrose, 'A Midsummer Night's Dream and the Shaping Fantasies of Elizabethan Culture: Gender, Power, Form', reproduced most conveniently in *New Historicism and Renaissance Drama*, ed. Richard Wilson and Richard Dutton (Harlow: Longman, 1992), pp. 109–30. For discussion between the relationship between the cult of Elizabeth and comic closure in general, see Peter Erickson, 'The Order of the Garter, the cult of Elizabeth, and class-gender tension in *The Merry Wives of Windsor*', in *Shakespeare Reproduced*, ed. Jean E. Howard and Marion F. O'Connor (London: Methuen, 1987), pp. 116–40, p. 130. Philippa Berry comments on the tension between the strong emphasis on marriage in Protestant ideology and Elizabeth's refusal of it, and offers a reading of *A Midsummer Night's Dream* as attempting to restore Elizabeth to 'the control of the patriarchy' (*Of Chastity and Power: Elizabethan Literature and the Unmarried Queen* [London: Routledge, 1989], p. 143) and as mounting a 'challenge [to] the Platonism of Elizabeth's cult by its emphasis upon female heterosexuality and the subordination of woman in marriage' (pp. 143–4). My own reading would agree that women are shown to be subordinated in marriage but would suggest that the implications of this fact may be a possible locus for debate, and hence that it is not being uncritically endorsed.

23. Hawkes (*Meaning by Shakespeare*, p. 20) comments that 'a motif of disfiguring, translating change is all-pervasive'.

24. Though Stephen Greenblatt suggests that the Fairies' use of field-dew at the end of the play is indeed evocative of the marriage blessing ('Resonance and Wonder', *Bulletin of the American Academy of Arts and Sciences*, 43 [1990], pp. 11–34; reprinted in Stephen J. Greenblatt, *Learning to Curse: Essays in Early Modern Culture* [London: Routledge, 1990], p. 163).

198   *The Shakespearean Marriage*

25. Christopher Brooke, *The Medieval Idea of Marriage* (Oxford: Oxford University Press, 1991), p. 231.
26. The importance of directing critical attention to the male characters as well as the female ones, even and perhaps especially for a feminist reading, has been stressed by, amongst others, Walter Cohen, who characterises as one of the achievements of American feminist criticism 'a psychoanalytically inspired sensitivity to the costs repeatedly exacted in the course of the plots not only from women but, given the constricting norms of male identity, from men as well' ('Political Criticism of Shakespeare', in *Shakespeare Reproduced*, p. 23). He goes on to question Linda Bamber's division into comic women, tragic men (p. 24).
27. William Shakespeare, *The Two Gentlemen of Verona*, ed. Clifford Leech (London: Methuen, 1969), V.IV.76–7. All further quotations from the play will be taken from this edition and reference will be given in the text.
28. For a discussion of this as a central concern in *The Two Noble Kinsmen*, see Kathleen McLuskie, *Renaissance Dramatists* (Atlantic Highlands, NJ: Humanities Press International, 1989), p. 13, and Bruce P. Smith, *Homosexual Desire in Shakespeare's England: A Cultural Poetics* (Chicago: University of Chicago Press, 1991), p. 72.

2 MARRIAGE IN THE MIDDLE

1. Juliet Dusinberre, *Shakespeare and the Nature of Women* (London: Macmillan, 1975), p. 73.
2. William Shakespeare, *Twelfth Night*, ed. J.M. Lothian and T.W. Craik (London: Methuen, 1975), V.I.154–9. All further quotations from the play will be taken from this edition and reference will be given in the text.
3. Stephen Greenblatt, *Shakespearean Negotiations* (Oxford: The Clarendon Press, 1988), p. 91.
4. See also Lisa Jardine, *Reading Shakespeare Historically* (London: Routledge, 1996), pp. 71–5, for an argument which emphasises status rather than gender in the play.
5. Eric S. Mallin, *Inscribing the Time: Shakespeare and the End of Elizabethan England* (Berkeley: University of California Press, 1995), p. 22.
6. Though for a very different argument which finds *Twelfth Night* essentially 'recuperative in terms of gender ideology', see Jean E. Howard, *The Stage and Social Struggle in Early Modern England* (London: Routledge, 1994), esp. p. 112.
7. Ejner J. Jensen, *Shakespeare and the Ends of Comedy* (Bloomington: Indiana University Press, 1991), p. 109.
8. Marianne Novy, *Love's Argument: Gender Relations in Shakespeare* (Chapel Hill, NC and London: University of North Carolina Press, 1984), p. 61.

9. William Shakespeare, *The Taming of the Shrew*, ed. Brian Morris (London: Methuen, 1981), IV.V.18–22. All further quotations from the play will be taken from this edition and reference will be given in the text.
10. See, for instance, Karen Newman, 'Renaissance Family Politics and The Taming of the Shrew', *English Literary Renaissance*, 16 (1986), pp. 86–100, and Laurie E. Maguire, ' "Household Kates": Chez Petruchio, Percy and Plantagenet', in *Gloriana's Face*, ed. S.P. Cerasano and Marion Wynne-Davies (Hemel Hempstead: Harvester Wheatsheaf, 1992), pp. 129–65, p. 148. Joel Fineman suggestively comments that 'Petruchio re-establishes the difference between the sexes by speaking the lunatic language of woman' ('The Turn of the Shrew', in *Shakespeare and the Question of Theory*, ed. Patricia Parker and Geoffrey Hartman [London: Methuen, 1985], pp. 138–59).
11. See Newman, 'Renaissance Family Politics', p. 99.
12. Juliet Dusinberre suggests it would also have been so to Puritans, who would see Kate's submission as excessive since woman was not 'made of the fete' (*Shakespeare and the Nature of Women*, p. 105). For some of the numerous and fascinating feminist responses to the play in general, and to Katherine's last speech in particular, see for instance Linda Bamber, *Comic Women, Tragic Men* (Stanford, CA: Stanford University Press, 1982), p. 35; Peter Erickson, *Rewriting Shakespeare, Rewriting Ourselves* (Berkeley: University of California Press, 1991), p. 23; Thomas Healy, *New Latitudes: Theory and English Renaissance Literature* (London: Edward Arnold, 1992), p. 174; Graham Holderness, *Shakespeare in Performance: The Taming of the Shrew* (Manchester: Manchester University Press, 1989), pp. 22–3, 116–17; Lisa Jardine, *Still Harping on Daughters* (Brighton: Harvester, 1983), pp. 60 and 113; Kate McLuskie, 'Feminist Deconstruction: The Example of Shakespeare's *Taming of the Shrew*', *Red Letters*, 12 (1982), pp. 33–40, pp. 38–9; Newman, 'Renaissance Family Politics', pp. 88 and 90; and Novy, *Love's Argument*, pp. 6–7.
13. Diane Elizabeth Dreher (*Domination and Defiance: Fathers and Daughters in Shakespeare* [Lexington: University Press of Kentucky, 1986], p. 52), argues that Baptista, like Polonius, is a bad father because he violates the conventions surrounding betrothal and marriage, but given that we must undoubtedly assume that only some part of characters' behaviour is to be taken as represented on stage, Baptista seems to me remarkably careful and full in his provisions for his daughters.
14. William Shakespeare, *The Taming of the Shrew*, ed. G.R. Hibbard (Harmondsworth: Pennguin, 1968), introduction, p. 35.
15. Graham Holderness and Bryan Loughrey, eds, *A Pleasant Conceited Historie, called The Taming of a Shrew* (Hemel Hempstead: Harvester Wheatsheaf, 1992), p. 89. The editors point out that 'Leah Marcus has suggested that one of the reasons for *A Shrew*'s exclusion from the Shakespeare canon is that it "hedges the play's patriarchal message with numerous qualifiers that do not exist in the Folio"' (introduction, p. 26).

200   *The Shakespearean Marriage*

16. For comment on this, see Newman, 'Renaissance Family Politics', p. 88.
17. This is commented on by Coppélia Kahn (*Man's Estate: Masculine Identity in Shakespeare* [Berkeley: University of California Press, 1981], p. 115), but in the context of a much less recuperative reading of the play than mine.
18. Newman, 'Renaissance Family Politics', p. 86; Newman also points to Kate's references to folk customs (p. 94), though Kate, unlike Petruchio, finds these disempowering rather than enabling.
19. William Shakespeare, *The Merchant of Venice*, ed. John Russell Brown (London: Methuen, 1955), I.III.90–1. All further quotations from the play will be taken from this edition and reference will be given in the text.
20. James Shapiro, *Rival Playwrights: Marlowe, Jonson, Shakespeare* (New York: Columbia University Press, 1991), p. 105.
21. Peter J. Smith, *Social Shakespeare* (Basingstoke: Macmillan, 1995), p. 175.
22. Barbara Everett, *Young Hamlet: Essays on Shakespeare's Tragedies* (Oxford: Clarendon Press, 1989), p. 41.
23. Lisa Jardine also sees Portia as mendacious elsewhere (*Reading Shakespeare Historically*, p. 63). Novy, however, sees her as an exemplar of mutuality and generosity (*Love's Argument*, p. 72).
24. Dreher, *Domination and Defiance*, pp. 132, 133 and 135.
25. See for instance Lynda E. Boose, 'The Father and the Bride in Shakespeare', *Publications of the Modern Language Association of America*, 97 (1982), pp. 325–47, p. 337.
26. Juliet Dusinberre (*Shakespeare and the Nature of Women*, p. 85) calls Portia's deference to Bassanio 'an act of courtesy, a ceremonial to the reality of love. In practice she retains total independence.'
27. William Shakespeare, *All's Well that Ends Well*, ed. G.K. Hunter (London: Methuen, 1959), I.I.1–2. All further quotations from the play will be taken from this edition and reference will be given in the text.
28. See Jardine, *Reading Shakespeare Historically*, p. 55. Jardine also remarks 'Throughout Act I Helena is curiously explicit about the carnal nature of her love for Bertram' (p. 178 note 25).
29. Peter Erickson, *Rewriting Shakespeare, Rewriting Ourselves* (Berkeley: University of California Press, 1991), p. 61.
30. Janet Adelman, *Suffocating Mothers* (London: Routledge, 1992), p. 79; Carol Thomas Neely also finds the comic conclusion highly problematic (*Broken Nuptials*, pp. 87–90), and A.P. Rossiter calls Bertram 'a weak, cowardly, mean-spirited, false, and ill-natured human being' (*Angel with Horns* [1961] [Harlow, Essex: Longman, 1989], p. 91).
31. Arthur Kirsch also sees 'at least the prospect that he may cherish her flesh as his own' (*Shakespeare and the Experience of Love* [Cambridge: Cambridge University Press, 1981], p. 142).
32. William Shakespeare, *The Comedy of Errors*, ed. R.A. Foakes (London: Methuen, 1962), I.I.104. All further quotations from the play will be taken from this edition and reference will be given in the text.

33. On the wife as working partner, see particularly Dusinberre, *Shakespeare and the Nature of Women*, p. 127.
34. Marilyn French sees Ephesus in this play as a classic location of what she terms the 'outlaw' feminine principle, 'identified with witchcraft, worship of a goddess, and sexual freedom... as well as with St Paul's discussion of the properties of marriage' (*Shakespeare's Divison of Experience* [London: Jonathan Cape, 1982], p. 77).
35. William Shakespeare, *The Merry Wives of Windsor*, ed. G.R. Hibbard (Harmondsworth: Penguin, 1973), I.I.22–3. All further quotations from the play will be taken from this edition and reference will be given in the text.

3 WHAT MAKES A MARRIAGE?

1. William Shakespeare, *Love's Labour's Lost*, ed. by Richard David (London: Methuen, 1951), I.I.96. All further quotations will be taken from this edition and reference will be given in the text.
2. C.L.Barber, *Shakespeare's Festive Comedy* (Princeton, NJ: Princeton University Press, 1959), p. 118.
3. William Shakespeare, *Much Ado About Nothing*, ed. A.R. Humphreys (London: Routledge, 1988), I.I.17–18. All further quotations from the play will be taken from this edition and reference will be given in the text.
4. See William Shakespeare, *Much Ado About Nothing*, ed. Holger Klein (Salzburg: Salzburg Studies in English Literature, 1992), p. 154, note 1, for commentary on this.
5. Jean E. Howard, *The Stage and Social Struggle in Early Modern England* (London: Routledge, 1992), pp.71 and 65. For an alternative view, see for instance Mary Beth Rose, who argues that Benedick and Beatrice achieve true self-knowledge when they fall in love (*The Expense of Spirit: Love and Sexuality in English Renaissance Drama* (Ithaca, NY: Cornell University Press, 1988), p. 39.
6. Peter J. Smith, *Social Shakespeare* (Basingstoke: Macmillan, 1995), p.31.
7. On their 'misogamy', see, for instance, A.P Rossiter, *Angel with Horns* [1961] (Harlow, Essex: Longman, 1989), p. 72.
8. For a development of this viewpoint, see, for instance, Carl Dennis, 'Wit and Wisdom in *Much Ado About Nothing*', *Studies in English Literature 1500–1900*, 13 (1973), pp. 223–37, Richard Henze, 'Deception in *Much Ado About Nothing*', *Studies in English Literature 1500–1900*, 11 (1971), pp. 187–201, and Arthur Kirsch, *Shakespeare and the Experience of Love* (Cambridge: Cambridge University Press, 1981), p. 57.
9. Lisa Jardine, *Reading Shakespeare Historically* (London: Routledge, 1996), p. 121.
10. As I write, the local paper reports a performance of the play at Kenilworth Castle which offered an interesting variation on this deferral: the actors playing Beatrice and Benedick joined their own real wedding onto the end of the play.

11. Alison Findlay argues that there is 'an implicit, perhaps even unconscious, antagonism to marriage in Don Pedro and Claudio' (Alison Findlay, *Illegitimate Power: Bastards in Renaissance Drama* [Manchester: Manchester University Press, 1994], p. 104).
12. Sheldon P. Zitner (William Shakespeare, *Much Ado About Nothing*, ed. Sheldon P. Zitner [Oxford: The Clarendon Press, 1993], introduction, pp. 24–5) and Holger Klein (*Much Ado*, ed. Klein, introduction, p. 25) both point out that Claudio and Hero also enact a binding formal betrothal in 2:1.
13. See also Kirsch, *Shakespeare and the Experience of Love*, pp. 44 and 55, for echoes of the marriage ceremony both in Claudio's repudiation of Hero and in Benedick's 'Enough, I am engag'd'.
14. Though Ian House argues that this play too subordinates women to the patriarchy: 'When Beatrice's voice is stopped by the voice of a paternalist society, when my Lady Tongue becomes a silent bride, there is a kind of death' (Ian House, '*Much Ado About Nothing*: A Line Restored to its Speaker', *Notes and Queries*, 239:4 (December 1994), p. 487). Carol Cook, in a highly perceptive and developed reading of the play, similarly sees a suppression of feminine values in the play's underlying logic, arguing that 'Beatrice's ostentatious flouting of conventional sexual roles is often only a concession to them at another level, and instead of challenging Messina's masculine ethos, she participates in its assumptions and values' (Carol Cook, '"The Sign and Semblance of Her Honor": Reading Gender Difference in *Much Ado About Nothing*', *Publications of the Modern Language Association of America*, 101 (1986), pp. 186–202, p. 190).
15. On the importance of pregnancy in the play, see Elizabeth Sacks, *Shakespeare's Images of Pregnancy* (Basingstoke: Macmillan, 1980), p. 53. Sacks also suggests that 'by the end of the play, we may safely assume, Mariana is pregnant' (p. 55).
16. William Shakespeare, *Measure for Measure*, ed. J.W. Lever (London: Methuen, 1965), I.I.10–13. All further quotations from the play will be taken from this edition and reference will be given in the text.
17. See for instance Lisa Jardine, *Still Harping on Daughters* (Brighton: Harvester, 1983), p. 99, note 21.
18. See Leah Marcus, *Puzzling Shakespeare: Local Reading and its Discontents* (Berkeley: University of California Press, 1988), pp. 178–82, on the ways in which the Duke's actions here can themselves be seen as arbitrary and incompatible with the new, stricter definition of marriage: '[t]he precipitous wedding ordered by the duke between Mariana and Angelo was also uncanonical unless, by some chance, they happened to be married in the parish church of one of them, or unless the duke's verbal "license" is taken to cancel out the usual rules.'
19. See for instance Kathleen McLuskie, 'The Patriarchal Bard: Feminist Criticism and Shakespeare: *King Lear* and *Measure for Measure*', in *Political Shakespeare*, ed. Jonathan Dollimore and Alan Sinfield (Manchester: Manchester University Press, 1985), pp. 88–108, and Richard Wilson, *Will Power: Essays on Shakespearean Authority* (Hemel Hempstead: Harvester Wheatsheaf, 1993), p. 130.

20. For a discussion of some staging choices, see, for instance, Michael D. Friedman, ' "O, let him marry her!" Matrimony and Recompense in *Measure for Measure*', *Shakespeare Quarterly* 46 (1995), pp. 454–64.
21. See also Jyotsna Singh, 'Interventions of History: Narratives of Sexuality', in Dympna Callaghan, Lorraine Helms and Jyotsna Singh, *The Weyward Sisters: Shakespeare and Feminist Politics* (Oxford: Basil Blackwell, 1994), pp. 7–58, pp. 44–5, on the possible presence of an equally silent Kate Keepdown.
22. Cindy Carlson suggests that 'Vincentio's universal panacea – or punishment of – marriage will make...consent to marriage, long thought to be the essence of marriage formation, irrelevant' ('Trials of Marriage in *Measure for Measure*', in *Shakespeare and History* (*Shakespeare Yearbook* 6) (New York: Edwin Mellen Press, 1996), pp. 355–81, p. 356. She also comments on the language of pregnancy in the play (p. 363).
23. Carol Thomas Neely argues that '[t]he marriages that conclude *Measure for Measure*...are enforced, joyless, and without promise' (*Broken Nuptials in Shakespeare's Plays*, p. 64).

4 THE FATE OF THE NATION: MARRIAGE IN THE HISTORY PLAYS

1. *The Second Part of King Henry IV*, ed. A.R. Humphreys (London: Methuen, 1966), IV.iv.68–73. All further quotations from the play will be taken from this edition and reference will be given in the text.
2. Stephen Greenblatt, 'Invisible Bullets: Renaissance Authority and its Subversion, *Henry IV* and *Henry V*', in *Political Shakespeare: New Essays in Cultural Materialism*, ed. Jonathan Dollimore and Alan Sinfield (Manchester: Manchester University Press, 1985), pp. 18–47, pp. 35–6. For comment on this speech and the play's obsession with language in general, see also Paola Pugliatti, *Shakespeare the Historian* (Basingstoke: Macmillan, 1996), p. 140.
3. William Shakespeare, *Henry V*, ed. Gary Taylor (Oxford: Oxford University Press, 1982), 3.4.7–46. All further quotations from the play will be taken from this edition and reference will be given in the text.
4. See the notes to the Oxford edition.
5. Jyotsna Singh, 'The Interventions of History: Narratives of Sexuality', in *The Weyward Sisters: Shakespeare and Feminist Politics*, ed. Dympna Callaghan, Lorraine Helms and Jyotsna Singh (Oxford: Basil Blackwell, 1994), pp. 7–58, p. 38.
6. Lisa Jardine, *Reading Shakespeare Historically* (London: Routledge, 1996), p. 9.
7. Quoted in Ralph A. Griffiths and Roger S. Thomas, *The Making of the Tudor Dynasty* (Gloucester: Alan Sutton, 1987), p. 31, an excellent source of information on the historical Catherine of Valois.
8. See Griffiths and Thomas, *Tudor Dynasty*, p. 32.

9. Leonard Tennenhouse, 'Strategies of State and Political Plays: *A Midsummer Night's Dream, Henry IV, Henry V, Henry VIII*', in *Political Shakespeare*, pp. 109-28, p. 121.
10. See Marie Louise Bruce, *The Usurper King: Henry of Bolingbroke 1366-99* (London: The Rubicon Press, n.d.), pp. 27-8 and 139-40.
11. See, for instance, Valerie Traub, *Desire and Anxiety: Circulations of Sexuality in Shakespearean Drama* (London: Routledge, 1992), pp. 55-6.
12. William Shakespeare, *Henry IV, Part 1*, ed. A.R. Humphreys (London: Methuen, 1960), II.IV.357-9. All further quotations from the play will be taken from this edition and reference will be given in the text.
13. For this parallel and the effect of the speech in general, see the Oxford edition, introduction, pp. 34-8.
14. For some illuminating responses to the scene, see for instance Coppélia Kahn, *Man's Estate: Masculine Identity in Shakespeare* (Berkeley: University of California Press, 1981), p. 81, Christopher Pye, *The Regal Phantasm: Shakespeare and the Politics of Spectacle* (London: Routledge, 1990), p. 32, and Robert Egan, 'A Muse of Fire: *Henry V* in the Light of *Tamburlaine*', *Modern Language Quarterly* 29 (1968), pp. 15-28, p. 27.
15. Anne Crawford, *Letters of the Queens of England 1100-1547* (Stroud: Alan Sutton, 1994), p. 116.
16. Christopher Marlowe, *Tamburlaine the Great*, ed. J.S. Cunningham (Manchester: Manchester University Press, 1981), I.ii.107-8.
17. On such links between the two characters, see James Shapiro, *Rival Playwrights: Marlowe, Jonson, Shakespeare* (New York: Columbia University Press, 1991), p. 100.
18. *Man's Estate: Masculine Identity in Shakespeare* (Berkeley: University of California Press, 1981), p. 55.
19. On the role of women and wives in *Richard II*, see Graham Holderness, *Shakespeare Recycled: The Making of Historical Drama* (Hemel Hempstead: Harvester Wheatsheaf, 1992), pp. 77-85. On the marriage of Margaret of Anjou in the *Henry VI* plays, see Theodora A. Jankowski, *Women in Power in the Early Modern Drama* (Urbana: University of Illinois Press, 1992), pp. 97-102; on women in history plays in general, see Phyllis Rackin, 'Anti-Historians: Women's Roles in Shakespeare's Histories', in *In Another Country: Feminist Perspectives on Renaissance Drama*, ed. Dorothea Kehler and Susan Baker (London: The Scarecrow Press, 1991), pp. 137-56.
20. Quoted in William Shakespeare, *Richard III*, ed. E.A.J. Honigmann (Harmondsworth: Penguin, 1968), introduction, p. 7. All quotations from the play are taken from this edition and reference will be given in the text.
21. William C. Carroll comments that 'it is the bloody butcher himself, Richard, who most clearly aligns himself with the ideology of legal and "natural" succession; and it is the re-sacramentalized emblem of "ceremonious" order, Richmond, who intervenes when the "chair" of state is not empty' (' "The Form of Law": Ritual and Succession in *Richard III*', in Edward Berry and Linda Woodbridge, eds, *True Rites*

and *Maimed Rites: Ritual and Anti-Ritual in Shakespeare and His Age* (Urbana: University of Illinois Press, 1992), pp. 203–19, p. 218.
22. Coppélia Kahn, 'The Providential Tempest and the Shakespearean Family', in *Representing Shakespeare: New Psychoanalytic Essays*, ed. Murray M. Schwartz and Coppélia Kahn (Baltimore: The Johns Hopkins University Press, 1980), pp. 217–43, p. 217.
23. Bruce, *Usurper King*, p. 140.
24. Kathleen McLuskie, *Renaissance Dramatists* (Atlantic Highlands, NJ: Humanities Press International, 1989), p. 157.
25. William Shakespeare, *King John*, ed. E.A.J. Honigmann (London: Methuen, 1954), II.i.94–8. All further quotations from the play will be taken from this edition and reference will be given in the text.
26. William Shakespeare, *Much Ado About Nothing*, ed. R.A. Foakes (Harmondsworth: Penguin, 1968), IV.1.6.
27. Juliet Dusinberre points to the fact that this is 'a sensational speeding up and telescoping of Holinshed's version' (*Shakespeare and the Nature of Women*, 2nd edition [Basingstoke: Macmillan, 1995], p. 296).

5 ROMAN MARRIAGE

1. See for instance Margaret Loftus Ranald, ' "As Marriage Binds, and Blood Breaks": English Marriage and Shakespeare', *Shakespeare Quarterly* 30:1 (Winter 1979), pp. 68–81, p. 78.
2. Marion Wynne-Davies, ' "The Swallowing Womb": Consumed and Consuming Women in *Titus Andronicus*', in *The Matter of Difference*, ed. Valerie Wayne (Hemel Hempstead: Harvester Wheatsheaf, 1991), pp. 129–51, p. 133.
3. This is made apparent twice in the play. See William Shakespeare, *Titus Andronicus*, ed. J.C. Maxwell (London: Methuen, 1953), IV.I.22 and IV.I.43. Future quotations from the play will be taken from this edition and reference will be given in the text.
4. *Shakespeare's Festive Tragedy* (London: Routledge, 1995), p. 145; see also p. 140.
5. Carol Thomas Neely, *Broken Nuptials in Shakespeare's Plays*, 2nd edition (Urbana, IL: Illini Books, 1993), preface, p. xiv.
6. On the concealment of Annabella's pregnancy, see Susan J. Wiseman, "'Tis Pity She's a Whore: Representing the Incestuous Body", in *Renaissance Bodies*, ed. Lucy Gent and Nigel Llewellyn (London: Reaktion Books, 1990), pp. 180–97.
7. Lynda E. Boose, 'The Family in Shakespeare Studies; or – Studies in the Family of Shakespeareans; or – The Politics of Politics', *Renaissance Quarterly*, 40 (1986), pp. 707–41, p. 729. In the latter part of my excerpt she is quoting from Peter Stallybrass.
8. Gordon McMullan, *The Politics of Unease in the Plays of John Fletcher* (Amherst: University of Massachusetts Press, 1994), p. 50.

9. Quoted in William W.E. Slights, 'Bodies of Texts and Textualized Bodies in *Sejanus* and *Coriolanus*', *Medieval and Renaissance Drama in England*, 5 (1991), pp. 181–93, p. 182.
10. Annabel Patterson, *Shakespeare and the Popular Voice* (Oxford: Basil Blackwell, 1989), p. 121. Patterson also provides other instances of the use of the body metaphor, by Sir Edwin Sandys and James I, where again all pronouns are masculine.
11. Slights, 'Bodies of Texts', p. 185. Slights acknowledges a debt here to Nancy J. Vickers. Thomas Sorge also considers the woman's place in the body metaphor ('The Failure of Orthodoxy in *Coriolanus*', in *Shakespeare Reproduced*, ed. Jean E. Howard and Marion F. O'Connor [London: Methuen, 1987], pp. 225–41, p. 226).
12. William Shakespeare, *Coriolanus*, ed. Philip Brockbank (London: Methuen, 1976), I.I.253. All further quotations from the play will be taken from this edition and reference will be given in the text.
13. Gail Kern Paster, in *The Body Embarrassed: Drama and the Disciplines of Shame in Early Modern England* (Ithaca, NY: Cornell University Press, 1993), comments both on Coriolanus' reluctance (p. 97) and on the analogous Petrarchanism of the imagery Antony uses to describe the corpse of Caesar (p. 111).
14. Ralph Berry, 'Sexual Imagery in *Coriolanus*', *Studies in English Literature 1500–1900*, 13 (1973), pp. 301–16, p. 313.
15. On the emotional dynamic of both these relationships, see particularly Madelon Sprengnether, 'Annihilating Intimacy in *Coriolanus*', in *Women in the Middle Ages and the Renaissance*, ed. Mary Beth Rose (Syracuse, NY: Syracuse University Press, 1986), pp. 89–111. For interesting commentary on the relationship between Coriolanus and Aufidius, see Berry, 'Sexual Imagery', pp. 309, pp. 312–13.
16. See, for instance, Bruce R. Smith, 'Making a Difference: Male / Male "Desire" in Tragedy, Comedy, and Tragi-comedy', in *Erotic Politics*, ed. Susan Zimmerman (London: Routledge, 1992), pp. 127–49, on the representation of homoerotic desire in this play.
17. Leonard Tennenhouse, '*Coriolanus*: History and the Crisis of Semantic Order', *Comparative Drama*, 10 (1976), pp. 328–46, p. 342.
18. Janet Adelman, *Suffocating Mothers* (London: Routledge, 1992), p. 161.
19. Naomi Conn Liebler, *Shakespeare's Festive Tragedy* (London: Routledge, 1995), p. 161.
20. Ibid.
21. Ibid. Liebler also points out (p. 15) that at least in Francis Bacon's version of the body legend the belly can be identified either with the populace or the aristocracy; Menenius' use of it as an emblem of the natural thus encodes a very conscious ideological choice.
22. Laura Levine, *Men in Women's Clothing: Anti-theatricality and Effeminization 1579–1642* (Cambridge: Cambridge University Press, 1994).
23. Adelman, *Suffocating Mothers*, p. 149; see also Juliet Dusinberre, *Shakespeare and the Nature of Women* (Basingstoke: Macmillan, 1975), p. 244.

24. Richard Wilson, *Will Power: Essays on Shakespearean Authority* (Hemel Hempstead: Harvester Wheatsheaf, 1993), pp. 97 and 113.
25. McMullan, *Politics of Unease*, p. 54.
26. See Patterson, *Shakespeare and the Popular Voice*, p. 68, and Michael D. Bristol, 'Lenten Butchery: Legitimation Crisis in *Coriolanus*', in *Shakespeare Reproduced*, pp. 207–24, p. 213.
27. OED does not record the word 'anus' in print until 1658, but Jonson uses it in *The Alchemist* (4.3.23). Peter Smith, in *Social Shakespeare* (Basingstoke: Macmillan, 1995), p. 215, note 84, also suggests this pun.
28. Carolyn Williams, ' "The Jealousy of Wars": Marlowe's *Tamburlaine* and Renaissance Parenthood', paper read at the 1995 Reading conference on Literature, Politics and History and not yet published, p. 25. I am very grateful to Carolyn Williams for kindly sending me a copy of this.
29. Wilson, *Will Power*, pp. 114 and 116.
30. Stanley Cavell, ' "Who Does the Wolf Love?": *Coriolanus* and the Interpretation of Politics', in *Shakespeare and the Question of Theory*, ed. Patricia Parker and Geoffrey Hartman (London: Methuen, 1985), pp. 245–72, p. 248.
31. Reprinted in Adelman, *Suffocating Mothers*.
32. See, for instance, McMullan, *Politics of Unease*, p. 52, Patterson, *Shakespeare and the Popular Voice*, pp. 135–46, Wilson, *Will Power*, Adelman, *Suffocating Mothers*, p. 147, and Jonathan Dollimore, *Radical Tragedy*, 2nd edition (London: Harvester Wheatsheaf, 1989).
33. Rufus Putney, 'Coriolanus and his Mother', *Psychoanalytic Quarterly*, 31 (1962), pp. 364–81, p. 364.
34. Liebler, *Shakespeare's Festive Tragedy*, p. 88.
35. William Shakespeare, *Julius Caesar*, ed. T.S. Dorsch (London: Methuen, 1955), II.I.70, IV.III.95, IV.III.211, IV.III.232, IV.III.236 and IV.III.303. All further quotations from the play will be taken from this edition and reference will be given in the text.
36. See Liebler, *Shakespeare's Festive Tragedy*, pp. 102–3, for the argument that both Caesar and, later, Portia, are seen as genitally mutilated. On the importance of fertility rites in Shakespearean tragedy, see Linda Woodbridge and Edward Berry, eds, *True Rites and Maimed Rites: Ritual and Anti-Ritual in Shakespeare and His Age* (Urbana: University of Illinois Press, 1992), introduction, pp. 5–9. In the same collection, Jeanne Addison Roberts notes Caesar's appeal to a male fertilising figure rather than a female one ('Shakespeare's Maimed Birth Rites', pp. 123–44, p. 135), while Mark Rose memorably terms the Rome of the play 'a city of statues' ('Conjuring Caesar: Ceremony, History, and Authority in 1599', pp. 256–69, pp. 263–4).
37. On the question of marriage in the creation of Cleopatra's image, see Lucy Hughes-Hallett, *Cleopatra: Histories, Dreams and Distortions* (London: Sphere, 1990), pp. 216–17. It was of a Victorian Cleopatra that a theatregoer is said to have remarked 'How unlike the home life of our own dear queen' (Hughes-Hallett, p. 258). Kim F. Hall comments that women writers of the Renaissance who treated Cleo-

208   *The Shakespearean Marriage*

patra 'never forget that her affair with Antony takes place in the shadow of an abandoned wife' (' "I rather would wish to be a blackmoor": Beauty, Race and Rank in Lady Mary Wroth's *Urania*', in *Women, 'Race', and Writing in the Early Modern Period*, ed. Margo Hendricks and Patricia Parker (London: Routledge, 1994), pp. 178–94, p. 182.

38. William Shakespeare, *Antony and Cleopatra*, ed. M.R. Ridley (London: Methuen,1954), I.I.20. All further quotations from the play will be taken from this edition and references will be given in the text.
39. Mary Sidney, *The Tragedie of Antonie*, in *Renaissance Drama By Women: Texts and Documents*, ed. S.P. Cerasano and Marion Wynne-Davies (London: Routledge, 1995), II.320 and II.480.
40. Smith, *Social Shakespeare*, p. 63. Smith credits the suggestion to Richard Wilson.
41. Carol Thomas Neely comments that 'In Octavia's absence the two men enact an Elizabethan betrothal ceremony; parodying the customary form for spousals, they take hands, deny "impediment", and vow love and fidelity to each other... This betrothal embodies the purpose of the marriage' (*Broken Nuptials*, p. 143); similarly, Laura Levine writes of 'The symbolic marriage that Caesar craves with Antony' (*Men in Women's Clothing: Anti-theatricality and Effeminization 1579–1642* [Cambridge: Cambridge University Press, 1994], p. 61).

6 TRAGIC MARRIAGE

1. Joanna Montgomery Byles, 'Tragic Alternatives: Eros and Superego Revenge in *Hamlet*', in *New Essays on Hamlet*, ed. Mark Thornton Burnett and John Manning (New York: AMS Press, 1994), pp. 117–34, p. 122.
2. Carol Thomas Neely also comments on how 'In the tragedies, maidens become wives' (*Broken Nuptials*, p. 22) and on the extent to which 'disrupted marriages are prominent in many of the tragedies' (p. 1). Marilyn French similarly remarks that 'Shakespeare's comedies and tragedies have similar events' (*Shakespeare's Division of Experience* [London: Jonathan Cape, 1982], p. 35), while Lawrence Danson comments that 'in comedy the catastrophe is a nuptial; in tragedy and romance, the nuptial is prologue' (' "The Catastrophe is a Nuptial": The Space of Masculine Desire in *Othello*, *Cymbeline* and *The Winter's Tale*', *Shakespeare Survey* 46 (1994), pp. 69–79, p. 74.
3. William Shakespeare, *Romeo and Juliet*, ed. T.J.B. Spencer (Harmondsworth: Penguin, 1967), I.1.20–2. All further quotations from the play will be taken from this edition and reference will be given in the text.
4. Naomi Conn Liebler, *Shakespeare's Festive Tragedy* (London: Routledge, 1995), p. 150. Another interesting instance of reading the play in terms of ritual is to be found in Barbara Everett, *Young Hamlet: Essays*

on Shakespeare's Tragedies (Oxford: The Clarendon Press, 1989), discussing the importance of Lammas (p. 115).
5. David Lindley, *The Trials of Frances Howard* (London: Routledge, 1993), p. 40.
6. Diane Elizabeth Dreher, *Domination and Defiance: Fathers and Daughters in Shakespeare* (Lexington: University Press of Kentucky, 1986), p. 60. Christopher Brooke further notes that 'Shakespeare unrolls at length the betrothal and prepares elaborately for the consummation; but makes shift with the ceremony off-stage' (*The Medieval Idea of Marriage* [Oxford: Oxford University Press, 1991], p. 246).
7. Jonathan Goldberg, 'Romeo and Juliet's Open Rs', in *Queering the Renaissance*, ed. Jonathan Goldberg (Durham, NC: Duke University Press, 1994), pp. 218–35, p. 219.
8. Dympna Callaghan, 'The Ideology of Romantic Love: The Case of *Romeo and Juliet*', in *The Weyward Sisters: Shakespeare and Feminist Politics*, ed. Dympna Callaghan, Lorraine Helms and Jyotsna Singh (Oxford: Basil Blackwell, 1994), pp. 59–101, p. 78. This essay offers a particularly interesting discussion of the play's representation of marriage.
9. Thomas Moisan, ' "O Any Thing, of Nothing First Create!": Gender and Patriarchy and the Tragedy of *Romeo and Juliet*', in *In Another Country: Feminist Perspectives on Renaissance Drama*, ed. Dorothea Kehler and Susan Baker (Metuchen, NJ and London: The Scarecrow Press, 1991), pp. 113–36, p. 120.
10. See David Lindley, *The Trials of Frances Howard* (London: Routledge, 1993), p. 166, for contemporary assumptions about this link.
11. Lynda E. Boose, 'The Father and the Bride in Shakespeare', *Publications of the Modern Language Association of America* 97 (1982), pp. 325–47, p. 329.
12. Janet Adelman, *Suffocating Mothers* (London: Routledge, 1992), p. 10.
13. Terence Hawkes, *Meaning by Shakespeare* (London: Routledge, 1992), p. 1.
14. Roland Mushat Frye, *The Renaissance Hamlet: Issues and Responses in 1600* (Princeton, NJ: Princeton University Press, 1984), pp. 79 and 82–3. Sharon Ouditt discusses critical approaches to Gertrude which focus on the inappropriateness of her remarriage in 'Explaining Woman's Frailty: Feminist Readings of Gertrude', in *Theory in Practice: Hamlet*, ed. Peter J. Smith and Nigel Wood (Buckingham: Open University Press, 1996), pp. 83–107, p. 102. See also Lisa Jardine, *Reading Shakespeare Historically* (London: Routledge, 1996), p. 45, on the play's representation of second marriage.
15. William Shakespeare, *Hamlet*, ed. Harold Jenkins (London: Methuen, 1982), I.ii.9. All further quotations from the play will be taken from this edition and references will be given in the text..
16. Lisa Jardine, *Still Harping on Daughters*, p. 72. Diane Elizabeth Dreher (*Domination and Defiance: Fathers and Daughters in Shakespeare* [Lexington: University Press of Kentucky, 1986], p. 61), sees the nunnery scene as a 'distorted marriage ceremony... an exchange of vows at this point would constitute a legal marriage'.

210 The Shakespearean Marriage

17. For interesting comment on Gertrude, see for instance Kay Stanton, 'Hamlet's Whores', in New Essays on Hamlet, pp. 167–88, esp. p. 167.
18. Naomi Conn Liebler, Shakespeare's Festive Tragedy (London: Routledge, 1995), p. 178. See also Liebler's discussion of tainted marriage rites and the dissolution of distinction, pp. 186–7; Boose ('The Father and the Bride', p. 329), points out the extent to which the nunnery scene constitutes a parody of a marriage.
19. Bridget Gellert Lyons, 'The Iconography of Ophelia', English Literary History 44 (1977), pp. 60–74, p. 72.
20. See Stanton, 'Hamlet's Whores', p. 176.
21. Diane Elizabeth Dreher sees Lear as feeling an 'emotional need [which] has long been recognized in Christian marriage ceremonies' (Domination and Defiance, p. 72); see also Boose, 'The Father and the Bride', p. 333. Everett (Young Hamlet, p. 79) comments interestingly on Lear's later characterisation of himself as 'like a smugge Bridegroome', a term that may perhaps be prompted in part by resentment of the play's actual bridegroom.
22. For this idea, see Coppélia Kahn, 'The Absent Mother in King Lear', in Rewriting the Renaissance, ed. Margaret W. Ferguson, Maureen Quilligan, and Nancy J. Vickers (Chicago: University of Chicago Press, 1986), pp. 33–49, p. 39; Kahn rightly credits the insight to Lynda Boose, who in turn has also commented elsewhere on the absence of mothers from the Lear and Gloucester families (' "The Getting of a Lawful Race": Racial Discourse in Early Modern England and the Unrepresentable Black Woman', in Women, 'Race' and Writing in the Early Modern Period, ed. Margo Hendricks and Patricia Parker (London: Routledge, 1994), pp. 35–54, p. 45. On absent mothers, see also Adelman, Suffocating Mothers, p. 104.
23. William Shakespeare, King Lear, ed. Kenneth Muir (London: Methuen, 1972), I.i.11–23. All further quotations from the play will be taken from this edition and references will be given in the text.
24. See, for instance, Kathleen McLuskie, 'The Patriarchal Bard: Feminist Criticism and Shakespeare: King Lear and Measure for Measure', in Political Shakespeare, ed. Jonathan Dollimore and Alan Sinfield (Manchester: Manchester University Press, 1985), pp. 88–108, p. 99. Dreher (Domination and Defiance, p. 71) thinks that Lear prefers Burgundy as a candidate, because he sees him as less of a rival).
25. William Shakespeare, Macbeth, ed. G.K. Hunter (Harmondsworth: Penguin, 1967), I.2.14–15. All further quotations from the play will be taken from this edition and references will be given in the text.
26. As John Wain asks in his introduction to Macbeth: A Casebook (Macmillan: Basingstoke, 1968, p. 12), 'Are the green boughs held by the soldiers... related to the May-day dances?' Malcolm Evans similarly points to the relationship between Macbeth and the forms of popular ritual (Signifying Nothing, 2nd edition [London: Harvester Wheatsheaf, 1989], p. 136).
27. At III.4.141–3, Macbeth uses a series of phrases which may, perhaps, be suggestive in this connection, saying to his wife, 'Come, we'll to

sleep. My strange and self-abuse / Is the initiate fear that wants hard use. / We are yet but young in deed'. Though OED does not record 'self-abuse' as signalling 'masturbation' until 1728, its close proximity to 'hard use' and 'deed', which often has a sexual connotation, might perhaps be thought to work towards an implication of a sterile sex act here. It is at any rate noticeable that Macbeth invites his wife to bed specifically to 'sleep'.

28. See, for instance, Carol Rutter, *Clamorous Voices: Shakespeare's Women Today* (London: The Women's Press, 1988), p. 56. Philip Franks' autumn 1995 production at the Sheffield Crucible had an empty pram by the stage throughout.
29. *Young Hamlet*, p. 103.
30. A.C.Bradley, *Shakespearean Tragedy* [1904] (Basingstoke: Macmillan, 1974), p. 316.
31. For the otherness of women in this play, see also Jonathan Goldberg, 'Speculations: *Macbeth* and Source', in Howard and O'Connor, eds, *Shakespeare Reproduced*, pp. 242–64, p. 258.
32. For a suggestive discussion of this see Adelman, *Suffocating Mothers* p. 135. Adelman suggests that Lady Macbeth may in fact be offering to feed the spirits, if they take her milk *as* their gall.
33. Anny Crunelle-Vanrigh, '*Macbeth*: Oedipus Transposed', *Cahiers Elisabéthains*, 43 (April 1993), pp. 21–33, p. 28.
34. Coppélia Kahn, *Man's Estate: Masculine Identity in Shakespeare* (Berkeley: University of California Press, 1981), p. 191.
35. William Shakespeare, *Macbeth*, ed. Nicholas Brooke (Oxford: Oxford University Press, 1990), p. 19.
36. See, for instance, Pierre Janton, 'Othello's Weak Function', *Cahiers Elisabéthains* 7 (April 1975), pp. 43–50; T.G.A. Nelson and Charles Haines, 'Othello's Unconsummated Marriage', *Essays in Criticism* 33 (1983), pp. 1–18; Norman Nathan, 'Othello's Marriage is Consummated', *Cahiers Elisabéthains* 34 (1988), pp. 79–82; Adelman, *Suffocating Mothers*, p. 66; and Arthur Kirsch, *Shakespeare and the Experience of Love* (Cambridge: Cambridge University Press, 1981), p. 23.
37. Stephen Greenblatt, *Renaissance Self-Fashioning: From More to Shakespeare* (Chicago: University of Chicago Press, 1980), p. 247. For comments along similar lines, though dealing with other parts of the play, see, for instance, Danson, ' "The Catastrophe is a Nuptial" ', p. 74, and Marianne Novy, *Love's Argument: Gender Relations in Shakespeare* (Chapel Hill, NC and London: University of North Carolina Press, 1984), p. 131.
38. Michael Hattaway, 'Fleshing his Will in the Spoil of her Honour: Desire, Misogyny, and the Perils of Chivalry', *Shakespeare Survey* 46 (1994), pp. 121–35, p. 132.
39. William Shakespeare, *Othello*, ed. M.R. Ridley (London: Methuen, 1958; reprinted Routledge, 1989), I.ii.21–8. All further quotations from the play will be from this edition and reference will be given in the text.
40. Mark Thornton Burnett comments that 'Marriage is envisaged by Othello as an unexciting responsibility and an unattractive inevit-

ability' (' "When you shall these unlucky deeds relate"': *Othello* and Story-telling', in *Longman Critical Essays: Othello*, ed. Linda Cookson and Bryan Loughrey [Harlow, Essex: Longman, n.d.], pp. 61–71, p. 69).

41. Some critics share this tendency: see, for instance, Margaret Loftus Ranald, *Shakespeare and His Social Context* (New York: AMS Press, 1987), pp. 135–52, on Desdemona as failing to adhere to Renaissance ideals of wifely conduct.
42. Michael D. Bristol, 'Charivari and the Comedy of Abjection in *Othello*', in *True Rites and Maimed Rites: Ritual and Anti-Ritual in Shakespeare and His Age*, ed. Linda Woodbridge and Edward Berry (Urbana: University of Illinois Press, 1992), pp. 75–97.
43. Juliet Dusinberre, in *Shakespeare and the Nature of Women* (Basingstoke: Macmillan, 1975), argues that Desdemona's general outspokenness would be regarded as justifiable within Puritan views on marriage (p. 84); Mary Beth Rose, in *The Expense of Spirit: Love and Sexuality in English Renaissance Drama* (Ithaca, NY: Cornell University Press, 1988), argues that 'Desdemona presents herself to the Senate as a hero of marriage' (p. 138).
44. I am indebted here to a lively debate on the electronic discussion group SHAKSPER, initiated by Jacob Goldberg and with subsequent contributions from David Evett, Daniel Lowenstein, Linda Vecchi, Richard Bovard and Sydney Kasten.
45. Virginia Mason Vaughan comments on the extent to which Desdemona's elopement deviated from the normal marriage practices of the Venetian aristocracy, which were highly formalised and endogamic (*Othello: A Contextual History* [Cambridge: Cambridge University Press, 1994], p. 28).
46. Virginia Mason Vaughan comments 'Desdemona is a true Venetian; true, that is, to the city's whore image by being unchaste, deceitful, and given to vice' (*Othello*, p. 32).

7 THE WEDDING OF THE DAUGHTER: MARRIAGE IN THE LAST PLAYS

1. William Shakespeare, *The Winter's Tale*, ed. J.H.P. Pafford [1966] (London: Routledge, 1988), I.II.1–3. All further quotations from the play will be taken from this edition and reference will be given in the text.
2. For a rather different view of the relationship between Paulina and St Paul, see Dorothea Kehler, 'Shakespeare's Emilias and the Politics of Celibacy', in *In Another Country: Feminist Perspectives on Renaissance Drama*, ed. Dorothea Kehler and Susan Baker (Metuchen, NJ and London: The Scarecrow Press, 1991), pp. 137–56, p. 165.
3. Carol Thomas Neely, *Broken Nuptials in Shakespeare's Plays*, 2nd edition (Urbana, IL: Illini Books, 1993), p. 209.

Notes 213

4. William Shakespeare, *Cymbeline*, ed. J.M. Nosworthy (London: Methuen, 1965), I.I.17–18. All further quotations from the play will be taken from this edition and reference will be given in the text.
5. Diane Elizabeth Dreher, *Domination and Defiance: Fathers and Daughters in Shakespeare* (Lexington: University Press of Kentucky, 1986), p. 48.
6. I note Jonathan Hope's recent support for the argument that 'the text of Pericles as we have it is a final draft by Wilkins of a collaboration between him and Shakespeare in which Wilkins contributed more to acts 1 and 2 than in the remainder of the play' (*The Authorship of Shakespeare's Plays* [Cambridge: Cambridge University Press, 1994], p. 152). However, in theme and structure it is so close to the other Last Plays that I have chosen to treat it whole.
7. William Shakespeare, *Pericles*, ed. F.D. Hoeniger (London: Methuen, 1963), Act I Chorus, 21–2. All further quotations from the play will be taken from this edition and reference will be given in the text.
8. See Jardine, *Still Harping on Daughters*.
9. See A.D. Wraight and Virginia F. Stern, *In Search of Christopher Marlowe*, 2nd edition (Chichester: Adam Hart, 1993), p. 308.
10. On her absence, see Stephen Orgel, 'Prospero's Wife', in *Rewriting the Renaissance*, ed. Margaret W. Ferguson, Maureen Quilligan, and Nancy J. Vickers (Chicago: University of Chicago Press, 1986), pp. 50–64, esp. pp. 51 and 54.
11. See William Shakespeare, *The Tempest*, ed. Anne Righter (Anne Barton) (Harmondsworth: Penguin, 1968), I.2.349–51. All further quotations from the play will be taken from this edition and reference will be given in the text.
12. For comment on this, see Jeanne Addison Roberts, 'Shakespeare's Maimed Birth Rites', in *True Rites and Maimed Rites: Ritual and Anti-Ritual in Shakespeare and His Age*, ed. Linda Woodbridge and Edward Berry (Urbana, IL: University of Illinois Press, 1992), pp. 123–44, p.134.
13. See Orgel, 'Prospero's Wife', p. 63, and also Frank Kermode's Arden edition note on the line.
14. Paul Brown suggestively comments on how the scarcity of formal marriage in Ireland was read as a mark of its lack of civilisation, and how *The Tempest*, by contrast, demonstrates 'the proper course of civil courtship' (Paul Brown, ' "This thing of darkness I acknowledge mine": *The Tempest* and the Discourse of Colonialism', in *Political Shakespeare*, ed. Jonathan Dollimore and Alan Sinfield [Manchester: Manchester University Press, 1985], pp. 48–71, pp. 56 and 63).
15. Michael Neill, '"Feasts Put Down Funerals": Death and Ritual in Renaissance Comedy', in *True Rites and Maimed Rites*, pp. 47–74, p. 67.
16. William Shakespeare and John Fletcher, *The Two Noble Kinsmen*, ed. N.W. Bawcutt (Harmondsworth: Penguin, 1977), Prologue, 1–10. All further quotations from the play will be taken from this edition and reference will be given in the text.

214   *The Shakespearean Marriage*

17. See also Kehler, 'Shakespeare's Emilias', p. 167.
18. William Shakespeare, *Henry VIII*, ed. A.R. Humphreys (Harmondsworth: Penguin, 1971), II.I.76. All further quotations from the play will be taken from this edition and reference will be given in the text.
19. On the print metaphor, see Stevie Davies, *The Idea of Woman in Renaissance Literature* (Brighton: Harvester, 1986), p. 108; Richard Wilson, *Will Power* (Hemel Hempstead: Harvester Wheatsheaf, 1993), p. 165; Terence Hawkes, *Meaning by Shakespeare* (London: Routledge, 1992), p. 23; and Ann Thompson, '"The warrant of womanhood": Shakespeare and Feminist Criticism', in *The Shakespeare Myth*, ed. Graham Holderness (Manchester: Manchester University Press, 1988), pp. 74–88, p. 85.

CONCLUSION

1. William Shakespeare, *Troilus and Cressida*, ed. Kenneth Palmer (London: Methuen, 1982), I.I.95. All further quotations from the play will be taken from this edition and reference will be given in the text.
2. *Young Hamlet: Essays on Shakespeare's Tragedies* (Oxford: The Clarendon Press, 1989), p.174.
3. See for instance *Titus Andronicus* II.I.89.
4. For the argument that Hector's language suggests some reciprocation of this feeling, see Eric S. Mallin, *Inscribing the Time: Shakespeare and the End of Elizabethan England* (Berkeley: University of California Press, 1995), p. 46.
5. *The Expense of Spirit: Love and Sexuality in English Renaissance Drama* (Ithaca, NY: Cornell University Press, 1988), p. 210.
6. William Shakespeare, *Timon of Athens*, ed. H.J. Oliver (London: Methuen, 1959), I.II.65, I.II.109, II.II.87–8, II.II.108, III.VI.75–7, IV.I.12–13, IV.III.43, IV.III.122, IV.III.385–6. All further quotations from the play will be taken from this edition and reference will be given in the text.
7. Margaret Loftus Ranald, '"As Marriage Binds, and Blood Breaks": English Marriage and Shakespeare', *Shakespeare Quarterly* 30:1 (Winter 1979), pp. 68–81, p. 81. On the question of English marriage, see also Anne Barton's essay on *Cymbeline* in her *Essays Mainly Shakespearean* (Cambridge: Cambridge University Press, 1994), which I did not read until this book was in press.

Index

Adelman, Janet, 62, 115, 116, 120, 136, 196, 200, 206, 207, 209, 210, 211
Anne Neville, Queen of England, 98
Aristotle, 18

Baines, Richard, 173
Baker, Susan, 204, 209, 212
Bakhtin, Mikhail, 112
Bamber, Linda, 198, 199
Barber, C.L., 67, 201
Barton, Anne, 214; see also Anne Righter
Barton, John, 103
Bassnett, Susan, 197
Belsey, Catherine, 5, 7, 193
Berger, Harry J., 194
Bergeron, David, 7, 193
Berry, Edward, 205, 207, 212, 213
Berry, Ralph, 114, 117, 206
Berry, Philippa, 197
Bloom, Allan, 112–3
Bohun, Mary, 90–91
Bono, Barbara J., 196
Boose, Lynda, 112, 135, 200, 205, 209, 210
Booth, Stephen, 194
Bovard, Richard, 212
Boy actors, 14
Braunmuller, A.R., 197
Bradley, A.C., 138, 148
Branagh, Kenneth, 88, 92
Bristol, Michael, 119, 151, 207, 212
Brockbank, Philip, 206
Brooke, Christopher, 29, 198, 209
Brooke, Nicholas, 149, 211
Brooks, Harold, 196
Brown, Paul, 213
Bruce, Marie Louise, 204, 205
Buc, Sir George, 103

Burbage, Richard, 95
Burnett, Mark Thornton, 208, 211–12
Byles, Joanna Montgomery, 133, 208

Callaghan, Dympna, 4, 6, 193, 203, 209
Calvin, John, 3
Carlson, Cindy, 203
Carroll, William C., 204
Catherine of Valois, 89–90, 92–3, 101
Catholicism, 3, 79
Cavell, Stanley, 120, 207
Cerasano, S.P., 193, 199, 208
Cohen, Walter, 198
Consent, age of, 1
Cook, Carol, 202
Cook, Ann Jennalie, 109, 192, 193, 194
Cookson, Linda, 212
Craik, T.W., 198
Crawford, Anne, 204
Cross-dressing, 14, 161
Crunelle-Vanrigh, Anny, 149, 211
Cunningham, J.S., 204
Cusack, Sinead, 15

Danson, Lawrence, 208, 211
David, Richard, 201
Davies, Kathleen M., 192
Davies, Stevie, 214
Dennis, Carl, 201
Devereux, Penelope and Dorothy, 10
Dolan, Frances, 2, 192, 193
Dollimore, Jonathan, 195, 202, 203, 207, 210, 213
Dorsch, T.S., 207
Downie, Penny, 25
Draper, J.W., 194

Dreher, Diane Elizabeth, 20, 54, 109, 134, 169, 193, 196, 199, 200, 209, 210, 213
Dubrow, Heather, 7, 193
Durant, David, 194
Dusinberre, Juliet, 4, 34, 193, 198, 199, 200, 201, 205, 206, 212
Dutton, Richard, 197

Edward III, 11, 194
Edward of Middleham, 98
Egan, Robert, 204
Elias, Norbert, 112
Elizabeth I, 25, 27, 89, 91, 172, 185
Elsom, John, 194
Erickson, Peter, 58, 197, 199, 200
Euripides,*The Bacchae*, 69
Evans, Malcolm, 195–6, 210
Everett, Barbara, 47, 148, 189, 200, 208, 210
Evett, David, 212

Ferguson, Margaret W., 210, 213
Findlay, Alison, 1, 192, 202
Fineman, Joel, 199
Fisher King, the, 58, 124
Fletcher, John, 112, 182, 185; and with Beaumont, Francis, 161–2
Foakes, R.A., 200, 205
Ford, John,*'Tis Pity She's a Whore*, 112
Forset, Edward, 112
Franks, Philip, 148, 211
French, Marilyn, 201, 208
Friedman, Michael D., 203
Frye, Roland Mushat, 136–7, 209

Garnier, Robert, 125
Gent, Lucy, 205
George, St, 115, 174
Goldberg, Jacob, 212
Goldberg, Jonathan, 8, 134, 193, 209, 211
Graham, Elspeth, 3, 192, 193
Greenblatt, Stephen, 36, 85–6, 149, 197, 198, 203, 211
Greene, Robert, *Pandosto*, 168
Grey, Lady Catherine and Lady Jane, 82

Griffiths, Ralph A., 203
Gruoch, Queen of Scotland, 147–8

Haines, Charles, 211
Hall, Kim F., 207–8
Hardwick, Bess of, 10
Hariot, Thomas, 86
Hartman, Geoffrey, 199, 207
Hattaway, Michael, 149, 197, 211
Hawkes, Terence, 136, 196, 197, 209, 214
Healy, Thomas, 199
Helms, Lorraine, 193, 203, 209
Hendricks, Margo, 208, 210
Henry IV, 90
Henry V, 90, 93, 101
Henry VI, 89–90
Henry VII, 89
Henze, Richard, 201
Hibbard, G.R., 45, 199, 201
Hinds, Hilary, 3, 192
Hobby, Elaine, 3, 192
Hoeniger, F.D., 213
Holderness, Graham, 6, 193, 199, 204, 214
Holinshed, Raphael, 11, 89, 97
Honigmann, E.A.J., 204, 205
Hope, Jonathan, 213
Houlbrooke, Ralph A., 192
House, Ian, 202
Howard, Frances, Countess of Essex, 9
Howard, Jean, 72, 197, 198, 201, 206, 211
Hughes-Hallett, Lucy, 207
Humphreys, A.R., 201, 203, 204, 214
Hunter, G.K., 200, 210

Ingram, Martin, 192
Isabeau of Bavaria, 92

James VI and I, 145–6, 206
Jankowski, 204
Janton, Pierre, 211
Jardine, Lisa, 5, 74, 87, 137, 172, 193, 195, 197, 198, 199, 200, 201, 202, 203, 209, 213
Jenkins, Harold, 209

Index

Jensen, Ejner, 39, 195, 198
Joan of Arc, 92, 94, 165
Joanna of Navarre, 90
Jones, Ernest, 138

Kahn, Coppélia, 95, 98, 149, 200, 204, 205, 210, 211
Kamps, Ivo, 193, 195
Kasten, Sydney, 212
Keeble, N.H., 192
Kehler, Dorothea, 204, 209, 212, 214
Kelly, Jude, 49
Kermode, Frank, 213
Kern Paster, Gail, 206
King Leir, 144
Kirsch, Arthur, 193, 194, 200, 201, 202, 211
Klein, Holger, 201, 202
Kusunoki, Akiko, 193

Latham, Agnes, 195
Leech, Clifford, 198
Lever, J.W., 202
Levin, Richard, 197
Levine, Laura, 116–18, 206, 208
Lewalski, Barbara Kiefer, 196
Liebler, Naomi Conn, 110, 115, 134, 139, 206, 207, 208, 210
Lindley, David, 9, 134, 192, 193, 194, 195, 209
Lindsay, Sir David of the Mount, 25
Llewellyn, Nigel, 205
Loncraine, Richard, 103
Lothian, J.W., 198
Loughrey, Bryan, 199, 212
Lowenstein, Daniel, 212
Lynch, Barry, 29
Lyons, Bridget Gellert, 140, 210

Macfarlane, Alan, 2, 9, 192, 194
Maguire, Laurie, 199
Malcolmson, Cristina, 194
Mallin, Eric, 39, 198, 214
Manningham, John, 95
Marcus, Leah, 199, 202
Marlowe, Christopher, 11, 94, 173; *Tamburlaine the Great*, 93, 118
Marriage

aristocratic, 9–11, 13, 121
clandestine, 45
ceremonies and customs, 1, 12, 17, 34–5, 42–3, 54–5, 76, 79, 82, 114, 134, 136–7, 183, 185, 188, 208 n. 41, 209 n. 6, 209 n. 16, 210 n. 18
companionate, 3–6
definition of, 1–2, 63, 83
per verba de futuro, 26, 82
per verba de praesenti, 82
Mandeville, Sir John, 159
Manning, John, 208
Maus, Katharine Eisaman, 195
Maxwell, J.C., 205
May, Steven, 194, 196
McKellen, Ian, 103
McLuskie, Kathleen, 5, 102, 193, 198, 199, 202, 205, 210
McMullan, Gordon, 112, 116, 205, 207
Moisan, Thomas, 135, 209
Montrose, Louis Adrian, 194, 196, 197
Morris, Brian, 199
Muir, Kenneth, 210

Nathan, Norman, 211
Neill, Michael, 213
Nelson, T.G.A., 211
Newman, Karen, 47, 199, 200
Nosworthy, J.M., 213
Novy, Marianne, 9, 40, 194, 198, 199, 200, 211

O'Connor, Marion, 197, 206, 211
Oliver, H.J., 195, 214
Olivier, Laurence, 95
Orgel, Stephen, 213
Ouditt, Sharon, 209
Outhwaite, R.B., 192

Pafford, J.H.P., 212
Palmer, Kenneth, 214
Parfitt, George, 194
Parker, Patricia, 199, 207, 208, 210
Patterson, Annabel, 112–13, 194, 206, 207
Pepys, Samuel, 90

Plutarch, 122
Porter, Cole, 117
Protestantism, 3, 6, 79
Pugliatti, Paola, 203
Puritanism, 3–5, 9, 79
Putney, Rufus, 120, 207
Pye, Christopher, 204

Quilligan, Maureen, 210, 213

Rackin, Phyllis, 192, 204
Ranald, Margaret Loftus, 190, 205, 212, 214
Richard III, 98
Ridley, M.R., 208, 211
Righter, Anne (Anne Barton), 213
Roberts, Jeanne Addison, 207, 213
Rose, Mark, 207
Rose, Mary Beth, 190, 192, 196, 201, 206, 212
Rossiter, A.P., 200, 201
Russell Brown, John, 200
Rutter, Carol, 14–15, 195, 211

Sacks, Elizabeth, 202
Sales, Roger, 194
Sandys, Sir Edward, 206
Scalingi, Paula Louise, 196
Schwartz, Murray M., 205
Sedgwick, Eve Kosofsky, 13, 194
Semiramis, 25, 196–7
Shakespeare, William
  All's Well That Ends Well, 16, 17, 34, 56–62, 66, 81, 158
  Antony and Cleopatra, 109, 125–32, 143, 152–3
  As You Like It, 16, 17–24, 26, 29, 56, 64, 69, 88, 92, 94, 104, 111, 162, 164
  The Comedy of Errors, 16, 34, 62–4
  Coriolanus, 69, 109, 110, 111–21, 122
  Cymbeline, 161, 168–71
  Hamlet, 18, 56, 58, 60, 62, 87, 100, 133, 135, 136–41, 158, 160, 182
  Henry IV, 90–1
  Henry V, 85–95, 108
  Henry VI, 94–5
  Henry VIII, 185–7
  his own marriage, 7
  Julius Caesar, 109, 121–5
  King John, 85, 95, 103–8, 128, 130
  King Lear, 18, 20, 133, 141–5, 152, 180
  Love's Labour's Lost, 16, 66–8
  Macbeth, 18, 111, 121, 133, 145–9, 160
  Measure for Measure, 16, 45, 48, 62, 66, 76, 77–84, 176
  The Merchant of Venice, 16, 34, 47–56, 69, 76
  The Merry Wives of Windsor, 16, 29, 34, 62, 64–5
  A Midsummer Night's Dream, 10–11, 13, 16, 17, 24–9, 32, 34, 47, 50, 59, 69, 76, 77, 109, 111, 116–17, 121, 182, 184
  Much Ado About Nothing, 13, 16, 66, 68–76, 78, 84, 106
  Othello, 18, 69, 100, 133, 135, 145, 149–60, 165, 160–70
  Pericles, 161, 162, 171–7, 178
  The Rape of Lucrece, 109
  Richard II, 95, 111
  Richard III, 85, 95–103, 108
  Romeo and Juliet, 28, 45, 50, 133–6, 188
  sonnets, 8, 12, 17, 106
  'The Phoenix and the Turtle', 8
  The Taming of the Shrew, 16, 34, 40–7, 51, 61, 72, 74, 94, 155, 159
  The Tempest, 111, 161, 177–81
  Timon of Athens, 190–1
  Titus Andronicus, 109–10
  Troilus and Cressida, 111, 188–90
  Twelfth Night, 16, 26, 34–40, 49, 56, 80, 109
  Two Gentlemen of Verona, 16, 18, 26, 29–33
  The Two Noble Kinsmen, 11, 13, 32, 182–5
  The Winter's Tale, 158, 161, 162–8, 171, 177, 178
Shapiro, James, 47, 200, 204
Sher, Antony, 101
Sidney, Mary, Countess of Pembroke,The Tragedie of Antonie, 125–6, 208

Index

Sidney, Sir Philip, 3, 62, 192
Sinfield, Alan, 195, 202, 203, 210, 213
Singh, Jyotsna, 86, 193, 203, 209
Slights, William, 113, 206
Smith, Bruce, 198, 206
Smith, Peter, 47, 72, 128, 195, 200, 201, 207, 208, 209
Sophocles, *Oedipus Tyrannus*, 171
Sorge, Thomas, 206
Spencer, T.J.B., 208
Sprengnether, Madelon, 206
Stallybrass, Peter, 205
Stanton, Kay, 210
Stern, Virginia F., 213
Stone, Lawrence, 2, 9, 194
Strong, Sir Roy, 197
Suetonius, 128

The Taming of a Shrew, 45
Taylor, Gary, 203
Tennenhouse, Leonard, 90, 114, 204, 206
Thacker, David, 29
Thomas Neely, Carol, 12, 66, 111, 166, 194, 196, 200, 203, 205, 208, 212
Thomas, Roger S., 203
Thompson, Ann, 214
Traub, Valerie, 196, 197, 204

Tristan and Iseult, 135, 204
Tudor, Owen, 89

Vaughan, Virgina Mason, 212
Vecchi, Linda, 212
Vickers, Brian, 195, 213
Vickers, Nancy, 206, 210

Wain, John, 210
Wayne, Valerie, 194, 196, 205
Webster, John, *The Duchess of Malfi*, 80, 112
Wilcox, Helen, 3, 192
Wilkinson, Robert, 112
Williams, Carolyn, 118, 207
Williams, Gwyn, 194
Wilson, Richard, 20, 116, 119–20, 193, 194, 196, 197, 202, 207, 208, 214
Wiseman, Susan J., 205
Wood, Nigel, 195, 209
Woodbridge, Linda, 13, 195, 205, 207, 212, 213
Wraight, A.D., 213
Wrightson, Keith, 2
Wynne-Davies, Marion, 109, 193, 199, 205, 208

Zimmerman, Susan, 193, 206
Zitner, Sheldon P., 202